FIVE PLAYS

FIVE PLAYS

Anton Chekhov

Translated by MARINA BRODSKAYA

with an Introduction by TOBIAS WOLFF

Stanford University Press
Stanford, California

Stanford University Press
Stanford, California

Printed in the United States of America on acid-free, archival-quality paper

Library of Congress Cataloging-in-Publication Data

Chekhov, Anton Pavlovich, 1860-1904.
 [Plays. English. Selections]
 Five plays / Anton Chekhov ; translated by Marina Brodskaya, with an introduction by Tobias
Wolff.
     p. cm.
 Includes bibliographical references.
 Newly translated from the Russian.
 ISBN 978-0-8047-6965-5 (cloth : alk. paper)--ISBN 978-0-8047-6966-2 (pbk. : alk. paper)
 1. Chekhov, Anton Pavlovich, 1860-1904--Translations into English. I. Brodskaya, Marina, 1957-
II. Title.
 PG3456.A19 2010
 891.72´3--dc22   2010032338

Designed by Bruce Lundquist
Typeset at Stanford University Press in 10/15 Minion

CONTENTS

Acknowledgments vii

Introduction ix
    TOBIAS WOLFF

Notes on the Translation xix
    MONIKA GREENLEAF

Note on Russian Names xxiii

IVANOV 1

THE SEAGULL 63

UNCLE VANYA 115

THREE SISTERS 161

THE CHERRY ORCHARD 225

Notes 275

ACKNOWLEDGMENTS

I've been most fortunate to have support and guidance from terrific scholars, writers, colleagues, friends, and family. My most heartfelt thank-you to my cast of extraordinary characters (mostly in alphabetical order): Rachel Anderson for directing an early draft of my translation of *The Cherry Orchard* at Stanford; Rosamund Bartlett of the Anton Chekhov Foundation; Elizabeth Beaujour of Hunter College; Stephen Boyd for helping me create a space of my own; my editor, Emily-Jane Cohen of Stanford University Press, for having faith in the project; Caryl Emerson for her stalwart support and valuable suggestions; Joseph and Marguerite Frank; Veronika Frenkel; John Gill, the computer whisperer of Stanford; Monika Greenleaf for her unwavering dedication and guidance and much more, and for her "Notes on the Translation"; Frank Gruber for his legal advice; my husband, Bill Guttentag, for his extraordinary patience and willingness to entertain questions at all hours; our children, Misha and Sasha, who may have already left the house but continue to provide me with life-sustaining questions and inspiration; my mother, Bella I. Usarowa, for leaving many things behind but not Chekhov's collected works in twelve volumes; Katie Hammerson; Pamela Ison; Charles Junkerman for the opportunity to offer the course on Chekhov and Acting; and Sharon Chatten, a master acting teacher, for co-teaching the course with me; Larry Moss; Robert Proctor for his support of the project; Mariana Raykov for putting up with countless revisions; Xenia Lisanevich and Sarah Crane Newman for their help with the production process; Bruce Lundquist and Rob Ehle for the design of the text and the cover; the late Elliot Mossman of the University of Pennsylvania; Varvara D. Kulkova; Keith Scribner; Robin Seaman; Frances Wren; and Tobias Wolff for his insightful comments and the beautiful "Introduction."

I have benefited greatly from your collective wisdom, and this translation is dedicated to all of you.

MB   *Stanford, May 2010*

INTRODUCTION

Tobias Wolff

Anton Chekhov's life was the epic novel he never wrote. His paternal grandparents were serfs. When by prodigies of cunning and thrift they scraped together almost enough money to buy their freedom, their master, in a fit of generosity, threw in a daughter for free. One of their sons, Pavel, hankering after riches and respectability, opened a grocery store in the muddy port town of Taganrog on the Sea of Azov. This Pavel was a declaiming bully, a beater of children, a sanctimonious choirmaster who sold his customers tainted food, then cheated them on weight and change. This Pavel was Chekhov's father.

When his children weren't minding the store he dragooned them into his choir and volunteered them for a numbing schedule of services, morning and night, day after day, piously basking in the admiration with which churchgoers regarded him and his model brood. It was a lesson in hypocrisy. Chekhov must have learned it well, because his work is bitter in its revelation of the selfish ends that religion can be made to serve, and canny in its recognition of the distance between the public presentation of a life and its private reality. As he writes of Gurov in "The Lady with the Pet Dog": "Judging others by himself, he did not believe what he saw, and always fancied that every man led his real, most interesting life under cover of secrecy as under cover of night. The personal life of every individual is based on secrecy, and perhaps it was partly for that reason that civilized man is so nervously anxious that personal privacy should be respected."

Of course Chekhov had no way of knowing then that this would be the capital he'd someday live on, this hard education in human nature. At the time he was sickly, tired, and intimidated. "In my childhood," he wrote, "there was no childhood."

In 1876, when Chekhov was sixteen, his father went bankrupt and stole out of town under a carpet to save himself from prison. He settled in Moscow with

nd five of his six children—all but Chekhov, who was left behind in
to make ends meet as best he could while finishing school. He kept
afloat by tutoring other boys and accepting the hospitality of relatives and
s. For a time he stayed with a Cossack family whose passion for the hunt
o extreme that when no more challenging prey came to hand they hunted
down their own chickens and cows. Chekhov's dependent condition rankled
him; it encouraged, he later said, slavish tendencies that he had to dedicate his
life to squeezing out—"drop by drop."

Chekhov did well enough in school to win a municipal scholarship for the
purpose of studying medicine in Moscow. He joined his family there in 1879,
and found them living in poverty; his father was no longer even living at home.
Chekhov spent a good part of his stipend setting them up in decent lodgings,
and before long he had effectively taken on the burden of support for the entire
household. He seems to have done this without rancor. Those who knew the Che-
khovs at that time later remarked on the raucous good humor of their life together.

This spirit owed much to Chekhov himself. He was a mimic, a prankster,
a wag. At a dull provincial wedding he amused himself by teaching one of the
bridesmaids to exclaim "You are so naïve!" at her suitors. He had a satirical eye
that found rich fare on the streets of Moscow and led him, almost inevitably, to
the writer's life. He began writing jokes and sketches to supplement his university
stipend. The sketches grew into stories. By the time Chekhov finished his medical degree in 1884 he had become a regular contributor to the popular comic
gazettes, and that same year he published his first collection of tales.

Chekhov was not inclined to take himself seriously as a writer. He considered the work he'd done to be superficial and hesitated to take it further, afraid
to risk for the sake of art his reliable income from the comic papers. It was a
matter of survival—his family needed the money. And now that he was a doctor
he felt an obligation to begin treating people. "Medicine," he wrote, "is my lawful wife and Literature is my mistress. When I get fed up with one, I spend the
night with the other." The joke by which he illustrates these competing claims
on his talents and time does not obscure the moral predicament Chekhov felt
himself to be in. He aspired to serve humanity and doubted that his writing had
a legitimate place in this aspiration.

Chekhov needed to be roused to some more serious conception of his possibilities as a writer. This encouragement took the form of a letter from D. V.
Grigorovich, an older writer of particular renown and influence, one of the

so-called Olympians. Grigorovich wrote Chekhov in the spring of 1886. In his letter he pronounced Chekhov the most talented writer of his generation and scolded him for not doing justice to his gift. Chekhov replied immediately with an outpouring of gratitude, flattery, explanations, and the promise to "undertake something serious." His letter is a touching reminder that those whom we call great were once poor mortals distracted by debt, doubtful, worried, ignorant of future triumphs, dying for a kind word.

Chekhov kept his promise to undertake something serious. This something became the long story "The Steppe," a lyrical evocation of a young boy's journey across the Russian heartland. It won the Pushkin Prize in 1888, but Chekhov, always his own most demanding reader, was not entirely happy with it. He considered it too episodic, loose-knit. In this judgment he was probably right, though wrong in his opinion that whatever its faults, it was "the best work I can do." He had in fact written better stories during the period of his supposed frivolity: "Heartache," for example, and "A Gentleman Friend," and the dire, masterful story "Dreams." The most important change was not so much in Chekhov's work as in his attitude toward his work, and toward himself as a writer. Henceforth, though Chekhov continued intermittently to practice medicine, he did so as a public service, sometimes even as a charity. It had become clear to him that his vocation was to write. He had a large and zealous audience. His work was moving in a direction that interested him, and he had won by now the goodwill of the Russian literary establishment: critics praised him; other writers treated him with respect; editors flooded him with letters of solicitation and advice, viciously slandering one another in hopes of maneuvering themselves into position for first crack at his manuscripts.

Chekhov settled in for the duration. He wrote steadily and seriously. By 1899, five years before his death and with some of his best work still to be written, he estimated his output at "more than ten thousand pages of stories and tales in twenty years of literary activity." This reckoning did not include reviews, reportage, occasional pieces, serials, and a vast body of trivial pseudonymous work that he had no wish to bring to public attention. He was thirty-nine years old.

At the end of his account Chekhov added, "I also wrote plays." Indeed he did. And the best of those plays, *The Seagull, Uncle Vanya, Three Sisters, The Cherry Orchard,* and *Ivanov*—here given fresh, vibrant expression by the translator Marina Brodskaya—changed our theater forever, and their charge of life still shows no sign of weakening.

To understand the peculiar character of Chekhov's plays and their abiding attraction for generations of actors and audiences, it is essential to recognize his evolving practice as a writer of short fiction. His stories are, to my mind, the greatest ever written.

He was not without his critics. John Galsworthy accused him of writing shapeless stories, "all middle like a tortoise." It is true that Chekhov's short fiction is unconventional in form, unlike that of, say, Tolstoy, whose stories have discernible beginnings in which the characters are introduced, gradually heightened situations in which the characters are tested and revealed, and endings that resolve these complications with rich, satisfying finality, suitable for the author's edifying purposes. Chekhov's stories are less obviously purposeful, and therefore less predictable; they tell us what we need to know by implication and indirection. They are not shapeless at all, but methodically shaped according to Chekhov's instinct for the essential in his revelation of character and social milieu. He was ruthless in cutting away customary inessentials—scene-setting, weather reports, landscape painting, and even the initial establishment of his characters' histories, trusting his readers to come to intelligent conclusions based on their observations and thus engaging their imaginations and understanding ever more deeply. He arrived at his method not by inadvertence but by the most unsparing, rigorous calculation. And this was as true of his dramatic work as of his fiction.

His first plays, like his first stories, were slight and traditional in form and subject matter—jokey, cleverly plotted sketches intended for the popular stage and conventional melodramas such as *The Wood Demon*. Even in parts of *Ivanov* we can see a residual attachment to the oversized gestures and thin, recognizable characterizations distinctive of this genre. But as with his fiction, Chekhov grew restless working under such constraints, however great the immediate rewards, and soon began testing the limits of dramatic art.

We see the fruits of these efforts in *The Seagull*, the first of the great plays, written in 1896. Nothing much happens, in the usual sense. A famous actress, Arkadina, dominates the stage, declaiming, making grand exits and entrances, living in a fog of self-absorption and frivolity even as her son, Treplev, rails against the dull, hidebound artistic establishment that has so richly blessed both her and her amoral lover, the writer Trigorin. Trigorin seduces the woman Treplev loves, their neighbor Nina, an aspiring actress, then abandons her and their child. In despair, Treplev shoots himself—offstage.

Indeed, most of what we might call "the action" takes place offstage. What we are left with is a sort of choral arrangement, with the characters revealing more and more of themselves not so much in what they say as in their peculiar tone and manner of saying it. And in their speech they often seem to be responding not to one another, but to some inner question or uncertainty or argument. They address each other at oblique angles. The effect is unsettling, dramatizing the isolation of these people—unsettling and not infrequently comical. Here Nina and Trigorin are discussing an experimental play of Treplev's in which she has performed:

NINA: A strange play, isn't it?

TRIGORIN: I didn't understand anything. Although I watched with interest. You acted with such sincerity. And the set was beautiful.

A pause.

There must be a lot of fish in this lake.

Fish! How unexpected, and how perfectly this nonsequitur captures Trigorin's indifference to what he has just seen. And yet Trigorin ultimately accepts Treplev's harsh judgment of his art and even his character:

TRIGORIN: . . . I never liked myself. I don't like myself as a writer . . . as far as everything else is concerned, I'm a fraud, a fraud through and through.

Thus, characteristically, Chekhov mitigates our impulse to condemn Trigorin by revealing his knowledge of his own mediocrity and moral vacuity, and showing as well the pain his self-understanding inflicts. Our judgment is hardly necessary; his own is severe enough.

We see this pattern repeated in all the great plays: the choral intertwining of voices, voices so distinct that they reveal the characters in all their complexity without the obvious devices of detailed personal histories and "plots" manifestly designed to bring everyone to some convenient point where the playwright's moral can be clearly seen; the anguish of self-knowledge—even Ivanov, surely one of the most maddening characters in all drama, suffers this burden to an exquisite degree, exciting our sympathy in spite of our impatience, an aspect of Chekhov's merciful way with his characters. Even Natasha in *Three Sisters*, as close to a villainess as we will find here—coarse, domineering, cruel, cuckolding her husband for all the world to see—has herself been the object of ridicule and disdain from the sisters who now suffer most from her ill will.

These plays are serious, but not grave. That is, their seriousness is never advertised, but felt as a pulse beneath the apparent ordinariness of the scenes as they pass; when a character does give voice to some lyrical outburst about the dignity of work, or the beauty and fragility of nature, or the glories awaiting those who will live hundreds of years hence, we come to understand that these fine sentiments—which in a more conventional play might signal a change in the speaker, perhaps even leading to some new, admirable undertaking—here remain in the realm of sentiment, of noble language whose utterance makes the speaker feel noble without costing him any real effort.

Indeed, that inability to move from the idea to the act is a signature aspect of Chekhov's characters, and accounts for the atmosphere of stasis, even paralysis, in the drawing rooms where they play out their lives. Liubov Ranevskaya of *The Cherry Orchard* knows exactly what she must do to save her estate, but she seems unable to do it, and as a result the calculating Lopakhin, the son of a serf, takes possession. Yet throughout the play we see that same Lopakhin trying to bring Ranevskaya to her senses, to help her do what is necessary, even at his own expense. We cannot condemn him. We have seen almost from the beginning how all this would end, and part of the interest of the play derives precisely from the inevitability of its outcome. Yet it is not a grim play. Its people are alive; they have charm and generosity, they feel as we feel, and are foolish as we are foolish, and pretend as we pretend that somehow we will be saved from our follies, from the fate we have created for ourselves.

Chekhov writes of Vassilyev in his short story "A Nervous Breakdown" that "he had a talent for humanity." It was this same talent in himself that we feel in these plays, and indeed in all of Chekhov's mature work. This is not to say that he was soft or sentimental. He wrote with sympathy, but without the usual flourishes of fine feeling by which writers identify themselves as Caring Souls. His eyes were on the facts of human conduct. He did not design his work to conform to the wish list of any party or creed. He did not seek to reassure the reader by forcing his plays and stories to uplifting conclusions, or by firing improbable insights and resolutions into the heads of his characters. He examined humanity, in short, with the same objectivity that a doctor must bring to the examination of a patient, counting it no favor to tell lies about his findings. "Man will become better," he wrote, "when you show him what he is like."

Not everyone appreciated this objectivity. Chekhov came under fire from ideologues of all kinds for failing to advance the Cause, whatever that might be. Simply to write the truth was not enough; the truth must serve the revolution. Not to take sides was a dereliction of responsibility. The radical critic N. K. Mikhailovsky wrote of Chekhov: "I seemed to see a giant walking down a road, not knowing where he was going or why." This criticism bothered Chekhov, more than he cared to admit, but he kept his independence. "I am not a liberal," he wrote, "not a conservative, not a gradualist, not a monk, not an indifferentist. I should like to be a free artist and nothing more."

Yet Chekhov's writings, however objective in technique and tone, are anything but morally neutral. They dramatize Chekhov's sympathy for the powerless and his loathing of oppression, not only the oppression of one class by another but also of wife by husband and husband by wife, servants by their masters, truth by falsehood, gentleness by violence. He hated bullies. And as much as he hated bullies he hated the cowardice that creates them, that makes us cringe before the possibilities of life. Chekhov was not a cynic; he believed in those possibilities. He did not always believe in our power to achieve them, but they gleam at the edges of even his darkest works, throwing light on the faces of the just and the unjust, giving them a wistful, expectant, familiar look.

For all his achievements in fiction and drama, Chekhov never entirely overcame his feeling that literature wasn't enough, that even more was expected of him. At his country home near the village of Melikhovo he regularly treated ailing peasants, as many as a thousand a year. He did relief work during outbreaks of cholera and famine. He helped organize and finance the construction of schools. He gave help of every kind to young writers and built, in his home town of Taganrog, a library and a museum. His anger over the injustice of the Dreyfus trial reached such a pitch that he quarreled with A. S. Suvorin, the conservative editor who had been his close friend and mentor in the early days, and in the same spirit he resigned his membership in the Russian Academy when Gorky's membership was revoked for political reasons. But of all the deeds and gestures that came to characterize Chekhov's impatience with the literary, meditative life, his need to do something, the most extravagant was his journey to the Siberian penal colony of Sakhalin Island.

"Sakhalin," Chekhov wrote, "is a place of unbearable sufferings, such as only human beings can endure." Yet beyond that fact outsiders knew almost nothing about the place, not even how many sufferers it held or in what particular ways they suffered. This ignorance seemed insupportable to Chekhov. "From the books I have been reading it is clear that we have let millions of people rot in prison, destroying them carelessly, thoughtlessly, barbarously; we drove people in chains through the cold across thousands of miles, infected them with syphilis, depraved them, multiplied criminals, and placed the blame for all this on red-nosed prison wardens . . . yet this is no concern of ours, we are not interested."

In hope of arousing some interest while satisfying his own curiosity, Chekhov set out for Sakhalin in April of 1890. He had before him over five thousand miles of some of the most forbidding terrain on earth. He traveled for a short distance by rail, until the tracks gave out. Then he jolted along by coach when he could, or by cart, or sledge. This was not always possible. The roads were unpaved and boggy, often to the point of disappearing altogether, so that Chekhov was forced to make a significant part of the journey on foot. He passed through blizzards and torrential rains. The heat and dust, he wrote, were "dreadful." The rivers were swollen, the ferrymen unreliable, the inns filthy, the food disgusting. But the tone of his letters is exultant rather than complaining: "I am content and thank God for having given me the strength and opportunity to make this journey. I have seen and lived through a great deal, and everything is exceedingly interesting and new to me, not as a man of letters but simply as a human being. The river, the forest, the stations, untamed Nature, the wildlife, the physical agonies caused by the hardships of travel, the delights of resting—altogether everything is so wonderful that I can't even describe it."

It took him almost three months to get to Sakhalin. He stayed on the island another three months, visiting the labor camps and prisons and small, hardscrabble holdings where some of the convicts were allowed to live with their families. He had set himself an impossible task: to take a personal, comprehensive census of every prisoner and settler on the island. That meant coming face-to-face with literally thousands of people. It was impossible but Chekhov did it, meeting along the way, often over dinner, some of the most notoriously blackhearted criminals in Russia. He kept a list of particulars on every convict, and later published an account of his findings: *The Island of Sakhalin: Travel Notes*. The book is a vision of almost complete darkness; only in the children of Sakhalin did he find any alternative to despair. Just before he left, he wrote his mother: "I've seen nothing for three months but convicts and people who can talk only of hard labor, convicts and the lash. What a dismal life!"

It has been suggested, logically enough, that the hardships of this expedition shortened Chekhov's life. By 1890 his lungs were causing him enough trouble to indicate that he had tuberculosis. But health is not a purely physical condition. It renews itself on spiritual resources as well, and in this respect Chekhov's journey to Sakhalin was cathartic and invigorating. It delivered him from a literary and personal life that seemed to him narrow, petty, incidental to the main drama. In taking on this great adventure, he was forced day by day to jettison his gloom and guilt—excess baggage in Siberia—while strengthening himself with faith and courage. A man like Chekhov suffers more from safety than from risk.

Chekhov sailed home by way of the Indian Ocean. After stopping in Ceylon—"The site of Paradise"—he wrote: "When I have children, I'll say to them, not without pride: 'You sons of bitches, in my time I had dalliance with a dark-eyed Hindu—and where? In a coconut grove, on a moonlit night!'"

Chekhov never had those children. In 1901 he married Olga Knipper, an actress with Konstantin Stanislavsky's Moscow Art Theater whom Chekhov had met when she played the lead in *The Seagull*, but his health had by then reached so fragile a state that he was forced to live in Yalta while his wife's career kept her in Moscow. Her one pregnancy ended in miscarriage. By the spring of 1904 Chekhov was failing rapidly, which did not keep him from thoughts of entering the Russo-Japanese War as a doctor. Instead he let himself be persuaded to go to the German health resort of Badenweiler, near the Black Forest, for treatment. On the night of June 29 he described to his wife an idea he had for a story. A few hours later he was dead. His body was sent back to Moscow in a railroad car marked Fresh Oysters. It arrived on a rainy, dreary day, and part of the crowd that had turned out for his funeral mistakenly attached themselves to another procession. The rest of the mourners followed Chekhov to Novodevichy Convent, where he was buried beside his father. Of this absurd business Maxim Gorky wrote, "Vulgarity triumphed over the coffin and the grave of her quiet but stubborn enemy, triumphed in every way."

But Gorky's righteous gravity seems misplaced (as gravity so often does), perhaps because the whole episode has the distinctive character of a Chekhov invention—antic, subversive to solemnity, miserably, desperately true to the frustration of human designs—as if, for a kind of last meal, he had been granted the boon of choreographing his own departure.

NOTES ON THE TRANSLATION

Monika Greenleaf

Chekhov famously called medicine his lawful wife and literature his mistress. In his literary work he also made a distinction between his stories, which came to him quickly and plentifully, and the five plays he wrote between 1887 and 1903, painstakingly feeling his way toward a theatrical form that didn't yet exist. These plays were in fact prophetic, and would necessitate the new directors' and actors' theaters of the twentieth century.

Chekhov is (together with Dostoevsky and Tolstoy) one of the three most frequently read and taught Russian writers in the English-speaking world. His plays are also a mainstay of the Anglo-American stage, beyond those of any other foreign writer. They have left an indelible imprint on modern dramatists from Tennessee Williams and Arthur Miller to Tom Stoppard, and on innovators of stagecraft from Stanislavsky and Meyerhold, through Brecht and Beckett, to Peter Brooks. Yet anyone who has taught Chekhov's plays or produced them theatrically, certainly anyone with a knowledge of the original texts, must have been frustrated by the marked defects of previous translations:

arbitrary omissions of whole passages;

gross and absurd mistranslations;

blatant insertions of text that is clearly not Chekhov;

use of stylistically impossible or anachronistic expressions for a character's class, historical period, gender, occupation, or state of mind;

failure to sense and render the elusive melody of each character's intonation, as well as the musical intertwinement of the ensemble's voices as the play progresses;

failure to understand and render Chekhov's quick changeability of tone, from lyrical and elegiac, to comic and farcical, to tragicomic and philosophical;

and finally, the distraction of dated or jarring British or American style.

Most English translations of Chekhov have been guided by specific goals—emotional unity, theatrical effectiveness, smooth integration into English or American idiomatic speech. Often the argument for a new translation is simply to update the currency of its idiom. Some are less translations than adaptations for the stage which miss the beauty of the original and the original shock of Chekhov's process of communication.

The unmistakable quality that runs like a bright thread through all of Chekhov's work is his surgical precision. Marina Brodskaya's translation allows us to discover Chekhovian precision and the impact of his strategic word choices, together with the light these shine on the fabric of modern drama and communication. Seemingly meaningless repetitions adding no new information, unconscious echoes passing from character to character, the seemingly superfluous aspects of language, become the driving force of the action. Translations that omit repetitions and substitute synonyms in essence eliminate the fine joins of Chekhov's design. Repeated phrasings and bouncing echoes are the secret handshake, the musical through-line and rhythm within the plays, making the characters part of one another's world, inextricably linked in ways unbeknownst to themselves. Brodskaya's alert attention also teases out riddling affinities and continuities among the five plays and their casts of characters: doctors who don't heal, inert brothers who never learn, estate managers who don't manage, lovers who don't . . .

The present translation's outer and inner precision make it as revelatory a text for reading as for theatrical performance. It is deeply attuned to the spirit of Chekhov's language and his compassionate observation of humans caught in the net of their own habits and blind spots, striving to stop, cause, or foresee the huge change that has already engulfed them. It also succeeds where many have failed in preserving Chekhov's unparalleled sense of humor. We laugh at the characters even as we see ourselves in them. Yet the translation transmits humor not only by jokes, but by shaping the intonation, timing, and delivery of the characters' utterances. This is a quality that is by and large overlooked in other translations, yet is of utmost importance to the intimate irony and integrity of the plays.

Here is one example of the way the translator's small choices engender widening reverberations. In *The Seagull*, the actress Arkadina addresses her son: "Мой милый сын, когда же начало?" *Moi milyi syn, kogda zhe nachalo?* ("My dearest son, when does it all begin?"). She is referring to the avant-garde play that he is struggling to stage. But her iambic rhythm, captured in this translation, reveals to us that the play, in which *she* is starring, has already begun. He asks, "A minute longer. A little patience," but she instead upstages him with her bravura rendition of Gertrude's speech to Hamlet: "My son! Thou turn'st mine eyes into my very soul." Arkadina makes it impossible for her son's play to begin, or to survive the competition with his mother and Shakespeare, essentially catching him in her Mousetrap. For if Treplev's play succeeded, it would make her and her art instantly obsolete.

Chekhov's characters, like his readers, may think of themselves as individuals and independent thinkers, but so much of what we say and think depends on what we hear uttered by others around us. The permeating influence of words, notions, and intonations of others enters our vocabulary and psyche. In Chekhov, the ricocheting echoes form a web, so that a line uttered by a character becomes a thread, and a first-rate translation, like fine stitching, preserves the seamless fabric. The words don't leave the universe; they reverberate.

Chekhov's play *Three Sisters* presents us with a close, parentless family of bright young women longing for escape from the seeming trap of their provincial lives. "To Moscow, to Moscow!" becomes the almost comical motto of their hunger for an idealized change that will elude them. In Act I, the dashing Vershinin's musing words, "We can't know now what will be considered sublime, important, and what—pitiful and ridiculous," arouse the longing household to leap out of their limited perspectives into some sublimer relation to time and change. Unnoticed, perhaps, the words also seep into Masha's dismissive description of Natasha, her brother's lower-class fiancée: "Oh, the way she dresses! It's not that it's ugly or out of fashion; it's just pitiful." A throwaway line, but let's follow its trajectory. Olga's similarly condescending remark on Natasha's green sash will eventually be echoed by the once "pitiful," now monstrously powerful Natasha, as she meticulously completes the expulsion of the three sisters from their family home and the destruction of their world. In other translations, that is where the thread ends, but this translation allows us to trace it further. Vershinin's musings echo one more time in Olga's wistful words, uttered just before the final curtain, "If only we could know, if only we could know." This fine detail is what brings the play full circle, while leaving the nature of that eternally desired "knowledge" just beyond our grasp.

A few months before he died Chekhov told the writer Ivan Bunin that he thought people might go on reading him for seven years. "Why seven?" asked

Bunin. "Well, seven and a half," Chekhov replied. "That's not bad. I've got six years to live." Over a hundred years later, Marina Brodskaya's fresh translation will allow readers, students, directors, and actors to reexperience Chekhov's vital, still-unanswered questions in the twenty-first century.

NOTE ON RUSSIAN NAMES

Russians do not have middle names. Instead, every Russian has a given name, a patronymic name, and a last name. Anton Pavlovich Chekhov. Chekhov is the family name that is passed through the father to his children. However, the feminine variant is slightly different from its male variant. In other words, the last name of Chekhov's sister is Chekhova; the same name but with an *a* that shows that the person is a woman. While Chekhov and Chekhova may not sound quite the same to an English-speaking audience, to the Russian ear they represent the same family/last name. In contemporary Russia, it is not unusual for a woman to keep her maiden name after marriage, although historically, wives took their husbands' last names. For example, Lev Nikolayevich Tolstoy's Anna Karenina acquired her last name as a result of her marriage to Alexei Karenin, Karenina being the feminine form of the last name Karenin. And in *Uncle Vanya*, too, Uncle Vanya's last name is Voinitsky and his mother's (married) name is Voinitskaya. Thus, Voinitsky and Voinitskaya are the same family name.

Patronymic names behave similarly. A patronymic is the person's father's first name with a suffix. The suffix depends on whether the bearer is a man or a woman. For example, Anton Pavlovich Chekhov's first name is Anton, and his patronymic is Pavlovich: Pavel, his father's first name, plus the suffix *ovich* for sons. Chekhov's sister's name and patronymic name is Maria Pavlovna: Pavel, her father's first name, plus *ovna* for daughters. And that is why the siblings' names Anton Pavl*ovich* Chekhov and Maria Pavl*ovna* Chekhov*a* are spelled a little differently.

In Russian culture, the last name, first name, and patronymic constitute a person's name. All three names are used in official documents, while first and patronymic names, when addressing somebody formally: for example, teachers, one's neighbors, often colleagues and superiors at work, those working in an official capacity, and in formal writing. First and patronymic names are not used when addressing one's children, parents, or close relatives.

In the prerevolutionary Russia of Chekhov's plays, masters do not address their servants by both their name and patronymic; they use either the first name or the patronymic. Using both would transgress class boundaries. Servants, on the other hand, can use first name and patronymic in addressing one another.

In addition to this formal mode of addressing one another, Russians have numerous nicknames and diminutives. For example, in *Ivanov*, the hero, Nikolai Ivanov, calls his wife Aniuta, which is a diminutive of Anna. Alexandra, a character in the same play, goes by several diminutives: Sasha, Shura, Shurochka. In *Three Sisters*, the nanny, Anfisa, calls one of the sisters Arinushka and the other Oliushka; both names are endearing and folksy versions of Irina and Olga. In *Uncle Vanya*, even the name in the title of the play, Vanya, is a diminutive of Ivan, a common first name akin to Johnny in English. Numerous diminutives of first names are part of the Russian language. For the purposes of this translation, however, here are the diminutives and alternate names used in each of the plays:

IVANOV

NIKOLAI: Kolya, Nikolasha, Nicolas (French)

ANNA: Aniuta, Anya

ALEXANDRA: Sasha, Shura, Shurochka

MIKHAIL: Misha, *Michel Michel*ich (mock French)

MARFA: Marfusha, Marfutka

ZINAIDA: Ziuziushka

GAVRIL: Gavriusha

MATVEY: Matiusha

THE SEAGULL

KONSTANTIN: Kostya

PYOTR: Petrusha

MARIA: Masha, Mashenka

EVGENY SERGEYEVICH: Evgeny Sergeyich (a more colloquial form of the patronymic)

YAKOV: Yasha

UNCLE VANYA

ELENA: Lenochka, *Hélène* (French)

SOFIA: Sonya, Sonechka

MARIA: Masha, Mashenka

IVAN: Vanya

THREE SISTERS

ANDREY: Andriusha, Andriushka, Andriushanchik (a very cloying
     diminutive)

ANDREY SERGEYEVICH: Andrey Sergeyich (a more colloquial form of the
     patronymic)

NATALYA: Natasha

OLGA: Olia, Olechka, Oliushka

MASHA: Mashka

IRINA: Irinushka, Arinushka (folksy variant)

THE CHERRY ORCHARD

LIUBOV: Liuba

VARVARA: Varya (Mikhailovna is her patronymic)

LEONID: Lionya

PYOTR: Petya

AVDOTIYA FEDOROVNA: Dunyasha

The selection of names, mostly last names, Chekhov featured in his plays
often sheds light on his characters:

IVANOV

IVANOV: a very common Russian name akin to the English name Johnson

SARRA: a strictly Jewish name in Russia

BABAKINA: *baba* (a peasant woman)

KOSYKH: squint-eye

EGORUSHKA: a diminutive of Egor (George), the patron saint of Russia
          and the name of A. P. Chekhov's paternal grandfather who had saved
          enough money to buy his family's freedom in 1841

THE SEAGULL

ARKADINA: rustic paradise, from Arcadus, the mythic king and son of Jupiter

TREPLEV: *trep* (prattle, rumple, number three)

SORIN: *sor* (rubbish, litter)

NINA ZARECHNAYA: Nina, from the old Slavic нинати (to dream)—a
dreamer; Zarechnaya, from the other side of the river

TRIGORIN: three mountains, or three peaks

EVGENY DORN: first name, of noble birth, "a genius of Eves," immediately
associated with Eugene Onegin, a connoisseur of fine things and a
favorite among women; last name, thorn as a variation of dorn

MEDVEDENKO: medved (bear), plus a suffix to indicate a Ukranian last name

UNCLE VANYA

SEREBRIAKOV: silver

ELENA: a Russian version of Helen as in Helen of Troy or *La belle Hélène* (an
operetta by Jacques Offenbach)

SOFIA: wisdom

IVAN VOINITSKY: a very common first name like John in English; the last
name—warring; *voina* (war)

ASTROV: aster, a flower without scent; astral

TELEGIN: horse cart

THREE SISTERS

PROZOROV: sagacious, clairvoyant; Иоанн Прозорливый (John the
Clairvoyant)

VERSHININ: peak, summit, apex

SOLYONY: salty, salted

TUZENBACH: a German-sounding name (in contrast to the rest of the names
in the play); *tuz* means ace

CHEBUTYKIN: a made-up last name somewhat related to the word *chepukha*
(nonsense)

FERAPONT: from the Greek, a servant

PROTOPOPOV: a protopope

THE CHERRY ORCHARD

LIUBOV RANEVSKAYA: Liubov: love; Ranevskaya: contains the word *rana* (wound)

ERMOLAI LOPAKHIN: first name, from the Greek Hermolaos, a messenger of the people; last name, a composite of parts of words for shovel, softie, groin, and blade

PISHCHIK: close to the word "squeak"

CHARLOTTA IVANOVNA: a combination of a foreign-sounding first name with a very common Russian patronymic

DUNYASHA (AVODOTIYA) AND VARVARA: peasant-sounding names; both names refer to martyrs in early Christian history

EPIKHODOV: funny-sounding name with the word "walk" in it

MB

FIVE PLAYS

IVANOV

A Drama in Four Acts

Characters

IVANOV, NIKOLAI ALEXEYEVICH, a permanent member of the local
government, Peasant Affairs division

ANNA PETROVNA, his wife, née Sarra Abramson

SHABELSKY, MATVEY SEMENOVICH, count, Ivanov's uncle on his
mother's side

LEBEDEV, PAVEL KIRILLYCH, chairman of the District Council

ZINAIDA SAVISHNA, his wife

SASHA, THEIR DAUGHTER, twenty years old

LVOV, EVGENY KONSTANTINOVICH, a young country doctor

BABAKINA, MARFA EGOROVNA, a rich merchant's daughter, young widow,
and landowner

KOSYKH, DMITRI NIKITICH, an excise tax clerk

BORKIN, MIKHAIL MIKHAILOVICH, a distant relative of Ivanov and
manager of his estate

AVDOTIYA NAZAROVNA, an old woman of uncertain occupation

EGORUSHKA, a freeloader at the Lebedevs

FIRST GUEST   SECOND GUEST   THIRD GUEST   FOURTH GUEST

PYOTR, Ivanov's servant

GAVRIL, the Lebedevs' servant

GUESTS OF BOTH SEXES, SERVANTS

The action takes place in one of the districts in Central Russia.

ACT ONE

The garden of Ivanov's country estate. To the left, a terrace and the facade of the house. One window is open. In front of the terrace—a broad semicircle of a lawn; to the left and right of it—paths leading into the garden. On the right—garden settees and small tables. On the last one, a lamp is burning. Evening is descending. As the curtain rises, sounds of a piano and cello duet being rehearsed come from the house.

I

Ivanov and Borkin.

Ivanov is sitting at a table reading a book. Borkin, in high boots and carrying a rifle, appears in the back of the garden. He is a little tipsy. Upon seeing Ivanov he tiptoes over toward him, and when he comes up very close to him, aims the rifle at his face.

IVANOV [*Noticing Borkin, flinches and jumps to his feet*]: Misha, for God's sake . . . You scared me . . . I'm upset as it is and you here with your stupid jokes . . . [*Sitting down*] You've scared me and you're so pleased with yourself . . .

BORKIN [*Bursts out laughing*]: All right, all right, I'm sorry . . . [*Sits down next to him*] I won't do it again . . . [*Taking off his cap*] It's hot. Can you believe, dear boy, I've just knocked off twelve miles in only three hours . . . I'm tired out. Here, feel my heart beating . . .

IVANOV [*Still reading*]: Fine, later . . .

BORKIN: No, feel it now. [*Takes Ivanov's hand and presses it against his chest*] Can you hear it? Thump-thump-thump. That means I have a heart murmur and I can die suddenly at any moment. Tell me, will you feel sorry if I die?

IVANOV: I'm reading now . . . , later . . .

BORKIN: No, seriously, will you feel sorry if I die suddenly? Nikolai Alexeyevich, will you feel sorry if I die?

IVANOV: Don't bother me!

BORKIN: Please, my dear man, tell me: will you feel sorry or not?

IVANOV: I'm sorry that you smell of vodka. Misha, that's disgusting.

BORKIN: Does it really smell? That's most unusual . . . But really, there's nothing unusual about it. In Plesniki, I bumped into a prosecutor and we downed, I confess, eight shots each or so. Strictly speaking, of course, drinking is very bad for you. It's bad for you, isn't it? Eh? Is it bad?

IVANOV: This is unbearable . . . Misha, don't you see this mockery . . .

BORKIN: All right, all right . . . my fault, my fault! Never mind, fine, you can sit here by yourself . . . [*Gets up and goes away*] You people are amazing; can't even talk to you . . . [*Comes back*] Oh, yes! I almost forgot . . . Eighty-two rubles, please! . . .

IVANOV: What eighty-two rubles?

BORKIN: To pay the workers tomorrow.

IVANOV: I don't have it.

BORKIN: Much obliged! [*Teasing*] I don't have it . . . Do we need to pay the workers? Do we?

IVANOV: I don't know. I don't have anything today. Wait till the first of the month when I get my salary.

BORKIN: Try talking to your kind of people! . . . The workers are coming for the money not on the first of the month but tomorrow morning! . . .

IVANOV: Then what can I do now? Rake me over the coals . . . And what a revolting habit you have of bothering me just as I sit down to read or write or . . .

BORKIN: Tell me, do we need to pay the workers or not? Ekh, that's what I'm talking about! . . . [*Waves his hand*] Some estate owners, damn it, landowners . . . Efficient farming . . . Two thousand acres and not a kopeck in his pocket . . . He has a wine cellar and no corkscrew . . . And what if I sell the troika[1] tomorrow! I will! I've already sold the oats in the field, and tomorrow I'll sell the rye. [*Marches up and down the stage*] You think I'm going to stand on ceremony with you? Do you? You've got the wrong fellow . . .

II

Same characters, Anna and Shabelsky (offstage).

Shabelsky's voice coming through the window: "Playing with you is simply impossible . . . You're more tone deaf than a gefilte fish. And your technique is ghastly."

ANNA [*Appearing at the open window*]: Who was that conversing just now? Was that you, Misha? Why are you marching like that?

BORKIN: Your "*Nicolas-voilà*"[2] will make you pick up the pace.

ANNA: Misha, tell them to put hay on the croquet lawn.

BORKIN [*Waves his hand*]: Leave me alone, please!

ANNA: Listen to that tone of voice . . . It's not becoming to you at all. If you want women to like you, don't ever get angry in their presence and don't put on airs . . . [*To her husband*] Nikolai, let's go gambol in the hay! . . .

IVANOV: Aniuta, it's bad for you to stand by the open window. [*Calling*] Get away, please . . . [*Yells out*] Uncle, shut the window!

The window shuts.

BORKIN: And don't forget also that in two days you need to pay the interest to Lebedev.

IVANOV: I know. I'll be at Lebedev's today and I'll ask him to wait . . . [*He looks at his watch*]

BORKIN: When are you going there?

IVANOV: Now.

BORKIN: Wait! Wait! . . . Isn't today Shurochka's[3] birthday? Tsk-tsk-tsk-tsk . . . And I forgot . . . You call that memory! [*Jumping*] I'll go, I will . . . [*Singing*] I'm going . . . I'll go take a bath, chew through some paperwork, take three drops of ammonia—and I'll be as good as new . . . My dearest and sweetest Nikolai Alexeyevich, sweetheart, you're always fretting, whining, always in gloomlandia,[4] but just think how much you and I could accomplish together! I'd do anything for you . . . Do you want me to marry Marfa Babakina? Take half of her dowry . . . No, not half—all of it, take it all! . . .

IVANOV: Stop spewing nonsense . . .

BORKIN: No, seriously! Do you want me to marry Marfusha?[5] The dowry— fifty-fifty . . . But why am I telling you this? Can you even grasp this? [*Teasing*] "Stop spewing nonsense!" You're a good man, intelligent, but you don't have what it takes—you know, no gumption, so to speak. If only we would spread our wings, make the devil himself jealous . . . You are crazy, a crybaby, but if you were a normal person, you'd have a million in a year. For instance, if I had twenty-three hundred rubles now, I'd have two hundred thousand in two weeks. You don't believe me? You think it's all nonsense? No, it's not nonsense . . . Give me twenty-three hundred rubles and I'll deliver twenty thousand in a week. Just across the river, Ovsianov's selling a strip of land, directly across from us, for twenty-three hundred rubles. If we buy it, then both riverbanks will be ours. And if both riverbanks are ours, then you see, we have a right to build a dam. Isn't that right? We'll build a mill, and as soon as we announce that we are putting a dam here, then everybody who lives down the river will cry *gevalt*,[6] and we'll say: *kommen-sie*[7]—if you don't want a dam, then pay up. You get it? The Zarevsky factory will give us five thousand; Korolkov—three thousand, and the monastery will give five thousand . . .

IVANOV: Misha, that's all shenanigans . . . If you don't want us to have a falling out, keep them to yourself.

BORKIN [*Sits down at the table*]: Of course! . . . I knew it! . . . You are not doing anything yourself, only tying my hands . . .

III

Same characters plus Shabelsky and Lvov.

SHABELSKY [*Coming out of the house with Lvov*]: Doctors are the same as lawyers, the only difference being that lawyers only rob you while doctors rob you and kill you . . . Present company excepted. [*Sits down on the small garden settee*] Charlatans, exploiters . . . Perhaps somewhere in Arcadia[8] you can find an exception to the rule, but . . . I've spent twenty thousand on treatments, and I have yet to meet a doctor who didn't strike me as a bonafide crook.

BORKIN [*To Ivanov*]: Well, you're not doing anything yourself, only tying my hands . . . That's why we've got no money . . .

SHABELSKY: Again, present company excepted . . . Maybe there are exceptions, although . . . [*He yawns*]

IVANOV [*Closing the book*]: What can you tell us, doctor?

LVOV [*Glancing at the window*]: Same thing as I told you this morning: she needs to go to the Crimea[9] immediately. [*Walking*]

SHABELSKY [*Snorts with laughter*]: To the Crimea! . . . Misha, why shouldn't you and I treat patients? It's so easy . . . Every time Madame Angot[10] or Ophelia gets a scratchy throat or starts coughing out of boredom, you take out a piece of paper and, in keeping with the laws of science, start prescribing: first, a young doctor, then a trip to the Crimea, and in the Crimea—a young Tatar . . .

IVANOV [*To the count*]: Oh, stop droning, you drone! [*To Lvov*] Going to the Crimea requires money. Even if, suppose, I find the money, she absolutely refuses to go . . .

LVOV: Yes, she does.

A pause.

BORKIN: Listen, Doctor, is Anna Petrovna really so sick that she must go to the Crimea? . . .

LVOV [*Glances at the window*]: Yes, she has consumption . . .

BORKIN: Oh! . . . that's not good . . . I've noticed a while back, just by looking at her face, that she isn't long for this world.

LVOV: But talk softly . . . you can hear it from the house.

A pause.

BORKIN: [*Sighing*] This life of ours . . . It's like a flower, budding sumptuously in a field; then along comes a jackass, eats it, and there's no more flower . . .

SHABELSKY: That's such nonsense, sheer nonsense . . . [*Yawning*] That's just nonsense and more of your schemes.

A pause.

BORKIN: Meanwhile, gentlemen, I've been teaching Nikolai Alexeyevich how to make money. I've shared a great idea with him, but, as usual, the gunpowder fell on damp soil. I can't drill it into him . . . Look at him: melancholy, spleen, sorrow, grief, and hopelessness . . .

SHABELSKY [*Gets up and stretches*]: You, brilliant noggin, are always coming up with schemes and teaching everyone but me how to live . . . Big brain, tell me how to live, show me the way . . .

BORKIN [*Getting up*]: I'm off to take a dip. Good-bye, gentlemen . . . [*To the count*] You've got twenty ways out . . . If I were you, I'd have twenty thousand in a week. [*Walks*]

SHABELSKY [*Follows him*]: How's that? Come on, teach me.

BORKIN: There's nothing to teach. It's very simple . . . [*Comes back*] Nikolai Alexeyevich, give me a ruble!

Ivanov hands him the money in silence.

Merci! [*To Shabelsky*] You are still holding many trump cards.

SHABELSKY [*Following him*]: Well, which ones?

BORKIN: If I were you, I'd have thirty thousand in a week, if not more. [*They walk out together*]

IVANOV [*After a pause*]: These superfluous people, superfluous talk; responding to stupid questions—doctor, all this has exhausted me to the point of illness. I've become irritable, short tempered, brusque, and petty to the point that I no longer recognize myself. I have headaches for days on end, insomnia, ringing in my ears . . . And there is no escape, positively none . . . None . . .

LVOV: I need to have a serious talk with you, Nikolai Alexeyevich.

IVANOV: Talk.

LVOV: It's about Anna Petrovna. She refuses to go to the Crimea, but she would go with you.

IVANOV [*Thoughtfully*]: Going together requires money. Besides, they won't give me a long vacation. I've already used up my vacation this year . . .

LVOV: Let's assume that it's true. Now, furthermore, the most important medicine for consumption is complete rest, and your wife doesn't know a moment's peace. She's worried constantly about your feelings towards her. Forgive me, I'm upset and will speak frankly. Your behavior's killing her.

A pause.

Nikolai Alexseyevich, I'd like to think better of you! . . .

IVANOV: That's all true . . . It is probably my fault, but my thoughts are all confused; my heart's paralyzed with laziness, and I'm incapable of understanding myself. I don't understand other people or myself . . . [*Glances at the window*] Someone could overhear us; let's take a walk.

They get up.

My dear friend, I'd tell it to you from the very beginning, but the story's long and complicated, and it'll take all night.

They walk.

Aniuta is a remarkable and extraordinary woman . . . She converted,[11] left her mother and father and all her riches for me, and were I to ask her for another hundred such sacrifices, she would do it without batting an eye. Well, whereas there's nothing remarkable about me, and I've made no sacrifices. Although it's a long story . . . The point of it is, my dear doctor, [*Hesitating*] . . . that—in short, I got married because I was passionately in love, and I swore to love her forever, but . . . five years later, she still loves me, whereas I . . . [*Spreads his hands in exasperation*] Here, you're telling me that she's dying, but I don't feel love or pity; I feel a kind of emptiness and exhaustion. From the outside I must look awful, but I myself don't understand what's happening to my soul . . .

They walk down a tree-lined alley.

I V

Shabelsky, then Anna Petrovna.

SHABELSKY [*Enters laughing uproariously*]: I swear, the man is not a crook, but a great thinker, a virtuoso! He deserves a monument. He combines modern-day pus in all its varieties: a lawyer, a doctor, a scrounger, and a cashier. [*Sits down on the lowest step of the terrace*] And come to think of it, he never went to the university, that's what's amazing . . . Just think what a genius of a scoundrel he could have been had he studied the humanities and absorbed a little culture! He says, "You could have twenty thousand in a week. You still have your trump ace: your title— count. [*Laughing uproariously*] Any bride with a dowry would marry you . . ."

Anna opens the window and looks down.

"Would you like me to fix you up with Marfa, he says?" *Qui est-ce que c'est Marfusha?*[12] Oh, that Marfusha . . . Balabalkina . . . the one who looks like a washerwoman.

ANNA: Count, is that you?

SHABELSKY: What is it?

Anna laughs.

[*With a Yiddish accent*] Vai you lahfink?

ANNA: I just remembered something you said. Remember what you said at lunch? A pardoned thief, a horse . . . How does it go?

SHABELSKY: A christened Yid, a pardoned thief, and a crippled steed—are all the same.

ANNA [*Laughing*]: You can't even make simple word-play without spite. You're a spiteful person. [*Seriously*] Count, I'm not joking, you're very mean.

Living in the same house with you is both boring and terrifying. Always grumbling, complaining, and everybody is always either a rascal or a scoundrel. Tell me honestly, Count, have you ever spoken well of anybody?

SHABELSKY: What kind of an examination is this?

ANNA: We've been living together under the same roof for five years, and I've yet to hear you speak nicely of people, without spitefulness or derision. What have people ever done to you? Do you really think that you're so much better than everybody?

SHABELSKY: I don't think that at all. I think I'm just as much a pig in a skull-cap and a rascal like the rest of them. *Mauvais ton*[13] and a has-been. I always chew myself out. Who am I? What am I? I used to be rich, free, a little happy, but now . . . a freeloader, a sponger, a faceless buffoon. I get indignant, I despise them, and they respond by laughing in my face; I laugh and they nod their heads mournfully and say, "The old man's off his rocker." . . . But most of the time, they don't hear or notice me . . .

ANNA [*Gravely*]: Here it goes again . . .

SHABELSKY: What?

ANNA: The owl. It hoots[14] every evening.

SHABELSKY: Let it hoot. It can't be any worse than it is already. [*Stretching*] Alas, my dearest Sarra, were I to win a hundred or two hundred thousand, I'd show you which end is up! I'd be gone in a flash. I'd leave this hole, this free bread, and I wouldn't come back here till the Day of Reckoning . . .

ANNA: And if you won, what would you do?

SHABELSKY [*Thoughtfully*]: First, I'd go to Moscow to hear the Gypsies sing. Then . . . then, I'd take off for Paris. I'd rent an apartment there and start going to the Russian Church there . . .

ANNA: And what else?

SHABELSKY: I'd spend days at my wife's grave, just thinking. And I'd sit there at the grave till I kicked the bucket. My wife's buried in Paris . . .

A pause.

ANNA: It's terribly boring. Should we play another duet, maybe?

SHABELSKY: All right. Get the sheet music ready.

V

Shabelsky, Ivanov, and Lvov.

IVANOV [*Appearing with Lvov in the alley*]: You, my dear friend, graduated only last year, and you're still young and full of energy, and I'm already thirty-five. Allow me to give you a piece of advice. Don't marry a Jew, a neurotic, or a bluestocking; instead, choose someone commonplace and ordinary, someone without pastel colors or grace notes. Build your life like a cliché. The more grey and monotonous the background, the better. My dear boy, don't wage war against thousands by yourself; don't tilt at windmills; don't bang your head against walls . . . May God spare you from all this efficient farming, extraordinary schools, and impassioned speeches . . . Lock yourself inside your shell and stick to whatever little thing God has set out for you to do . . . It's warmer, healthier, and more honest that way. Because the life I've been through—it exhausts you! Oh, how it exhausts you! . . . So many mistakes, injustices, so much absurdity! [*Upon seeing the count, speaks angrily*] Uncle, you're always in my face, won't ever let me have a one-on-one conversation!

SHABELSKY [*In a tearful voice*]: God damn, no refuge anywhere! [*Jumps up and runs into the house*]

IVANOV [*Yelling after his uncle*]: I'm sorry, my fault! [*To Lvov*] Why did I have to insult him? Yes, I'm positively coming undone. I've got to do something about myself. I've got to . . .

LVOV [*Agitated*]: Nikolai Alexeyevich, I've listened to you and . . . and, forgive me, but I'm going to speak frankly, and straight to the point. In your voice, in your intonation, not to mention your words, there's so much empty egoism and cold-heartedness . . . Someone close to you is dying because she's close to you; her days are numbered, and you . . . you don't have love, you walk around, give advice, and show off . . . I can't express it; I don't have the gift for words but . . . but I find you deeply unsympathetic! . . .

IVANOV: Maybe . . . Maybe you're right . . . You can see it better from the outside . . . It is very possible that you understand me. Probably it's all very much my fault . . . [*Listens to something*] I think the horses are ready. I'll go get dressed. [*Walks towards the house and then stops*] Doctor,

you don't like me and you don't hide it. That does your heart credit . . .
[*Walks into the house*]

LVOV [*Alone*]: That damn temperament . . . Again I missed the chance to have
the right kind of talk with him. I simply can't stay calm when speaking
with him! As soon as I open my mouth, I feel [*Points to his chest*] that
something starts churning and choking me, and the tongue gets stuck
in my throat. Oh, I hate that Tartuffe, that high-minded crook, with all
my heart . . . There, he's leaving . . . His poor wife is happy only when
he's by her side; she lives and breathes him and begs him to spend an
evening with her, but no . . . he can't do that . . . He feels crammed and
smothered at home, you see. Such hopelessness; if he were to spend
even one evening at home, he might put a bullet though his head. Poor
thing . . . he needs his freedom to do another vile thing . . . Oh, I know
why you go to the Lebedevs every evening! I know!

VI

Lvov, Ivanov (in hat and coat), Shabelsky, and Anna Petrovna.

SHABELSKY [*Walking out of the house with Ivanov and Anna Petrovna*]: In the
end, it's heartless, *Nicolas*! . . . You go out every evening, and we're left
here alone. We go to bed out of boredom at eight o'clock every evening.
It's a disgrace, not a life! And why is it that you can go and we can't?
Why?

ANNA: Leave him alone, Count. Let him go, just let him . . .

IVANOV [*To his wife*]: How can you go anywhere, ill as you are? You're ill and
you're not allowed to be outside after sunset . . . Ask the doctor here.
You're not a child, Aniuta, think about it . . . [*To the count*] And you,
what do you want to go there for?

SHABELSKY: To hell itself, into the jaws of crocodiles, only not to stay here.
I'm bored. I've lost my mind from boredom! Everybody's fed up with
me. You leave me at home to keep her company, but all I do is gnaw her
and eat her alive!

ANNA: Leave him alone, Count. Leave him! Let him go if it amuses him so
much.

IVANOV: Anya, why this tone of voice? You know that I don't go there to amuse
myself! I need to talk to Lebedev about the promissory note.

ANNA: I don't see why you need to justify yourself. Go! Who's stopping you?

IVANOV: For God's sake, ladies and gentlemen, let's not devour each other. Is it really that necessary?

SHABELSKY [*Tearfully*]: *Nicolas*, my dear boy, please take me with you! I'll see the crooks and the fools there and it may distract me a little. You know that I haven't gone anywhere since Easter!

IVANOV [*Irritated*]: Fine, let's go! I'm fed up with all of you!

SHABELSKY: Yes? Well; *merci, merci* . . . [*Takes him merrily by the arm and leads him aside*] Can I wear your straw hat?

IVANOV: Yes; only hurry, please!

The count runs into the house.

I'm so fed up with all of you! But no, oh, my God, what am I saying? Anya, the tone I use with you is completely uncalled for. I never used to be like this. Well, good-bye, Anya. I'll be back around one.

ANNA: Kolya, my dear, stay home!

IVANOV [*Agitated*]: My darling, my love, my poor girl, I beg you, don't prevent me from going out in the evening. It's cruel and unfair of me, but allow me this unfairness! Staying at home is torture for me! As soon as the sun goes down, I feel hopeless. So hopeless! Don't ask me what causes it. I don't know myself. I swear, I don't! I feel it here, and then at the Lebedevs' I feel it even worse; I come back home and I feel it here again, and it's like this all night long . . . It's utter torture! . . .

ANNA: Kolya . . . why don't you stay? We'll talk as before . . . We'll have supper together and then we'll read . . . The grumbler and I have learned many duets for you . . . [*She embraces him*] Stay! . . .

A pause.

I don't understand you. It's been going on for a year now. Why have you changed so much?

IVANOV: I don't know, I don't know . . .

ANNA: And why don't you want me to go out with you in the evening?

IVANOV: If you need to know, then I'll tell you. It's a little cruel to be saying this, but it's better to say it . . . When I feel hopeless, then I stop loving you. I run away from you as well. In other words, I have to leave the house.

ANNA: Hopeless? I see, . . . I see. You know, Kolya, try to sing and laugh and get upset as before . . . Stay and we'll laugh, drink brandy,[15] and we'll chase away your hopelessness in no time. Do you want me to sing? Or let's go sit in your study, in the darkness, like we used to, and you'll tell me all about why you feel hopeless . . . You have such doleful eyes! I'll look into them and cry, and we'll both feel better . . . [*Laughs and cries*] Or, Kolya, how does it go? The flowers repeat themselves every spring, but the joys don't? Yes? Well, then go, go . . .

IVANOV: Pray to God for me, Anya! [*Walks, then stops and thinks briefly*] No, I can't. [*Goes out*]

ANNA: Go then . . . [*Sits down at the table*]

LVOV [*Paces up and down the stage*]: Anna Petrovna, make it a rule: as soon as the clock strikes six, go inside and don't come out till morning. The evening dampness is bad for you.

ANNA: Yes, sir.

LVOV: What's this "Yes, sir"? I'm serious.

ANNA: But I don't want to be serious. [*Coughs*]

LVOV: See—you're coughing already . . .

VII

Lvov, Anna Petrovna, and Shabelsky.

SHABELSKY [*Comes out of the house in his hat and coat*]: Where is Nikolai? Are the horses ready? [*Walks quickly over to Anna and kisses her hand*] Sleep well, my lovely! [*Makes a face and speaks with a Jewish accent*] Gevalt! Shcoose me, pleece! [*Leaves quickly*]

LVOV: Buffoon!

A pause; the sounds of an accordion are heard in the distance.

ANNA: It's so boring! . . . There, the coachmen and the cooks are having a ball, and I . . . I'm like—abandoned . . . Evgeny Konstantinovich, what are you doing marching there? Come over here and sit down! . . .

LVOV: I can't stay seated.

A pause.

ANNA: They're playing a game in the kitchen. [*She sings*]
"Siskin, siskin, where were you?
Down the hill I drank a few."[16]

A pause.

Doctor, do you still have your mother and father?

LVOV: My father died, but my mother's still alive.

ANNA: Do you miss your mother?

LVOV: I've no time to miss her.

ANNA [*Laughing*]: The flowers repeat themselves every spring, but the joys don't. Who told me this? God, who was it . . . I think it was Nikolai himself. [*Listens*] The owl's hooting again!

LVOV: So let it hoot.

ANNA: I'm beginning to think, Doctor, that life has shortchanged me somehow. Millions of people, who may not be better than me, are happy and don't pay anything for their happiness. I, on the other hand, have paid for everything, decidedly for everything! . . . And so dearly, too! Why charge me such exorbitant interest? . . . My dear, you're all so careful with me, mincing your words, afraid to speak the truth; but do you think I don't know what my illness is? I know it perfectly well. Anyway, talking about it is boring. [*With a Yiddish accent*] Shcoose me, pleece. Do you know how to tell jokes?

LVOV: No, I don't.

ANNA: And Nikolai does. And it's beginning to amaze me just how unfair people can be: why not respond to love with love and why do they pay for truth with lies? Tell me, how long will my mother and father hate me? They live fifty-five miles away, and yet day and night, and even in my sleep, I sense their hatred. And what am I supposed to make out of Nikolai's feeling hopeless? He says that he doesn't love me only in the evenings, when he's feeling hopeless. I understand and accept it, but imagine he stopped loving me altogether! Of course that's impossible, but what if? No, no, I shouldn't even think about it. [*Sings*] "Siskin, siskin, where were you? . . ." [*Shivers*] What scary thoughts I have! . . . Doctor, you aren't married and can't yet understand . . .

LVOV: You are amazed . . . [*Sits next to her*] No, I, I'm amazed by you, you surprise me! Well, tell me, spell it out for me, how did someone smart, honest, practically a saint, allow herself to be so openly lied to and dragged into this den of thieves? Why are you here? What do you have in common with this cold and heartless . . . but enough about your husband! What do you have in common with this vulgar and vapid milieu? My God! . . . And this perpetually grumbling, rusted-out and crazy

count, or that old weasel, Misha, that crook of all crooks, with his foul
face? . . . Explain to me, why are you here? How did you end up here? . . .

ANNA [*Laughing*]: He used to say the same thing . . . Exactly the same . . . Only
his eyes are big and, when he gets excited talking about something, they
glow like coals . . . Keep talking, keep talking! . . .

LVOV [*Gets up and waves his hand*]: What can I say? Go inside . . .

ANNA: You say that Nikolai is this that and the other. How can you possibly
know him? Do you think you can get to know someone in half a year?
Doctor, he's a remarkable man, and I'm so sorry you didn't know him
two or three years ago. He's out of sorts, says nothing, does nothing,
but before . . . It was so lovely! . . . I fell in love with him at first sight.
[*Laughs*] I took one look at him and the mousetrap went slam! He said:
come . . . I cut myself off from everybody, like, you know, you cut off
rotten leaves with scissors, and came . . .

A pause.

But now something's not right . . . Now he goes to the Lebedevs to
distract himself with other women, and I . . . sit in the garden listening
to the owl's hooting . . .

The Watchman's tapping is heard.[17]

Tell me, Doctor, do you have any brothers?

LVOV: No.

Anna sobs.

What's wrong now? What is it?

ANNA [*Getting up*]: Doctor, I can't, I'll go there . . .

LVOV: Where?

ANNA: Where he is . . . I'll go . . . Tell them to harness the horses. [*Runs inside
the house*]

LVOV: No, I absolutely refuse to treat anyone under these conditions! Not only
are they not paying me a kopeck, but they're turning my soul inside
out! . . . No, I refuse! Enough! . . . [*Goes inside the house*]

Curtain.

ACT TWO

A drawing-room in the Lebedevs' house; straight ahead—the door to the garden; on the left and on the right—doors. Antique and expensive furniture. The chandelier, candelabras, and paintings—everything is covered with dust covers.

I

Zinaida Savishna, Kosykh, Avdotiya Nazarovna, Egorushka, Gavril, the Maid, Elderly Women Guests, Young Women, and Marfa Babakina.

Zinaida is sitting on the sofa; on either side of her, in armchairs, are elderly women guests; seated on the chairs are the young guests. In the background, by the door to the garden, a card game is on; among the players: Kosykh, Avdotiya Nazarovna, and Egorushka. Gavril stands by the door on the right. The maid is passing around a tray of sweets. During the entire act guests circulate from the garden through the door on the right and go back out. Marfa comes in through the door on the right and walks up to Zinaida Savishna.

ZINAIDA [*Happy*]: Darling, Marfa Egorovna . . .

BABAKINA: Hello, Zinaida Savishna! It's my honor to offer you my best wishes on your newborn . . .

They kiss.

I hope to God . . .

ZINAIDA: Thank you, my darling; I'm so happy . . . Well, how's your health?

BABAKINA: Much obliged by you. [*She sits down on the sofa*] Hello young people! . . .

The guests get up and take a bow.

FIRST GUEST [*Laughing*]: "Young people"—are you so old?

BABAKINA [*Sighing*]: No use competing with the young . . .

FIRST GUEST [*Laughing respectfully*]: Please, what are you talking about . . . It's your title—widow; otherwise you could beat any gal by a mile.

Gavril serves Babakina her tea.

ZINAIDA: Why do you serve it like that? You could bring some jam at least. Gooseberry maybe . . .

BABAKINA: Don't you worry about it. Much obliged by you.

A pause.

FIRST GUEST [*To Marfa*]: Did you come here by way of Mushkino?[18]

BABAKINA: No, toward Zaimishche.[19] The road's better there.

FIRST GUEST: Well, then.

KOSYKH: Two of spades.

EGORUSHKA: I pass.

AVDOTIYA: Pass.

SECOND GUEST: Pass.[20]

BABAKINA: Lottery-loans, my dear, Zinaida Savishna, are on the up and up again. Imagine: the first draw costs two hundred and seventy already, and the second's just short of two hundred and fifty . . . It's never been like this . . .

ZINAIDA [*Sighing*]: It's good for those who already have a lot of them . . .

BABAKINA: I'm no so sure, dear; although they're expensive, investing in them isn't profitable. Insurance alone will do you in.

ZINAIDA: Maybe so, but still, my dear, one always hopes . . . [*Sighs*] God's merciful . . .

THIRD GUEST: I'm of the opinion, *mesdames*, that is, as far as I'm concerned, to have capital at the present time is very unprofitable. Securities give low dividends, and putting money into circulation is extraordinarily dangerous. The way I see it, *mesdames*, someone who has capital finds himself in a much more precarious position, *mesdames*, than someone who . . .

BABAKINA [*Sighs*]: So true!

First Guest yawns.

How can you yawn in the presence of ladies?

FIRST GUEST: *Pardon, mesdames,* it was by accident.

Zinaida gets up and goes out through the door on the right; a long period of silence.

EGORUSHKA: Two of diamonds.

AVDOTIYA: I pass.

SECOND GUEST: Pass.

KOSYKH: Pass.

BABAKINA [*Aside*]: My God, it's ghastly boring here!

II

All the same characters. Zinaida and Lebedev.

ZINAIDA [*Coming in with Lebedev through the door on the right; softly*]: Why did you plop yourself here? Like a prima donna! Go sit with the guests! [*She goes back to her old place*]

LEBEDEV [*Yawning*]: Oh, dear, sinners that we are! [*Upon seeing Marfa*] My goodness, look at the fruit jelly here! Turkish delight! . . . [*Greets her*] How is your most precious? . . .

BABAKINA: Much obliged by you.

LEBEDEV: Well, thank goodness! . . . Thank goodness! [*He sits down in an armchair*] Well, well . . . Gavril!

Gavril brings him a shot of vodka and a glass of water. He drinks the vodka and then drinks the water.

FIRST GUEST: To your health! . . .

LEBEDEV: What health?! . . . I haven't kicked the bucket yet, thank you very much for that. [*To his wife*] Ziuziushka,[21] where's our newborn?

KOSYKH [*In a plaintive voice*]: Tell me: why did we end up without a single trick? [*Jumps up*] Why the hell did we lose the game, damn it?

AVDOTIYA [*Jumps up; sternly*]: Because, my dearie, don't play if you don't know how. Who gave you the absolute right to play someone else's suit? And that's why you get stuck with your pickled ace! . . .

They both leave the table and run forward.

KOSYKH [*In a plaintive voice*]: But ladies and gentlemen . . . I had in diamonds: the ace, king, queen, a run of diamonds, the ace of spades and one, you see, just one puny heart; and she, damn it, couldn't make a little slam. I said no-trumps . . .

AVDOTIYA [*Interrupting him*]: No, I said no-trumps! You said: two no-trumps . . .

KOSYKH: That's outrageous! . . . But . . . you had . . . I had . . . you had . . . [*To Lebedev*] Think about it, Pavel Kirillych . . . I had in diamonds: the ace, king, queen, a lineup . . .

LEBEDEV [*Stops his ears with his fingers*]: Get away from me . . . please get away . . .

AVDOTIYA [*Yelling*]: No, I said no-trumps!

KOSYKH [*Fiercely*]: I'll be damned, a scoundrel and anathema if I ever sit down
to play with this dried-up anchovy again! [*Goes quickly into the garden*]
The Second Guest follows him. Egorushka is left alone at the table.

AVDOTIYA: Phew! . . . He makes my blood boil! . . . Anchovy! . . . A dried-up
anchovy yourself!

BABAKINA: Grandma, you, too, are mean . . .

AVDOTIYA [*Raises her arms in surprise upon seeing Marfa*]: Sweetheart!
My beauty! She's right here, and I'm blind as a bat, can't even see
her . . . My darling . . . [*She kisses her on the shoulder and sits down next
to her*] My joy! Let me take a look at you, my white swan! *T'foo, t'foo,
t'foo . . .*[22] we don't want to put an evil eye on her! . . .

LEBEDEV: Oh, here you go, singing the praises . . . You'd better find her a
husband . . .

AVDOTIYA: And I will! I won't lay my bones to rest, sinner that I am, until I
find a husband for her, and for Sasha, too! . . . I won't lay my bones to
rest . . . [*A sigh*] Only where do you find them, husbands, nowadays?
There, look at them, sitting there, feathers all up, like wet roosters! . . .

THIRD GUEST: A rather poor comparison. In my opinion, *mesdames,* if young
men nowadays prefer the bachelor lifestyle, then it's, so to speak, social
conditions to blame . . .

LEBEDEV: Come, come! No philosophizing! I can't stand it!

III

Same characters and Sasha.

SASHA [*Enters and comes over to her father*]: It's so beautiful outside, and you,
ladies and gentlemen, are sitting here in this stuffy room.

ZINAIDA: Sasha, dear, don't you see that Marfa Egorovna's here?

SASHA: I'm sorry. [*Comes over to Babakina and greets her*]

BABAKINA: You've turned up your nose lately; I wish you'd come visit me
sometime. [*They kiss*] Many happy returns, darling . . .

SASHA: Thank you. [*She sits down next to her father*]

LEBEDEV: Well, Avdotiya Nazarovna, suitable men nowadays are hard to come
by. Not to mention husbands, worthwhile best men are nowhere to
be found. I must say, I don't want to offend anyone, but young people

nowadays, God bless them, are all sourpusses—overcooked! They can't dance, can't talk; they don't even know how to drink right . . .

AVDOTIYA: Well, drink they are all happy to; just offer . . .

LEBEDEV: Anyone can drink—a horse can drink . . . But try drinking right! . . . In our time, we'd mess with lectures all day long, but as soon as the evening came, we'd head straight for the fire and keep it up till dawn . . . We'd dance, entertain the girls, and this too. [*With his hand cupped he tips it towards his mouth*[23]] We wagged our tongues about this and that and used to philosophize, too, until our tongues gave out . . . But nowadays the young people—[*Waves his hand*] I don't get it . . . Neither fish nor fowl. In the whole district there's just one worthwhile fellow, and he's already married [*Sighs*] and, it seems, he's started going crazy . . .

BABAKINA: Who's that?

LEBEDEV: Nikolasha Ivanov.

BABAKINA: Yes, he's a fine man, but so unhappy! [*Makes a face*]

ZINAIDA: How would you, my dear, expect him to be happy? [*She sighs*] The poor man, he made such a mistake! He married his Yid counting, poor soul, that her mother and father would give him mounds of gold, but it turned out just the opposite . . . The moment she converted, her parents disowned her, pronounced the curse upon her . . . And he didn't get even a kopeck. He regrets it now; only it's too late . . .

SASHA: Mama, that's not true.

BABAKINA: Sasha, dear, what do you mean it's not true? Everyone knows it. Why would he marry a Jew if there was nothing to be gained? Not enough Russian girls around? No, he's made a big mistake, my dear, he has . . . [*Lively*] And what she has to put up with now! It's a joke. He comes home and straight to her: "Your mother and father have duped me! Get out of my house!" But where can she go? Her mother and father won't take her back; she'd work as a maid, but she never learned to work . . . He nags her and nags her day and night until the count steps in. If it hadn't been for the count, he would have done her in a long time ago . . .

AVDOTIYA: And sometimes he shuts her up in the cellar and—"eat garlic, you so and so" . . . She eats and eats till it starts coming out of her.

Laughter.

SASHA: Papa, but that's a lie!

LEBEDEV: So what if it is? Let them talk rot if they want to . . . [*He calls loudly*] Gavril! . . .

Gavril brings him another glass of vodka and a glass of water.

ZINAIDA: That's why the poor man is broke. His affairs, my dear, are in a terrible shape. If it weren't for Borkin's keeping an eye on the estate, he and his Yid would have nothing to eat. [*Sighs*] And God alone knows how hard-hit we've been because of him! Would you believe, my dear, that for three years he's owed us nine thousand!

BABAKINA [*Horrified*]: Nine thousand! . . .

ZINAIDA: Yes. My Pashenka lent it to him. He doesn't know who you can lend money to and who you can't. I'm not even talking about the principal; if he'd only pay the interest on time! . . .

SASHA [*Emotionally*]: Mama, you've said this a thousand times before!

ZINAIDA: What's it to you? Why stick up for him?

SASHA: How do you have it in your heart to say these things about someone who hasn't done you any harm? Tell me, what's he done to you?

THIRD GUEST: Alexandra Pavlovna, allow me to say two words! I respect Nikolai Alexeyevich, and it's always been an honor, but, *entre nous*,[24] I think he's an opportunist.

SASHA: Congratulations—if that's what you think!

THIRD GUEST: As proof, I'll share with you a fact which has been related to me by his attaché or, so to speak, *cicerone*,[25] Borkin. Two years ago, in the midst of the anthrax epidemic, he bought a lot of cattle, took out an insurance policy on it . . .

ZINAIDA: Yes, yes, yes! I remember it. I heard about it from someone.

THIRD GUEST: He took out this insurance policy, and then, mind you, infected the cattle with the plague and collected on the insurance.

SASHA: Oh, that's just nonsense! Such nonsense! No one bought and infected any cattle! It was Borkin himself who came up with that idea and went around boasting about it. When Ivanov learned about it, Borkin spent two weeks begging forgiveness. He's guilty of not having the will to chase that Borkin away, and of trusting people too much! Everything he's ever owned has been pilfered from him, plundered, and anyone who has ever wanted to has already profited from his generosity.

LEBEDEV: Shura,²⁶ hothead! That's enough!

SASHA: Why are they talking nonsense? It's so boring and boring! Ivanov this, Ivanov that—you can't talk about anything else. [*She goes toward the door, then comes back*] I am amazed! [*To the young men*] I am amazed by your patience, ladies and gentlemen! Aren't you bored sitting here? The air is stiff with boredom! For heaven's sake, do something, entertain the girls, budge! Well, if you don't have a topic other than Ivanov, then try laughing, singing, or dancing at least . . .

LEBEDEV [*Laughing*]: Go ahead, give it to them!

SASHA: Well, listen, do me a favor! If you don't want to dance or sing or laugh; if that's so boring, then, please, I beg you, pull yourselves together, and if only just once in your life, say something for the fun of it; something witty and clever, say it even at the risk of sounding impolite or improper, as long as it's something funny and new! Or all together do something small, barely noticeable, something even barely heroic, so that the girls looking at you could all go "Ah!" Listen, you want them to like you, then why aren't you doing something to make them like you? Ladies and gentlemen! There's something not right with all of you, all of you, all of you! The flies are dropping dead from boredom looking at you, and the lamps are spewing smoke. You're not it, not it! . . . I've said it a thousand times and I'll continue saying that you're not it, not it, not it! . . .

IV

Same characters, Ivanov and Shabelsky.

SHABELSKY [*Coming in with Ivanov through the door on the right*]: Who's making a speech here? Is that you, Sasha, dear? [*He laughs and squeezes her hand*] Many happy returns, my angel! May God postpone your final hour and safeguard you from being born the second time . . .

ZINAIDA [*Joyfully*]: Nikolai Alexeyevich, Count!

LEBEDEV: Aha! Look who's here . . . Count!

SHABELSKY [*Seeing Zinaida and Marfa Babakina, he stretches his arms in their direction*]: Two banks on one couch! . . . A lovely sight! [*Greets Zinaida*] Hello, Ziuziushka! [*To Marfa Babakina*] Hello, sugarplum! . . .

ZINAIDA: I'm so glad, Count. You're such a rare guest! [*Calls*] Gavril, bring tea! Please, have a seat. [*She gets up and goes out through the door on the right but comes back right away and looks concerned. Sasha sits down in her previous place. Ivanov silently greets everyone.*]

LEBEDEV [*To Shabelsky*]: Where did you come from? What forces bring you here? A real surprise! Why, Count, you're a rascal! That's no way to behave! [*Leads him by the hand towards the front of the stage*] How come you don't come see us? Are you angry with us?

SHABELSKY: How can I get here? On a broomstick? I don't have my own horses, and Nikolai doesn't take me with him; he makes me stay home and keep Sarra company. Send the horses for me and I'll come . . .

LEBEDEV [*Waving his hand*]: Yes, sure! . . . My dear Ziuziushka would rather die than give me horses. My dear, dear old friend, you are closer and dearer to me anybody else! You and I are all that's left from the old guard! "In you I love the old torments and my old youth that's long been gone."[27] . . . Joking aside, but look at me, I'm almost crying. [*He kisses the count*]

SHABELSKY: Let go, let go! You reek like a wine cellar . . .

LEBEDEV: My dear, you can't imagine how bored I am here without my friends! I'm ready to hang myself from this hopelessness! [*Whispers*] Ziuziushka, with her moneylending, has chased away all decent company, and all we have now is these Zulus[28] . . . these Bobkins and Dobkins . . . Well, drink your tea . . .

Gavril serves the count his tea.

ZINAIDA [*Preoccupied, to Gavril*]: Why do you serve like that? You could bring out some jam . . . Gooseberry maybe . . .

SHABELSKY [*Laughing uproariously; to Ivanov*]: Didn't I tell you? [*To Lebedev*] I made a bet with him on the way here that as soon as we get here Ziuziushka would start offering us gooseberry jam . . .

ZINAIDA: You, Count, you're still the same mocker! [*She sits down*]

LEBEDEV: We made twenty vats of it; what are we going to do with it?

SHABELSKY [*Sits down near the table*]: Still saving, dear Ziuziushka? Well then, do you have an itty-bitty million yet?

ZINAIDA [*Sighing*]: From the outside, you'd think there's no one richer, but where's the money coming from? Idle talk, that's all . . .

SHABELSKY: Oh, sure! We all know that . . . We know how you don't know how to play a game of checkers[29] . . . [*To Lebedev*] Pasha, tell me honestly, have you saved up a million?

LEBEDEV: I don't know. Ask Ziuziushka . . .

SHABELSKY [*To Babakina*]: This fat little sugarplum here will soon have a million too! She's getting cuter and chubbier not by the day but by the hour! Which means there's lots of money . . .

BABAKINA: Much obliged to you, Your Excellency; only I don't like being made fun of.

SHABELSKY: My dear bank, who's making fun of you? It's just a wail of the soul, lips parting from excess of passion . . . My love for you and Ziuziushka is immense . . . [*Happily*] Sheer delight! A bliss! I can't look at either one of you with indifference . . .

ZINAIDA: Count, you're still the same as always. [*To Egorushka*] Egorushka, dear, put out the candles! Why waste candles if you aren't playing? [*Egorushka flinches; then he puts out the candles and sits down again. She turns to Ivanov*] How's the health of your spouse?

IVANOV: It's bad. The doctor said today that she for certain has consumption . . .

ZINAIDA: You don't say! Oh, what a shame! . . . [*She sighs*] And we all love her so much . . .

SHABELSKY: Such nonsense, just nonsense, sheer nonsense! She doesn't have consumption; it's all the doctor's ploys and quackery. The medic likes to hang around and so he comes up with consumption. It's a good thing the husband isn't jealous.

Ivanov waves his hand impatiently.

As for Sarra herself, I don't believe her single word or gesture. I've never in my life trusted doctors, lawyers, or women. That's all nonsense, sheer nonsense, the doctor's ploys and quackery!

LEBEDEV [*To Shabelsky*]: You are really something, Matvei! . . . Playing a misanthrope and fussing over it like a fool crazy over a new toy. You seem fine, but as soon as you open your mouth it's all bitter as if your tongue or your bowels were all twisted up . . .

SHABELSKY: What do you want me to do? Kiss up to all these crooks and scoundrels?

LEBEDEV: Where do you see crooks and scoundrels?

SHABELSKY: Present company excepted, of course, but . . .

LEBEDEV: That's some *but* . . . That's all for show.

SHABELSKY: For show . . . It's a good thing that you have no ideology.

LEBEDEV: What ideology? All I do is sit here waiting to kick the bucket any minute. That's my ideology. At our age, my dear, we don't have time to worry about ideology. There . . . [*He calls out*] Gavril!

SHABELSKY: You've already "gavriled" plenty . . . Look at your nose, it's all red!

LEBEDEV: That's all right, my friend, I'm not getting married today.

ZINAIDA: Doctor Lvov hasn't been to see us in a long time. He's forgotten us.

SASHA: My antipathy. Honesty personified. He can't ask for water or light a cigarette without first showing off his remarkable honesty. He could be walking or talking but "I'm an honest man" is writ large on his face! He's such a bore.

SHABELSKY: Narrow-minded, simple medico! [*Teasing*] "Make way for honest labor!" He shrieks like a parrot every step of the way and thinks that he's another Dobroliubov.[30] If you don't shriek, you're a scoundrel. A remarkably deep thinker! If a peasant is rich and lives a good life then he's a scoundrel and exploiter. I wear a velvet jacket and my valet dresses me—I'm a scoundrel and a proponent of serfdom. He's so honest, oh, so honest, he's bursting with honesty. He doesn't know what to do with himself. He scares me even . . . Yes, he does . . . He would, out of his sense of duty, punch you in the kisser and stab you in the back.

IVANOV: I'm exhausted dealing with him, but I find him sympathetic; he's got a lot of sincerity.

SHABELSKY: Some sincerity! Yesterday evening he comes up to me and out of nowhere blurts out: "Count, I find you deeply unsympathetic!" Thank you very much! And not just says it, but says it tendentiously: his voice quivers, his eyes burn, and he is shaking all over . . . To hell with this wooden sincerity! So he thinks I'm disgusting and repulsive; well, that's natural . . . I know it, but why say it to my face? I'm worthless, but still, no matter what, I have grey hair . . . This mindless, ruthless honesty!

LEBEDEV: All right, all right, all right! . . . You were young once yourself and you know how it is.

SHABELSKY: Yes, I was young and stupid, pretended to be Chatsky[31] in my time, denounced crooks and scoundrels, but I never called a thief a thief to his face, or talked about a rope in the house of the hanged. I was well brought up. But this stupid medico of yours would think himself at the top of his game and in seventh heaven if only he could get a chance to poke me in the ribs or punch me in the kisser, all on principle and for the sake of common humanistic ideals.

LEBEDEV: All young men are hard to handle. I had an uncle, a Hegelian . . . he would invite a house full of people, then after a few drinks, he would get up on a chair, like this, and start: "You're all ignorant! You are the forces of evil! The dawn of a new life!" Blah-blah-blah . . . And he'd keep on berating them, berating them . . .

SASHA: And the guests?

LEBEDEV: Nothing, really . . . They listen and keep on drinking. Once, though, I challenged him to a duel . . . imagine that, my own uncle. It was over Francis Bacon. I was sitting where Matvey is, if I remember correctly, and my uncle and the late Gerasim Nilych were standing over here, about where Nikolasha is . . . And then, my dear, Gerasim Nilych asks me a question . . .

Enter Borkin.

V

Same characters and Borkin. [Dressed like a dandy and carrying a package, Borkin comes in through the door on the right singing and bouncing. A murmur of approval.]

YOUNG LADIES: Mikhail Mikhailovich! . . .

LEBEDEV: *Michel Michelich!* Himself!

SHABELSKY: The life of the party!

BORKIN: Here I am! [*He runs up to Sasha*] Noble signorina, allow me to be so bold and wish the whole universe many happy returns on the birth of such an exquisite flower as yourself . . . As a token of my elation, allow me to offer you [*He hands her the package*] these fireworks and sparklers of my own manufacture. May they illuminate the night the same way you light up the shadows in the kingdom of darkness. [*He bows theatrically before her*]

SASHA: Thank you very much . . .

LEBEDEV [*Laughing uproariously, to Ivanov*]: Why do you still keep this Judas?

BORKIN [*To Lebedev*]: To Pavel Kirillych, sir! [*To Ivanov*] To my patron . . . [*Sings*] *Nicolas-voilà,* hey ho hey! [*He greets everybody in turn*] The most

estimable Zinaida Savishna! Oh, Divine Marfa Egorovna . . . The most
ancient Avdotiya Nazarovna . . . Your Highest Excellency, Count . . .

SHABELSKY [*Bursts out laughing*]: The life of the party . . . As soon as he came
in, the atmosphere got thinner. Have you noticed?

BORKIN: Whew! I'm exhausted . . . I think I've said hello to everyone. Well,
what's new, ladies and gentlemen? Anything knock-you-off-your-feet
juicy? [*Speaking quickly to Zinaida*] Oh, Mamasha, I have something
to tell you . . . On my way here . . . [*To Gavril*] Please, Gavriusha, bring
me some tea but no gooseberry jam! [*To Zinaida*] On the way here, I
saw, down by the riverbank, peasants stripping bark off of your willows.
Why not lease the willows?

LEBEDEV [*To Ivanov*]: Why do you still keep this Judas?

ZINAIDA [*Startled*]: You're right, I've never thought about that! . . .

BORKIN [*Flexing his fingers*]: I can't sit still . . . Mamasha, what should I come
up with next? Marfa Egorovna, I'm in such a good mood today. [*He
sings*] I'm exalted! "Once more I stand before you . . ."³²

ZINAIDA: Come up with something, because everybody's bored.

BORKIN: Ladies and gentlemen, why are you looking so down in the mouth;
sitting there like members of a jury! . . . Let's do something. What would
you like? Forfeits, hide-and-seek, tag, dancing, or the fireworks?

YOUNG LADIES [*Clapping their hands*]: Fireworks! Fireworks! [*They run out
into the garden*]

SASHA [*To Ivanov*]: Why do you look so bored today? . . .

IVANOV: I've got a headache, Shurochka, and I'm bored . . .

SASHA: Let's go into the drawing room.

*They go out through the door on the right; all the guests go out into the
garden with the exception of Zinaida and Lebedev.*

ZINAIDA: That's what I call—a young man: got here less than a minute ago
and has already cheered everyone up. [*Turns down the large lamp*]
While they're all in the garden, there's no reason to waste the candles.
[*She snuffs the candles*]

LEBEDEV [*Following her*]: Ziuziushka, we really ought to give our guests something to eat . . .

ZINAIDA: Look at all the candles; no wonder people are saying that we're so
rich. [*Snuffs candles*]

LEBEDEV [*Following her*]: Ziuziushka, why don't you give them something to eat; they are young and probably hungry by now, poor things . . . Ziuziushka . . .

ZINAIDA: The count didn't finish his tea. A waste of sugar. [*Goes out through the door on the left*]

LEBEDEV: Ugh! . . . [*Goes out to the garden*]

VI

Ivanov and Sasha.

SASHA [*Coming in with Ivanov through the door on the right*]: Everyone's out in the garden.

IVANOV: That's how it is, dear Sasha. I used to work hard and think hard, and never felt exhausted; now I don't do anything and don't think about anything, and I'm tired, body and soul. My conscience weighs on me day and night; I feel terribly guilty, but what it is I'm guilty of I don't know. And now, my wife's illness, lack of money, eternal backbiting, gossip, unwanted conversations, stupid Borkin . . . I loathe my house and living there's worse than torture for me. To be honest with you, even my wife's company has become unbearable, and she loves me. You and I are old friends, and you won't be upset at me for being honest. I came here to cheer up a bit, but I'm bored here too, and I long again to go home. Forgive me, but I'll slip out quietly.

SASHA: I understand you, Nikolai Alexeyevich. The trouble with you is that you're lonely. You need someone by your side, someone to love and someone who'd understand you. Only love can restore you.

IVANOV: What's next, Shurochka! The last thing the old wet rooster like me needs is a new love affair! May God save me from this misfortune! No, my clever girl, it's not about love. I swear to God that I can endure it all: this feeling hopeless, psychosis, financial ruin, loss of a wife, early onset of old age, and loneliness, but what I won't put up with is self-mockery. I'm dying of shame just thinking that a strong, healthy man like me has turned into either a Hamlet or a Manfred, or one of those superfluous people . . . who the hell knows! There're pathetic people who're flattered when others call them Hamlets or superfluous, but for me—it's humiliation! My pride rebels; the shame crushes me and I suffer . . .

SASHA [*Joking and through tears*]: Nikolai Alexeyevich, let's run away to America!

IVANOV: I'm too lazy to walk to the doorway, and you're saying America . . .

They walk over to exit into the garden.

Really, Shura, how hard it must be for you to live here! It frightens me to see the people around you: Whom will you marry? The only hope is that a student or a lieutenant passing through kidnaps you and takes you away . . .

VII

Zinaida [Enters through the door on the right holding a jar of jam].

IVANOV: I'm sorry, Shurochka, I'll catch up with you . . .

Sasha goes out into the garden.

Zinaida Savishna, I've a favor to ask you . . .

ZINAIDA: What is it, Nikolai Alexeyevich?

IVANOV [*Hesitatingly*]: You see, the thing is that the interest on the promissory note is due the day after tomorrow. I'd be much obliged if you could either grant me an extension or let me add the interest to the principal. I don't have any money right now . . .

ZINAIDA [*Frightened*]: Nikolai Alexeyevich, what are you talking about? What kind of business is this? No, no, don't even think about it, and for God's sake, don't torment a poor woman . . .

IVANOV: I'm sorry . . . I'm very sorry. [*He goes out into the garden*]

ZINAIDA: Phew, my goodness, he's made me so uneasy! I'm all trembling . . . all trembling . . . [*Goes out through the door on the right*]

VIII

KOSYKH [*Comes out of the door on the left and crosses the stage*]: In diamonds I had: the ace, king, queen, and a run of diamonds, the ace of spades, and one . . . one small heart, and she—God damn her—couldn't declare a little slam! [*Goes out the door on the right*]

IX

Avdotiya Nazarovna and the First Guest.

AVDOTIYA NAZAROVNA [*Coming out of the garden with First Guest*]: Ugh, I'm
    ready to tear her to pieces, this skinflint . . . I've been here since five
    o'clock and you think she'd offer a piece of rusty herring! . . . Oh, this
    house! . . . Oh, this household! . . .

FIRST GUEST: It's so boring here; I'm ready to start banging my head against
    the wall! Oh, my God, these people! Being this bored and hungry will
    make you howl like a wolf and prey on people.

AVDOTIYA: I'm ready to tear her to pieces, sinner that I am.

FIRST GUEST: I'll down a drink, grandma, and then I'm off—home! I don't
    need your marriageable girls. What's god damn love if we haven't had a
    drop since lunchtime.

AVDOTIYA: Let's go and look for some, maybe . . .

FIRST GUEST: Shh! Quiet! I think there's schnapps in the sideboard in the
    dining room. We'll put the screws to Egorushka . . . Shh!

    They go out through the door on the left.

X

Anna and Lvov [Enter through the door on the right].

ANNA: It's all right, they'll be happy to see us. There's no one here. They must
    all be out in the garden.

LVOV: Why in the world did you bring me here to these vultures? This is no
    place for you and me! Honest people should not be exposed to this
    atmosphere.

ANNA: Listen up, Mr. Honesty; when escorting a lady it's bad manners to talk
    to her about your own honesty the entire way! Maybe it's honest, but
    it's boring, to say the least. Never talk to women about your own vir-
    tues. Let them figure it out for themselves. My Nikolai, when he was like
    you, in the company of women he used to simply sing songs and tell tall
    tales, and yet every woman knew very well what kind of person he was.

LVOV: Oh, please, don't talk to me of your Nikolai; I understand him very well!

ANNA: You're a good man, but you don't understand anything. Let's go into
    the garden. He would never say: "I'm an honest man!" or "This atmo-
    sphere's suffocating. Vultures! Owls' nest! Crocodiles!" He'd leave the

menagerie alone, and if he was outraged by something, the most I ever heard him say would be: "Oh, I was so unreasonable today!" or "Aniuta, I feel so sorry for that man!" Like that, see; but you . . .

They go out.

XI

Avdotiya and First Guest.

FIRST GUEST [*Coming in through the door on the left*]: It's not in the dining room, so it must be in the pantry somewhere. We ought to sound out Egorushka. Let's go through the drawing room.

AVDOTIYA: I'm ready to tear her to pieces!

They go out through the door on the right.

XII

Babakina, Borkin, and Shabelsky. [Babakina and Borkin run in from the garden laughing. Shabelsky comes mincing behind them, laughing and rubbing his hands.]

BABAKINA: It's so boring! [*Bursts out laughing*] It's so boring! Everyone looks stiff as a poker! I'm bored stiff. [*She skips about*] I need to stretch my legs . . .

Borkin grabs her by the waist and kisses her on the cheek.

SHABELSKY [*Laughs and snaps his fingers*]: Damn it! [*Cackling*] In a way . . .

BABAKINA: Let go, let go of my hands; you're shameless! The count might think God knows what! Leave me alone! . . .

BORKIN: Angel of my soul, carbuncle of my heart! . . . [*Kisses her*] Lend me twenty-three hundred rubles! . . .

BABAKINA: No, no, no . . . As you wish, but when it comes to money—much obliged by you . . . No, no, no! . . . Oh, let go of my hands! . . .

SHABELSKY [*Mincing near them*]: Sugarplum . . . She has a certain appeal . . .

BORKIN [*In a serious tone*]: Well, that's enough. Let's discuss the deal. We'll talk frankly and businesslike. Give me a straight answer; none of those subtleties and none of your tricks: yes or no? Listen! [*Points to Shabelsky*] He needs money, a minimum of three thousand a year income. You need a husband. Do you want to be a countess?

SHABELSKY [*Laughing uproariously*]: An amazing cynic!

BORKIN: Do you want to be a countess? Yes or no?

BABAKINA [*All excited*]: The things you say, Misha, really . . . And you don't do these things off the top of your head . . . If the count wishes, he can himself, and . . . and—I don't know, I don't know how just like that, all of a sudden . . .

BORKIN: Come on, no need to cloud these things! It's a business deal . . . Yes or no?

SHABELSKY [*Laughing and rubbing his hands*]: Really, why not, huh? Damn it, should I do this vile thing, huh? Sugarplum . . . [*Kisses her on the cheek*] So lovely! . . . Fresh as a cucumber! . . .

BABAKINA: Wait, wait, you got me all emotional . . . Go away, go away! No— don't leave! . . .

BORKIN: Hurry! Yes or no? We have to go . . .

BABAKINA: You know what, Count, why don't you come stay with me for three days or so . . . We have fun at my house, not like here . . . Come over tomorrow . . . [*To Borkin*] No, is this a joke?

BORKIN [*Angry*]: Why joke when it's a serious matter?

BABAKINA: Wait! Wait . . . Oh, I feel faint! I feel faint! A countess! I feel faint! . . . I'm about to faint . . .

Borkin and the count are laughing as they take her arm in arm, and kissing her on the cheeks take her out through the door on the right.

XIII

Ivanov, Sasha, and later Anna Petrovna. [Ivanov and Sasha run in from the garden.]

IVANOV [*Clutches his head in desperation*]: It can't be! Shurochka, don't, don't! . . . Oh, please, don't! . . .

SASHA [*Passionately*]: I love you madly . . . My life has no meaning without you, no happiness or joy! You're everything to me . . .

IVANOV: Why? What for? My God, I don't understand anything . . . Dear Shurochka, please, don't! . . .

SASHA: When I was little, you used to be my only joy; I loved you and your soul like myself, and now . . . I love you, Nikolai Alexeyevich . . . I'd follow you to the ends of the earth, wherever you want; into the grave even; only, for God's sake, hurry, or I'll suffocate . . .

IVANOV [*Breaks into a fit of joyous laughter*]: So what is it then? It means to begin life anew? Does it, Shurochka? My joy! [*He draws her close to him*] My youth, my fresh beginning . . .

Anna comes in from the garden and upon seeing her husband and Sasha, stops completely petrified.

Back to life then? Yes? Back to my work?

A kiss. After the kiss, Ivanov and Sasha turn around and see Anna.

[*In horror*] Sarra!

Curtain.

ACT THREE

Ivanov's study. A desk littered with papers, books, official envelopes, knick-knacks, revolvers; next to the papers—a lamp, a decanter with vodka, a plate with pickled herring, pieces of bread, and cucumbers. On the walls—maps, paintings, rifles, pistols, sickles, whips, and so on. It's noontime.

I

Shabelsky, Lebedev, Borkin, and Pyotr. [Shabelsky and Lebedev sit at the opposite ends of the desk. Borkin straddles a chair in the middle of the room. Pyotr stands by the door.]

LEBEDEV: France's position is unambiguously clear . . . The French know what they want: they want to crack those Krauts, that's all, but Germany, my friend, sings a different tune. Germany has plenty of other thorns to worry about besides France . . .

SHABELSKY: Such nonsense! . . . I think that both Germany and France are cowards . . . They're just giving each other the finger in their pockets. Take my word for it, taunting each other is as far as they'll go. They'll never fight each other.

BORKIN: I say, why fight? Who needs military buildup, congresses, expenditures? You know what I would do? I'd collect all the dogs in the country, inoculate them with a good dose of Pasteur's venom,[33] and then let them loose in the enemy's territory. The enemy would be foaming at the mouth within a month.

LEBEDEV [*Laughing*]: The head looks small but it teems with grand ideas like the ocean with fish!

SHABELSKY: A virtuoso!

LEBEDEV: Come on, Michel Michelich, you are funny! [*After laughing*] Well, Jomini and Jomini, but not a word about vodka! *Repetatur!*[34] [*He fills up three shot glasses*] To our health . . .

> *They drink and eat.*

This sweet little herring here is the appetizer of all appetizers.

SHABELSKY: No, a cucumber's better . . . The scientists, since the creation of the world, have tried to but haven't come up with anything more clever than a pickled cucumber . . . [*To Pyotr*] Pyotr, go get some more and tell them in the kitchen to fry up four onion pies. And make sure they're hot.

> *Pyotr goes out.*

LEBEDEV: Caviar goes well with vodka, too. You know how? You have to know how . . . Take one quarter of pressed caviar, a couple of shallots, olive oil; mix it all together and top it off . . . you know, with a little lemon . . . To die for! The smell alone will knock you out.

BORKIN: Fried gudgeon[35] goes well with vodka, too. It's just that you need to know how to fry it. First you clean it, then dip it in bread crumbs, and fry till it's really dry, so that it's crunchy when you chew it—crunch, crunch, crunch . . .

SHABELSKY: The appetizer was good at Babakina's yesterday: porcini mushrooms.

LEBEDEV: Of course . . .

SHABELSKY: And they cooked it a special way, too. You know, with onion and bay leaf, and all kinds of spices. When they took off the lid, the steam, the smell . . . sheer ecstasy!

LEBEDEV: Well, then? *Repetatur*, gentlemen!

> *They drink.*

Here's to our health . . . [*He looks at his watch*] Looks like I'll have to leave before Nikolasha gets back. It's time for me to go. So you're saying they were serving mushrooms at Babakina's, but our mushrooms are not anywhere near ready. Tell me, Count, why the hell have you been going over to Marfutka's so much?

SHABELSKY [*Nodding at Borkin*]: He wants me to marry her . . .

LEBEDEV: To marry! . . . How old are you?

SHABELSKY: Sixty-two.

LEBEDEV: Just the age to get married. And Marfa's just right for you!

BORKIN: It's not about Marfa; it's about Marfa's pounds sterling.

LEBEDEV: So you're after Marfa's pounds sterling . . . Would you like a rooster's egg too?

BORKIN: Just wait, he'll get married and stuff his pockets, and then you'll see a rooster's egg, too. You'll be licking your chops . . .

SHABELSKY: Look, he took it seriously. The genius here thinks I'm going to listen to him and marry her . . .

BORKIN: Why not? Are you not sure now?

SHABELSKY: You're out of your mind . . . When was I ever sure? Ha! . . .

BORKIN: Thank you very much . . . Much obliged to you! So you want to let me down? I will marry, I won't marry . . . who the hell knows, and I gave her my word of honor already! So you will not marry her?

SHABELSKY [Shrugs his shoulders]: He took it seriously . . . He's amazing!

BORKIN [Indignant]: Then why muck up a decent woman? She's nuts over your title; can't eat or sleep . . . You think it's a joke? Is that fair?

SHABELSKY [Snaps his fingers]: Well, should I do this vile thing? Eh? To spite myself! I just might do it. Word of honor . . . What a hoot it'll be!

Enter Lvov.

II

LEBEDEV: We greet you, Aesculapius[36] . . . [He offers Lvov his hand and then sings] "Doctor, sir, please, save my soul, I'm scared to death to die!"[37]

LVOV: Has Nikolai Alexeyevich come back yet?

LEBEDEV: Not yet. I've been waiting for him for over an hour myself.

Lvov walks impatiently along the stage.

Well, my dear, and how's Anna Petrovna's health?

LVOV: It's bad.

LEBEDEV [Sighing]: May I go and pay my respects?

LVOV: No, please don't. I think she's sleeping . . .

A pause.

LEBEDEV: Such a nice, lovely woman . . . [Sighs] On Shurochka's birthday, when she fainted at our place, I took one look at her face and I knew that the poor woman didn't have long to live. I don't understand why she fainted that day. I run in and see her: all pale, lying on the floor, and Nikolasha, also pale kneeling beside her, Shurochka all in tears. After that, Shurochka and I walked around in a daze for a week.

SHABELSKY [*To Lvov*]: Tell me, most honorable high priest of science, which scholar discovered that ladies with a chest condition benefit from frequent visits by a young doctor? That's a remarkable discovery! Would you classify it as allopathic or homeopathic?

Lvov wants to respond, but makes a gesture showing disdain instead and walks away.

What a scathing look . . .

LEBEDEV: What's gotten into you to say these things! Why did you have to insult him?

SHABELSKY [*Irritated*]: Why does he have to lie? Consumption, no hope, she's dying . . . He's lying! I can't stand it!

LEBEDEV: What makes you think he's lying?

SHABELSKY [*Gets up and starts pacing*]: I can't believe that a person could just suddenly die. Let's not talk about it!

III

KOSYKH [*Runs in panting*]: Is Nikolai Alexeyevich home? Hello! Is he home? [*Shakes hands quickly with everyone*]

BORKIN: No, he isn't.

KOSYKH [*Sits down and jumps up again*]: In that case good-bye! [*He drinks a shot of vodka and eats something quickly*] I must be going . . . Business, you know. I'm tired out . . . I can barely stand up straight . . .

LEBEDEV: Where are you hailing from?

KOSYKH: From Barabanov's. We bridged all night; just finished . . . I lost my shirt . . . That Barabanov's lousy at cards. [*In a tearful voice*] Listen to this: I'm playing hearts . . . [*Turning to Borkin, who jumps away from him*] He plays a diamond, and I'm playing a heart, he plays a diamond . . . And so, not a single trick. [*To Lebedev*] We're playing out four clubs. I have the ace, the queen on hand, the ace, and ten of spades . . .

LEBEDEV [*Stopping up his ears*]: Spare me, for Christ's sake, please, spare me!

KOSYKH [*To Shabelsky*]: You see . . . I had the ace, the queen of clubs, the ace, and a ten of spades . . .

SHABELSKY [*Pushes him away with his hands*]: Go, I don't want to hear this!

KOSYKH: And all of a sudden—a disaster: the ace of spades gets trumped in the first round.

SHABELSKY [*Grabbing a revolver*]: Move away or I'll shoot! . . .

KOSYKH [*Waving his hands*]: Damn . . . Not a single person to talk to . . . living here like in Australia or something: no common interests, no camaraderie . . . Everyone for himself . . . Well, I must be going . . . it's time . . . [*Grabs his cap*] Time is precious . . . [*He offers his hand to Lebedev*] I pass! . . .

Laughter. Kosykh walks out and in the doorway bumps into Avdotiya Nazarovna.

IV

AVDOTIYA [*Shrieks*]: You damn near knocked me down!

EVERYBODY: A-a-ahh! The ubiquitous!

AVDOTIYA: That's where you are, and I have been looking for them all over the house. Hello to you, my boys, my falcons! Greetings, welcome . . . [*Greets everyone*]

LEBEDEV: Why did you come here?

AVDOTIYA: On a special matter, my dear. [*To the count*] A matter concerning Your Excellency. [*She bows to the count*] I am supposed to pay respects and to inquire after your health . . . And my little doll's asked me to tell you that if you don't come to see her by this evening, she'll cry her eyes out. She says, dear, take him aside and whisper it in his ear in secret. But why in secret? We're all friends here. And we're not stealing chickens; it's by law and love, and civil consent. And although I never drink, on this occasion, sinner that I am, I'll have a drink!

LEBEDEV: And I will too. [*Filling the shot glasses with vodka*] You wear well, you old magpie! I've known you as an old woman for about thirty years now . . .

AVDOTIYA: I've stopped counting . . . buried two husbands, and would marry a third, but no one wants to take me without a dowry. I had eight children or so . . . [*She takes a shot glass*] Well, with God's help, we started a good thing here, and with God's help we'll finish it right! They'll live in happiness and we'll look at them and be merry. Peace and happiness to them . . . [*She drinks*] This vodka's strong!

SHABELSKY [*Laughing loudly, to Lebedev*]: The oddest thing about it is that they really think that I'm ... It's amazing! [*Gets up*] Wait, Pasha, should I do this vile thing? To spite myself ... Just like—here, eat that, you old dog! Pasha, eh?

LEBEDEV: It's all empty talk, Count. You and I need to think about kicking the bucket. Marfutkas and the pound sterling passed us by a long time ago ... Our time's over.

SHABELSKY: No, I'll do it! Word of honor I will!

Enter Ivanov and Lvov.

V

LVOV: All I'm asking you is to give me five minutes.

LEBEDEV: Nikolasha! [*He walks towards Ivanov and kisses him*] Hello, my friend ... I've been waiting for you for a whole hour.

AVDOTIYA [*Bows*]: Hello, dear Sir!

IVANOV [*Bitterly*]: Gentlemen, you've turned my library into a pub again! I've asked each and every one of you a thousand times not to do that! [*He walks up to the table*] There, you even spilled vodka on the papers ... crumbs ... cucumbers ... It's disgusting!

LEBEDEV: I'm sorry, Nikolasha, I'm sorry ... Forgive me. I have to talk to you, my friend, about one especially important matter ...

BORKIN: And I do too.

LVOV: Nikolai Alexeyevich, may I have a word with you?

IVANOV [*Pointing to Lebedev*]: He, too, wants me. I'll get to you next ... [*To Lebedev*] Well, what is it?

LEBEDEV: Gentlemen, it's confidential. Kindly ...

Shabelsky goes out with Avdotiya, followed by Borkin, and then Lvov.

IVANOV: Pasha, you may drink as much as you want, it's your illness, but please don't turn my uncle into an alcoholic. He didn't use to drink. It's bad for him.

LEBEDEV [*Frightened*]: My dear boy, I didn't know ... I didn't even think about it ...

IVANOV: God forbid, if this old child dies, it's not you but me who is going to be worse off ... Now, what is it?

A pause.

LEBEDEV: You see, my dear friend . . . I don't know how to begin so that it doesn't come out so heartless. Nikolasha, my heart aches, I'm blushing, I'm mumbling, but my dear boy, put yourself in my shoes; you see, I'm a slave, a Negro, spineless . . . Forgive me . . .

IVANOV: What is it?

LEBEDEV: My wife's sent me . . . Do me a favor, please pay her the interest! You see, she won't stop badgering, baiting, and berating me! Get her off your back for God's sake!

IVANOV: Pasha, you know that I don't have the money now.

LEBEDEV: I know, but what can I do? She doesn't want to wait. If she takes you to court, how will Shurochka and I ever face you again?

IVANOV: My own heart aches, Pasha, and I wish I could sink into the ground, but . . . but where can I get it? Teach me: where? There's only one thing left for me to do: wait till the fall when I sell my wheat.

LEBEDEV [Screams]: She doesn't want to wait!

A pause.

IVANOV: Your situation's unpleasant, delicate, but mine is even worse. [He paces while thinking] And there's nothing I can do . . . There's nothing to sell . . .

LEBEDEV: Go to Milbach[38] and ask him; he owes you sixteen thousand.

Ivanov makes a hopeless gesture with his hand.

You know, Nikolasha . . . I know you'll get angry with me, but . . . do it out of respect for the old drunk! As a friend . . . Look at me as a friend . . . We were both students once, liberals . . . We share interests and ideals . . . We both studied at Moscow University . . . Alma mater . . . [He takes out his wallet] Here's my secret stash; at home not a soul knows about it. Take it as a loan . . . [He takes out the money and puts it on the table] Forget the pride; look at it as a friend . . . I'd borrow money from you, word of honor I would . . .

A pause.

There's the money on the table: eleven hundred. Go see her today and hand it to her yourself. "Here you go, Zinaida Savishna, may you choke on it!" Only, watch out, for God's sake, don't let anyone know that you borrowed it from me! If not, that gooseberry jam of mine will make mincemeat out of me! [He looks intently at Ivanov's face] All right, all right, don't. [*He quickly takes the money from the table and hides it in his pocket*] Don't! It was a joke . . . Forgive me for Christ's sake!

A pause.

Feeling crummy, huh?

Ivanov waves his hand.

Well, what are you going to do? . . . [*He sighs*] It's your time of bitterness and sorrow. A person, my dear, is the same as a samovar: it doesn't always sit cold on a shelf; sometimes when you put hot coals inside, it goes—pshh . . . pshh! It's a damn stupid comparison, but I can't think of a better one . . . [*Sighs*] Hard times temper the soul. I don't pity you, Nikolasha, you'll get out of this scrape; it's a grind, but you'll have flour in the end. Still, it's a shame and it bothers me to hear others talk . . . Tell me, where in the world do these rumors come from! There's so much gossip about you in town that you'd think the prosecutor's on his way to pay you a visit . . . They're saying you're a killer, a robber, and a bloodsucker . . .

IVANOV: That's nothing, but my head hurts though.

LEBEDEV: It's all because you think too much.

IVANOV: I think nothing at all.

LEBEDEV: Nikolasha, just forget about it and come see us. Shurochka loves you, understands and appreciates you. She's a good and honest person. Not after me or her mother, she takes after somebody other . . . Sometimes I look at her, and I can't believe that a fat-nosed drunk like me could have such a treasure. Go, talk to her about intelligent things and—you'll cheer up. She's a loyal and sincere person . . .

A pause.

IVANOV: Pasha, dear, please, leave me alone . . .

LEBEDEV: I understand, I understand . . . [*Glances hurriedly at his watch*] Yes, I see. [*Kisses Ivanov*] Good-bye. I still have to make it to a school consecration. [*He walks towards the door, and then stops*] She's intelligent . . . Yesterday, Shurochka and I were talking about gossip. [*He laughs*] And she fired off an aphorism: "Papa, fireflies," she said, "shine at night only to make it easier for the night birds to see and feed on them, and good people exist in order to give gossip and slander something to feed on." How do you like that? A genius! George Sand! . . .

IVANOV [*Stopping him*]: Pasha! What's happening to me?

LEBEDEV: I wanted to ask you that myself, but, I confess, I was embarrassed. I don't know, my friend! On the one hand, I thought that the scrape you're in has gotten the better of you, but on the other hand, I know you are not the kind to . . . you know . . . You don't give in to troubles. It's something else, Nikolasha, but what exactly—I don't know!

IVANOV: I don't understand myself. It seems . . . but on the other hand, no!

A pause.

You see, what I wanted to say is this. I had a worker once, Semyon, you remember him. Once, at threshing-time, he decided to show off his strength before the girls, and he heaved two sacks of rye on his back, and something snapped. He died soon thereafter. I think something snapped in me, too. High school, university, then the house, elementary schools, and those projects . . . I didn't believe in God like everyone else and I didn't marry like everyone else, I got excited and I took risks; my money, you know yourself, I threw it right and left; I was happy and suffered like no one else in this district. All this, Pasha, is my sacks of rye . . . I heaved them on my back, and my back cracked. At twenty, we're all heroes; we take up anything; and by thirty, we become exhausted and useless. How do you explain this exhaustion? Though maybe that's not it . . . ! Not it, not it! . . . Go, Pasha, God bless, you must be fed up with me.

LEBEDEV [*Lively*]: You know what? The milieu is getting to you, my friend!

IVANOV: It's stupid and stale, Pasha. Go!

LEBEDEV: That's true, it's stupid. I see now myself that it's stupid. I'm going, I'm going . . . [*He goes out*]

VI

IVANOV [*Alone*]: A worthless, pitiful, and bad person is what I am. You have to be pitiful, worn out and a wino like Pasha to love and respect me. My God, how I despise myself! How deeply I detest my own voice, my footsteps, my hands, these clothes, my thoughts. Isn't it ridiculous, isn't it a crying shame? Less than a year ago I was still strong and healthy, full of energy, tireless, and excited; I worked with these same two hands, and when I spoke I moved even the ignorant ones to tears, I cried when I saw suffering, I grew indignant when I encountered evil. I knew what inspiration was; I understood the beauty and poetry of quiet nights when you sit at your desk working day and night, letting dreams take over. I believed in God, I looked to the future like into my mother's eyes . . . And now, oh my God! I'm exhausted, I don't have faith, and I spend days and nights doing nothing. My brain, my feet, my hands don't obey me. The estate is going to the dogs, the trees are falling under the axe. [*Cries*] My land looks at me like an orphan. I expect nothing, I pity nothing; my heart trembles at the thought of tomorrow . . . And this story with Sarra? I promised her eternal love, prophesied happiness, and promised a future the likes of which she never even dreamed of. She believed me. For five years now, I've only been watching her withering under the weight of her sacrifices, losing the battle with her conscience; but God knows, not a single look or word of reproach! And so? I fell out of love with her . . . How? Why? What for? I don't know. Here, she's suffering; her days are numbered; and I, like the worst coward, run away from her pale face, her sunken chest, her pleading eyes . . . It's shameful, just shameful!

A pause.

Sasha, a young girl, is touched by my misfortunes. She tells me, practically an old man, that she loves me, and I lose my head, forget about everything in the world, and as if enchanted by music, shout: "New life! My joy!" But the next day I believe in this new life and joy as little as I believe in house spirits . . . What's wrong with me? What abyss am I pushing myself into? Where did this weakness come from? What's become of my nerves? As soon as my sick wife does something that wounds my pride, or a servant doesn't do something to my liking, or my gun misfires—I lose my temper, become rude, and completely unlike myself . . .

A pause.

I don't, I don't understand, I don't understand it! I'll put a bullet through my head! . . .

Enter Lvov.

LVOV: I need to talk to you, Nikolai Alexeyevich!

IVANOV: I don't have the stamina to have these talks every day.

LVOV. Are you willing to listen to me?

IVANOV: I listen to you every day and to this day I still don't understand: what is it you want from me?

LVOV: I'm speaking clearly and unequivocally, and only someone without a heart would have trouble understanding me . . .

IVANOV: My wife's dying—I know that; I'm irreparably guilty before her—I know that as well; I also know that you're honest and direct. What more do you need?

LVOV: I'm outraged by human cruelty . . . A woman is dying. She has a mother and father whom she loves, and she'd like to see them before she dies; they know very well that she's dying and that she still loves them, but that damn cruelty; it's as if they want to shock everyone with their religious zeal; they still curse her! You're the person she has sacrificed everything for—her family nest, her conscience, and you for obvious reasons and in the open go gallivanting to the Lebedevs' every evening!

IVANOV: Oh, I haven't been there for two weeks . . .

LVOV [Not listening to him]: With people like you, you have to speak directly, not in the roundabout way, and if you don't wish to hear what I have to say, then don't listen! I call things as I see them . . . You need her death for new heroic feats; fine, but can't you wait? If you only let her die peacefully without chipping away at her with your open cynicism, do you think that Miss Lebedev with her dowry would leave you? If not now, then in a year or two, you, my amazing Tartuffe, you could turn the girl's head and take over her dowry just the same as now . . . What's the hurry? Why do you need your wife to die now and not in a month or in a year?

IVANOV: This is torture . . . You're a very bad doctor if you think that a person can control himself ad infinitum. It takes a great deal of effort on my part not to respond to your insults.

LVOV: Come on! Who are you trying to fool? Take off your mask.

IVANOV: Wise man, think about it: you think that it's so easy to understand me! Don't you? I married Anna to get a large dowry . . . They didn't give me the dowry, I missed the mark, and now I'm trying to do her in so that I could marry another one and take her dowry . . . It's so simple and easy . . . Isn't it? The man is a simple and uncomplicated machine . . . No, doctor, inside each one of us there are far too many wheels, bolts, and valves to be able to judge each other based on first impression or by two or three external traits. I don't understand you, you don't understand me, and we don't understand ourselves. One can be an excellent doctor—and at the same time not know people at all. Don't be so sure of yourself, and admit it.

LVOV: Do you really think that you're not transparent enough for me to see right through you and that I lack the smarts to tell the difference between honesty and dishonesty?

IVANOV: Obviously, we'll never see eye to eye . . . I'm asking you for the last time; please, answer me without prefacing it: what exactly do you want from me? What are you after? [*Irritated*] And whom do I have the honor of addressing: my prosecutor or my wife's doctor?

LVOV: I'm a doctor, and as a doctor I demand that you change your behavior . . . It's killing Anna Petrovna!

IVANOV: But what am I to do? What? If you understand me better than I understand myself, then tell me unequivocally: what am I to do?

LVOV: At least, don't be so open in your actions.

IVANOV: Oh, my God! Do you really understand yourself? [*He drinks water*] Leave me alone. I'm to blame a thousand times over; I'll answer before God; but no one's given you the right to torture me every day . . .

LVOV: And who's given you the right to insult my truth in me? You've tortured and poisoned my soul. Before I came to this town, I knew that there were crazy and stupid people who got infatuated easily, but I never thought that there would be people deliberately criminal, intentionally guiding their will in the direction of evil . . . I used to respect and love people, but when I saw you . . .

IVANOV: I've heard it before!

LVOV: Have you? [*Upon seeing Sasha, who comes in dressed in a riding habit*] Now, I hope, we finally understand each other very well! [*Shrugs his shoulders and leaves*]

VII

IVANOV [*Shocked*]: Shura, you?[39]

SASHA: Yes, me. Hello. You weren't expecting me? Why haven't you been to see us for so long?

IVANOV: Shura, for God's sake, it's not prudent! Your visit may have a terrible effect on my wife!

SASHA: She won't see me. I came in through the back entrance. And I'm leaving. I'm worried: are you well? Why haven't you come to see us in so long?

IVANOV: My wife's already been insulted; she's practically dying, and you're coming here. Shura, Shura, it's insensitive and cruel of you!

SASHA: What was I to do? You haven't been to see us in two weeks, haven't replied to my letters. I'm worn out. I thought that you might be ill or suffering unbearably here, or dead. I haven't had a single good night's sleep . . . I'm leaving . . . At least tell me: are you well?

IVANOV: No, I'm not; I'm tormenting myself and everyone's tormenting me without end . . . I can't do it anymore! And now you're here! It's so unhealthy, so insane! Shura, it's all my fault, my fault!

SASHA: You're so fond of using these pitiful and awful words! It's your fault? Is it? Yours? Then tell me exactly what it is.

IVANOV: I don't know, I don't know . . .

SASHA: That's not an answer. Every sinner must know what his sin is. Have you been maybe forging banknotes?

IVANOV: That's not funny!

SASHA: Is it your fault that you fell out of love with your wife? Perhaps, but a person can't control his feelings, you didn't want to fall out of love with her. Is it your fault that she saw me when I declared my love for you? No, you didn't want her to see that . . .

IVANOV [*Interrupting her*]: And so on, and so forth . . . Fell in love, fell out of love, lost control of his feelings—these are all commonplaces, clichés . . . they won't help . . .

SASHA: Talking to you is exhausting. [*She looks at a painting*] The dog's painted so well! Was it from life?

IVANOV: From life. And this love affair of ours—so trite and clichéd: He lost his heart and his footing. She appeared strong and cheerful and offered him a helping hand. It's all pretty and resembles the truth in novels only, but in real life . . .

SASHA: It's the same in real life, too.

IVANOV: Oh, I see your fine understanding of life! My whining instills religious awe in you, you think that you've found the second Hamlet in me; but I think that my psychosis with all its trimmings is good material for a laugh, that's all! One should be doubled over laughing looking at my contortions here, but instead you're screaming—help! Save someone, perform a feat. Oh, I'm so angry with myself today! I can sense that this tension I'm feeling today will get resolved somehow . . . I'm either going to break something or . . .

SASHA: That's exactly what you need. Break something, smash it, or scream. You're upset with me, it was stupid of me to come here. Well then, show your indignation, yell at me, stomp your feet. Well? Start getting upset . . .

A pause.

Well?

IVANOV: You're a funny one!

SASHA: Excellent. It looks like we're smiling! Kindly deign to smile one more time!

IVANOV [*Laughing*]: I've noticed: when you start saving me and talking sense into me, you get this most naïve look on your face, and the pupils get so big as if you're watching a comet. Wait, there's dust on your shoulder. [*He brushes dust off her shoulder*] A naïve man is a fool. But you women, you know how to act naïve in a way that actually comes across as sweet and gentle, and nice, and not as stupid as you might think. Only why do you all do the same thing? As long as a man is healthy, strong, and happy, you pay no attention to him; but as soon as he starts rolling downhill and starts telling a tale of woes, you throw yourselves at him! Is it any worse to be a wife to a strong and brave man than to be a sick-nurse to some tear-jerking failure of a man?

SASHA: It's worse!

IVANOV: But why? [*Laughing uproariously*] Darwin doesn't know about it; otherwise, he'd make mincemeat out of you! You're ruining the human race. Pretty soon, thanks to you, only whiners and lunatics will be born into this world.

SASHA: There're a lot of things men don't understand. Any young woman would prefer a failure to a success because she's seduced by active love . . . Do you understand? Active. Men are busy with work and for them love is always in the background. To talk to her, to take a walk with her in the garden, to have a good time, shed a tear at her grave—that's all. For us, love is life. I love you; and that means that I dream of finding a cure for your feeling hopeless, and how I'm going to follow you to the ends of the earth . . . You're on top of the world and so am I; you're in the dumps and so am I. For me, the greatest happiness would be to spend all night copying your papers, or guarding your sleep, or walk with you hundreds of miles. I remember, three years ago, during harvest time, you came by all covered in dust, sunburned and worn out, and asked for a drink of water. I brought you a glass, but you had already fallen dead asleep on the couch. You slept twelve hours, and all that time I stood guard at the door so no one would come in. And I was so happy! The more work it takes, the better the love, or, you see, the stronger you feel it.

IVANOV: Active love . . . Hmm . . . it's a wasting disease, schoolgirl philosophy; or maybe that's the way it's supposed to be . . . [*Shrugs his shoulders*] Who the hell knows! [*Cheerfully*] Shura, I swear, I'm a decent person! . . . Judge for yourself, I've always liked to philosophize, but I'd never ever say: "Our women are depraved," or "a woman has taken a wrong turn." I was only grateful, that's all! Yes, that's all! My dear girl, you're so funny! And I'm a silly blockhead! Making good Christians uneasy day and night with my tales of woe. [*He laughs*] Boohoo! Boohoo! [*Moves away quickly*] But you must go, Sasha! We lost track of time . . .

SASHA: Yes, it's time to go. Good-bye! I don't want your honest doctor, out of his sense of duty, to report to Anna Petrovna that I was here. Listen to me: go to your wife and stay, just stay there . . . If you have to stay a year, then stay a year. Ten years—then stay ten years. Do your duty. Grieve with her and beg forgiveness, and cry—all this is how it's supposed to be. And the main thing—don't neglect your work.

IVANOV: Once again, I feel like I've stuffed myself on a poisonous mushroom. Again!

SASHA: Well, God bless you! Don't even think about me! If in two weeks you drop me a line—I'll be grateful. But I'll keep writing to you . . .

Borkin sticks his head in the door.

VIII

BORKIN: May I, Nikolai Alexeyevich? [*Upon seeing Sasha*] I'm sorry, I didn't see you . . . [*Comes in*] Bonzhoor! [*He takes a bow*]

SASHA [*Embarrassed*]: Hello . . .

BORKIN: You've gained a little weight and added to your looks.

SASHA [*To Ivanov*]: So I'm going, Nikolai Alexeyevich. I'm going. [*She goes out*]

BORKIN: A wondrous vision! I came looking for prose and stumbled on poetry . . . [*Sings*] "You appeared to me like a bird to the light . . ."[40]

Ivanov, agitated, paces up and down the stage.

[*Sits down*] She does, *Nicolas*, have that something or other that the others don't. Wouldn't you agree? Something unusual . . . something phantasmagorical . . . [*He sighs*] Come to think of it, she's the richest bride in town, but her mother is such a battle-axe that no one will want to get involved. After she dies, however, everything will be Shurochka's, but until then, she'll give her about ten thousand, a curler and an iron, and will demand eternal gratitude. [*He fumbles in his pockets*] I'll have one *de los makhores.*[41] Would you care for some? [*He offers his cigar case*] They are good . . . Quite smokable.

IVANOV [*Enraged, comes up to Borkin*]: Get out of my house this instant! This instant!

Borkin starts getting up and drops the cigar.

Get out this instant!

BORKIN: *Nicolas*, what does this mean? Why are you upset?

IVANOV: Why? Where did you get these cigars? You think that I don't know why and where you take the old man every day?

BORKIN [*Shrugs his shoulders*]: What do you care?

IVANOV: A scoundrel is what you are! These dastardly schemes of yours that you have been blabbing around town have made me dishonest in everyone's eyes. We have nothing in common, and I'm asking you to leave my house immediately! [*Paces quickly*]

BORKIN: I know that you're irritated and that's why I'm not upset with you. Insult me all you want . . . [*He picks up his cigar*] But it's time to quit this melancholy. You're not a schoolboy anymore . . .

IVANOV: What did I just tell you? [*Shaking*] Are you toying with me?

Enter Anna Petrovna.

IX

BORKIN: See, Anna Petrovna's here . . . I'm leaving. [*He leaves*]

Ivanov stops near the table and stands there with his head hanging low.

ANNA [*After a pause*]: Why was she here?

A pause.

I'm asking you: Why was she here?

IVANOV: Don't ask me, Aniuta . . .

> *A pause.*

I'm deeply sorry. You can punish me all you want; I'll bear it all, but . . . don't ask me . . . I have no strength to talk.

ANNA [*Angrily*]: Why did she come here?

> *A pause.*

Oh, so that's how you are! Now I understand you. Finally, I can see the kind of person you are. Dishonest and low . . . Do you remember you came and lied that you loved me . . . I believed you, left my mother and father, my faith, and followed you . . . You lied to me about truth and goodness, and about your honest plans, and I believed your every word . . .

IVANOV: I never lied to you, Aniuta . . .

ANNA: I lived with you five years, pining away and getting ill, but I loved you and never left you for one minute . . . You were my idol . . . And now? All this time you have been openly deceiving me . . .

IVANOV: Aniuta, don't say something that's not true. I've made mistakes, but I've never lied to you, not once . . . You've no right to reproach me for that . . .

ANNA: Now I understand everything . . . You married me thinking that my mother and father would forgive me and give me money . . . That's what you thought . . .

IVANOV: Oh, my God! Aniuta, you're trying my patience . . . [*Crying*]

ANNA: Be quiet! As soon as you saw that there was no money, you changed your game . . . Now I remember everything and I understand. [*She cries*] You never loved me; you've never been faithful to me . . . Never! . . .

IVANOV: Sarra, that's a lie! . . . You can say whatever you want, but don't insult me with a lie . . .

ANNA: A dishonest and low person—that's what you are . . . You owe Lebedev money and now, to wiggle out of paying back the debt, you want to turn his daughter's head and deceive her just like you once deceived me. Isn't that true?

IVANOV [*Panting*]: For God's sake, stop it! I can't control myself . . . I'm choking with ire and I . . . I may insult you . . .

ANNA: You've always lied shamelessly, and not only to me . . . Always blaming Borkin for your dishonest actions, but now I know who's behind them . . .

IVANOV: Stop it, Sarra, go away, I'm burning to say something dreadful! I'm itching to say something dreadfully insulting . . . [*He yells*] Stop it, you Yid! . . .

ANNA: I won't stop . . . You've been lying to me too long to stop now . . .

IVANOV: So you won't stop? [*He struggles with himself*] For God's sake . . .

ANNA: Go and deceive that Lebedev girl now . . .

IVANOV: Then know that you . . . are dying . . . The doctor's told me that you're dying . . .

ANNA [*Sits down and speaks in a crestfallen voice*]: When did he say that?

A pause.

IVANOV [*Clutching his head*]: It's all my fault! Oh, my God, it's all my fault! [*He sobs*]

Curtain.

About a year has elapsed between the third and fourth acts.

ACT FOUR

One of the drawing rooms at the Lebedevs' house. In the front—an arch separating a drawing room from the reception room; to the right and left— doors. Antique bronzes and family portraits. The décor is festive. A piano; on top of the piano—a violin; a cello stands nearby. During the entire act, guests walk about in the reception room dressed in formal evening dress.

I

LVOV [*Enters and looks at his watch*]: It's after four. The blessing is about to begin . . . They'll give the blessing and then take them to get married. So that's the triumph of truth and virtue! He didn't succeed in robbing Sarra, so he tortured her and drove her into the grave, and now he's found another one. He'll wear a double face before this one until he robs her, and once he robs her, he'll drive her into the same place as poor Sarra. That's an old kulak story . . . [42]

A pause.

He's in seventh heaven with happiness, and will live to a ripe old age, and will die with a clear conscience. No, I'll smoke you out! When I rip that damn mask off of you and when everyone finds out just what you really are, you'll plunge from seventh heaven headfirst into a pit so deep that the devil himself won't be able to drag you back out! I'm an honest man and my job is to stand up and help the blind see. I finish my duty and tomorrow I'm leaving this damn town! [*Thinks*] But how to do it? Talking to the Lebedevs is pointless. Challenge him to a duel? Create a scandal? My God, I'm nervous like a boy and I've lost the ability to think. What am I to do? A duel?

II

KOSYKH [*Comes in; joyfully to Lvov*]: Yesterday I declared a little slam in clubs, and made a grand slam! But this Barabanov spoiled my tune again! We're playing. I say: "No trumps." He—pass. Two of clubs. He again—pass. Two of diamonds . . . three of clubs . . . and, can you imagine: I declare a slam, and he's not showing me his ace. Had the rascal showed me the ace, I would've declared a grand slam with no trumps . . .

LVOV: Forgive me, I don't play cards and for that reason am unable to share your enthusiasm. Is the blessing soon?

KOSYKH: Must be soon. They're bringing Ziuziushka back to her senses. She's screaming her head off, doesn't want to let go of the dowry.

LVOV: Not the daughter?

KOSYKH: No, the dowry. And she feels bad. Once they're married, he won't have to pay back his debt. You can't take your son-in-law to court.

III

BABAKINA [*Dressed in all her finery, struts across the stage past Lvov and Kosykh, who snorts into his fist. Marfa turns around*]: So stupid!

Kosykh touches her waist with his finger and burts out laughing.

Peasant! [*She walks out*]

KOSYKH [*Bursts out laughing*]: That broad is off her rocker! Before worming her way to "Her Excellency," she was a broad like any other; now you can't come near her! [*Mockingly*] "Peasant!"

LVOV [*Agitated*]: Listen, tell me, truthfully, what's your opinion of Ivanov?

KOSYKH: He's useless. Lousy at cards. Last year at Lent, we sit down to play: myself, the count, Borkin, and him. I deal the cards . . .

LVOV [*Interrupting*]: Is he a good person?

KOSYKH: Him? That wheeler-dealer! That weasel, he's been to hell and back.
He and the count are tight as thieves and good at sniffing out what no
one's keeping an eye on. He ran into trouble with that Yid; had his hope
dashed, and now he's stealing up to Ziuziushka's coffers. I'll bet you
anything, and may I be anathema three times if within a year he doesn't
put Ziuziushka in the poorhouse. He—Ziuziushka, and the count—
Babakina. They'll take the money and live in a pot of honey. Doctor,
why are you so pale today? You look terrible.

LVOV: Oh, it's all right. I had a little too much to drink yesterday.

IV

LEBEDEV [*Entering with Sasha*]: We'll talk here. [*To Lvov and Kosykh*] Zulus,
go with the girls to the reception room. We need to talk in private.

KOSYKH [*Walking by Sasha, he snaps his fingers enthusiastically*] Pretty as a
picture! A trump queen!

LEBEDEV: Keep walking, you caveman; keep walking!

Kosykh and Lvov go out.

Sit down, Shurochka, dear, like this . . . [*He sits down and looks around*]:
Listen carefully and with all due respect. The thing is this: your mother's
making me tell you this . . . You understand? I'm not speaking for myself
but your mother's making me do it.

SASHA: Papa, make it short!

LEBEDEV: You are to get a dowry of fifteen thousand rubles in silver . . . Here . . .
I don't want any discussion about it later! Wait! Be quiet! That's just a
taste of what's to come. Your dowry's fifteen thousand, but considering
that Nikolai Alexeyevich owes your mother nine thousand, it is sub-
tracted from your dowry . . . Well, and then also . . .

SASHA: Why are you telling me all this?

LEBEDEV: Your mother's making me!

SASHA: Leave me alone! If you had any respect at all for me, or yourself, you'd
never allow yourself to talk to me like that. I don't need your dowry!
I've never asked for it and never will!

LEBEDEV: What are you jumping all over me for? Remember Gogol's two
rats[43] first sniffed around and then went away, and you, *émancipée*, are
jumping all over me before sniffing.

SASHA: Leave me alone, both of you, and don't offend my ears with your petty calculations.

LEBEDEV [*Losing his temper*]: Ugh! Either I stab myself or kill someone else! One's been bawling all day for all she's worth, niggling, nagging, counting every coin, and the other's so intelligent, so humane, damn it, so emancipated, she can't understand her own father! I'm offending her ears! But before I came here to offend your ears, they [*He points to the door*] sliced and diced and quartered me there. She can't understand it! Her head was turned and her mind hasn't returned . . . Damn it! [*Walks toward the door, and stops*] I don't like it, I don't like anything about you two!

SASHA: What is it you don't like?

LEBEDEV: I don't like anything! Nothing at all!

SASHA: What?

LEBEDEV: Yes, sure, I'm going to sit down and start spelling it out for you. I don't like anything, and I don't even want to see your wedding! [*He goes up to Sasha and speaks tenderly*] Forgive me, Shurochka, dear; maybe your wedding is all intelligent and honest, high-minded, with principles, but there's something not right about it, something not right! It's not like other weddings. You're young, innocent, pure like a crystal, and he's—a widower, all tattered and frayed. And I don't understand him, but never mind. [*He kisses his daughter*] Shurochka, forgive me, but something's suspect about it. People have been talking much too much about it. First, his Sarra dies and then all of a sudden somehow he decides to marry you . . . [*Quickly*] But, I'm being like an old woman; I've turned into an old crinoline skirt. Don't listen to me. Listen to no one but yourself.

SASHA: Papa, I feel it myself that it's not it . . . Not it, not it, not it . . . If you only knew how hard it is for me! It's unbearable! I feel embarrassed and scared admitting this to you. Papa, dear, for God's sake, cheer me up a little . . . teach me what to do.

LEBEDEV: What is it? What?

SASHA: I've never been so scared before! [*She glances around her*] I think that I don't understand him and that I'll never understand him. He hasn't smiled at me once since I became his fiancée; he hasn't even looked me straight in the eyes. He's constantly complaining and feeling remorseful about something, hinting that he is guilty of something, and his trembling . . . I'm exhausted! There are even moments sometimes when I think . . . that I don't love him as much as I should. And when he comes to see us or when he talks to me, I get bored. Papa, dear, what does it all mean? I'm scared!

LEBEDEV: My darling girl, my only child, listen to your old father. Refuse to marry him!

SASHA [*Frightened*]: No, how can you say that!

LEBEDEV: Really, Shurochka. So there will be a scandal, the tongues will wag in the county; but it's better to put up with a scandal than to ruin the rest of your life.

SASHA: Don't say that, papa, don't. I don't even want to hear that! I have to chase away these dark thoughts. He's a good, unhappy, not easy to understand person, and I will love him and understand him, and get him back on his feet. I'll do my task. I've made up my mind!

LEBEDEV: It's not a task; it's insanity.

SASHA: Enough. I've just confessed to you things that I wasn't ready to admit to myself. Don't tell anyone. Let's just forget it.

LEBEDEV: I don't understand anything. Either I've lost my marbles to old age, or else you've become all too clever for me, only for the life of me, I don't understand anything.

V

SHABELSKY [*Coming in*]: God damn everybody, myself included! It's outrageous!

LEBEDEV: What do you need?

SHABELSKY: No, really, seriously, I've got to do something so vile, so despicable as to turn not just my own but everybody's stomach. And I'll do it! Word of honor! I've already asked Borkin to tell everyone today that I'm engaged. [*He laughs*] Everyone's a scoundrel and now I'll be one too.

LEBEDEV: I'm fed up with you! Listen, Matvey, all this talking will get you carted off, forgive my saying so, to the madhouse!

SHABELSKY: And what makes a madhouse any worse than a white house or a red house?[44] Be my guest and take me there right now. Be my guest. They're all scoundrels, worthless, stupid little people, I'm disgusted with myself and I don't believe a word I'm saying . . .

LEBEDEV: You know something, my friend? Why don't you stuff your mouth full of oakum, light it, and blow smoke at people. Or, better yet, take your hat and go home. It's a wedding here; people are having a good time, and you caw-caw like a crow. Please . . .

Shabelsky leans towards the piano and sobs.

Good gracious, Matiusha! Matvey! Count! What's the matter? Matiusha, dear, my angel . . . I offended you. Well, forgive the old dog . . . Forgive the drunk . . . Have some water . . .

SHABELSKY: I don't need it. [*Raises his head*]

LEBEDEV: Why are you crying?

SHABELSKY: It's all right . . .

LEBEDEV: Matiusha, don't lie to me. . . . Why? What is it?

SHABELSKY: I just looked at the cello and . . . remembered the little Yid . . .

LEBEDEV: Oh, this is not the time to remember! May she rest in peace, God rest her soul, but now's not the time to remember her . . .

SHABELSKY: We used to play duets together . . . A marvelous and extraordinary woman!

Sasha sobs.

LEBEDEV: What's with you? Don't cry! My God, the two of them are bawling, and I . . . and I . . . Move away from here at least, don't let the guests see you!

SHABELSKY: Pasha, when the sun's shining, even a cemetery can be a happy place. When you have hope, even old age is good. But I have no hope, not a single one!

LEBEDEV: Well, you aren't doing so well . . . No children, no money, and no . . . Well, but what are you going to do! [*To Sasha*] What's the matter with you?

SHABELSKY: Pasha, give me some money. I'll pay you back in the beyond. I'll go to Paris, look at my wife's grave. I've given away a lot in life, half of my fortune and that's why I have a right to ask now. Besides, I'm asking a friend . . .

LEBEDEV [*Confused*]: My dear, I haven't got a kopeck! But, all right, all right! In other words, I can't promise anything, but you see . . . all right, all right! [*Aside*] They wore me out!

VI

Enter Babakina.

BABAKINA: Where is my beau? Count, how dare you leave me alone? You are terrible! [*She hits Shabelsky on the arm with her fan*]

SHABELSKY [*In disgust*]: Leave me alone! I hate you!

BABAKINA [*Dumbfounded*]: What? Huh?

SHABELSKY: Get away!

BABAKINA [*Falls into an armchair*]: Ah! [*Cries*]

ZINAIDA [*Enters crying*]: Someone's here . . . I think it's the best man. It's time for the blessing . . . [*She sobs*]

SASHA [*Imploringly*]: Mama!

LEBEDEV: Oh, now everyone's bawling! A quartet! Enough, turn off the waterworks! Matvey! . . . Marfa Egorovna! . . . Or, I . . . I'm going to cry too . . . [*Cries*] Oh, my God!

ZINAIDA: If you don't need your mother, if you don't listen to her . . . then I'll give you the pleasure of my blessing . . .

Enter Ivanov; he is wearing tails and gloves.

VII

LEBEDEV: That's the last thing we need! What is this?

SASHA: Why are you here?

IVANOV: I'm sorry, ladies and gentlemen, I need to talk to Sasha in private.

LEBEDEV: You are not supposed to see the bride before the wedding! It's time for you to go to the church!

IVANOV: Pasha, please . . .

Lebedev shrugs his shoulders; he, Zinaida Savishna, the count, and Babakina leave.

VIII

SASHA [*Sternly*]: What is it you need?

IVANOV: I'm choking with anger, but I can speak calmly. Listen. I was just getting ready for the wedding, I looked at myself in the mirror, and I have grey in my temples . . . Shura, don't do it! While there's still time, we must end this senseless comedy . . . You're young, innocent, your whole life's ahead of you, whereas I . . .

SASHA: This is nothing new; I've heard it a thousand times before and I'm fed up with it! Get yourself to the church instead of making people wait!

IVANOV: I'll go home now, and you'll tell your family that there's not going to be a wedding. Tell them something. It's time to be sensible. I've played Hamlet and you the exalted maiden—and that's enough.

SASHA [*Flaring up*]: What's this tone? I'm not listening.

IVANOV: But I'm talking, and I'll continue talking!

SASHA: Why did you come? Your whining is turning into mockery!

IVANOV: Oh, no, I'm not whining! A mockery? Yes, I'm mocking. If only I could mock myself a thousand times more and make the whole world roar with laughter, I would do it! I looked at myself in the mirror—and it was as if a cannonball exploded in my conscience! I made a laughingstock of myself and the shame almost drove me insane. [*He laughs*] Melancholy indeed! Noble hopelessness! Instinctive grief! All I need is to start writing poems. Whining, spreading my hopelessness with tales of woe, all knowing full well that the life force is gone; I'm rusted out and my life is over; I've succumbed to cowardice and am up to my ears in this vile melancholy—and to realize that when the sun's shining brightly, when even an ant carrying his load feels happy—no, thank you very much! To see how some take you for a charlatan, others feel sorry for you; still others offer a helping hand, and the fourth—and that's the worst of them all—listen in awe to your every sigh, looking at you as if you're the second Mohammed, waiting with bated breath for you to proclaim a new religion to them . . . No, thank God, I still have my pride and my conscience! I was laughing at myself on the way here, and I thought that the birds and the trees were laughing, too . . .

SASHA: That's not anger; that's craziness!

IVANOV: Is that what you think? No, I'm not crazy. I can now see things in their true light, and my mind's as clear as your conscience. We love each other, but our wedding will not take place! I can rant and rave or mope as much as I want, but I have no right to destroy others! With this whining I poisoned my wife's last year. Since you've become my fiancée, you forgot how to laugh and have aged five years. Your father, for whom everything used to be crystal-clear in life, thanks to me, no longer understands people. Wherever I go—a meeting, paying a visit, hunting, I usher in boredom, gloom, and resentment. Wait, don't interrupt me!

I'm harsh and brutal, but forgive me, I'm choking with anger, and I can't speak otherwise. I never lied or slandered life, but since becoming a grumbler, I, against my own will and unnoticeably to myself, slander it, protest against my fate, complain, and everyone listening to me gets infected with the same loathing for life and begins to slander it too. And the tone! It's as if I'm doing nature a favor by existing. To hell with me!

SASHA: Wait . . . From what you've just said it sounds that you are fed up with whining and that it's time to start a new life! . . . Fine then! . . .

IVANOV: I see nothing fine about it. And what new life? I have perished irretrievably! It's time for both of us to see that. A new life!

SASHA: Nikolai, come to your senses! What makes you think that you have perished? What's this cynicism? No, I don't want to talk or listen . . . Go to the church!

IVANOV: I've perished!

SASHA: Don't yell; the guests might hear you!

IVANOV: If a sensible, educated, and healthy person starts telling a tale of woe for no apparent reason, and rolling downhill, he's rolling unstoppably and he's beyond salvation! Well, where's my salvation? In what? I can't drink—wine gives me a headache; I don't know how to write bad poetry; and worshipping my spiritual laziness and seeing an exalted meaning in it—is not for me. Laziness is laziness, and weakness is weakness—I have no other names for them. I've perished, perished—and there's nothing to talk about. [Looks over his shoulder] Someone could interrupt us. Listen. If you love me, then help me. Immediately, right now, refuse me! Quickly . . .

SASHA: Oh, Nikolai, if you only knew how you've exhausted me! How you are torturing my soul! Kind and intelligent person, judge for yourself—how can you ask me to do such things? Each day you give me a new task and each day the task is more difficult than the day before . . . I wanted active love, but this is agonizing love!

IVANOV: And when you become my wife, the tasks will get even harder. Refuse me! Don't you see: it's not love; it's the stubbornness of your honest nature. You took upon yourself to resurrect the person in me, to save me, and you felt flattered because you were performing a feat . . . Now you're ready to retreat, but this false feeling prevents you. Don't you understand!

SASHA: Your logic is cruel and strange! Well, how can I refuse you? How could I? You have no mother, no sister, and no friends . . . You're ruined, your estate's been plundered, and you're being slandered all around . . .

IVANOV: It was stupid of me to come here. I should have followed my plan . . .

Enter Lebedev.

IX

SASHA [*Runs towards her father*]: Papa, for God's sake, he ran in here like a madman and he's been torturing me! He demands that I refuse him, he doesn't want to destroy me. Tell him that I don't want his generosity! I know what I'm doing.

LEBEDEV: I don't understand anything . . . What generosity?

IVANOV: There will be no wedding!

SASHA: Yes, there will be! Papa, tell him that there will be a wedding!

LEBEDEV: Wait, wait! . . . Why don't you want the wedding?

IVANOV: I explained it to her, but she doesn't want to understand me.

LEBEDEV: No, not to her, explain it to me, and explain it so that I can understand! Oh, Nikolai Alexeyevich! May God be your judge! You've managed to confuse our lives to the point that I feel I'm living in a museum of curiosities;[45] I look around and I don't understand anything . . . What have I done to deserve this? . . . What do you want me, an old man, to do with you? Challenge you to a duel maybe?

IVANOV: There's no need for a duel. All you need is a head on your shoulders and to understand the Russian language.

SASHA [*Walking up and down the stage in great agitation*]: It's awful, just awful! Just like a child!

LEBEDEV: I'm at a loss for words, that's all. Listen, Nikolai! You think that everything is right and reasonable and in keeping with the rules of psychology, but I say it's a disaster and a scandal. Listen to me, an old man, for the last time! This is what I'm going to tell you: calm yourself down! Look at things like everyone else. It's not complicated. The ceiling is white; the boots are black; the sugar is sweet. You love Sasha and she loves you. If you love her—stay; if you don't—go; we won't hold it against you. It's that simple! You're both healthy, intelligent, ethical people; well fed, thank God, and clothed . . . What more do you need? No money? Who cares! Money can't buy happiness. . . . Of course, I understand, Nikolai, your estate's mortgaged, you can't pay the interest, but I'm the father and I understand . . . Her mother, never mind her, she can do as she pleases; she's not giving any money, so be it. Shurka says that she doesn't need a dowry! It's all principles, Schopenhauer . . . That's all such nonsense . . . I have ten thousand stashed away in the bank. [*Glances around him*] Not a soul knows about it . . . My grand-mother's . . . It's for both of you . . . Take it, only promise to give Matvey two thousand or so . . .

The guests begin to assemble in the reception room.

IVANOV: Pasha, there's no point talking about it. I'm following my conscience.

SASHA: And I'm following my conscience. You can say whatever you want, but I'm not letting you go. I'll go get mama. [*She walks out*]

X

LEBEDEV: I don't understand anything . . .

IVANOV: Listen, poor fellow . . . I'm not about to start telling you whether I'm an honest man or a scoundrel, of sound mind or insane. I can't get through to you. I used to be young, passionate, sincere, and intelligent; I loved, hated, and believed not like everyone else. I worked and hoped enough for ten people, tilted at windmills, and beat my head against walls. Not aware of my limitations, I heaved too heavy a burden onto my back and the back started cracking, and the sinews pulled. I was in a hurry to spend myself on youth alone; I was intoxicated, excited, and I worked; far too much. And tell me, could I have done it any other way? There're so few of us and there's so much work, so much! My God, how much! And now, the life I was fighting is getting back at me with a vengeance! I'm a broken man! At thirty with a hangover, I'm old, already in a dressing gown. With a heavy head and a lazy spirit, exhausted, strained and broken; without faith, without love, without goals I wander aimlessly like a shadow among people, and I don't know who I am, why I live, what I want. And I already think that love is just gibberish, caresses are nauseating; that there's no point in work; that song and impassioned speeches are stale and trite. And everywhere I go I usher in dejection, deadly boredom, displeasure, loathing for life . . . I've perished irretrievably! Before you stands a man who at thirty-five is already exhausted, disillusioned, crushed by his own worthless feats, burning with shame, and mocking his own weakness . . . Oh, how the pride's rising up in me and how the rage is choking me! [*Staggering*] Here, I've done myself in! I'm even staggering . . . I've gotten weak. Where's Matvey? Tell him to take me home.

Voices from the ballroom: "The best man is here!"

XI

SHABELSKY [*Entering*]: Wearing someone else's old and worn-out tails . . . no gloves . . . and all these derisive glances, stupid jokes, and these grins . . . Disgusting little people!

BORKIN [*Comes in quickly with a bouquet; he is wearing tails with a best-man flower in the buttonhole*]: Ugh! Where in the world is he? [*To Ivanov*] They've been waiting a long time for you at the church, and you're here philosophizing! What a comedian! Really, a comedian! You're not going with the bride; you're going separately with me; I'll come back for the bride from the church. Can't you understand even that? Decidedly, a comedian!

LVOV [*Comes in and to Ivanov*]: Oh, you're here? [*Loudly*] Nikolai Alexeyevich Ivanov, I declare for all to hear that you're a scoundrel!

IVANOV [*Coldly*]: Much obliged!

General confusion.

BORKIN [*To Lvov*]: Dear sir, this is low! I challenge you to a duel!

LVOV: Mister Borkin, I consider it demeaning to speak with you, not to mention to duel! Mister Ivanov, however, can receive satisfaction whenever he pleases!

SHABELSKY: Dear sir, I'll fight you! . . .

SASHA [*To Lvov*]: Why? Why did you insult him? Gentlemen, please, I want him to explain: why?

LVOV: Alexandra Pavlovna, I didn't insult him without evidence. I came here as an honest man to open your eyes, and I beg you to hear me out.

SASHA: What can you possibly tell me? That you're an honest man? The whole world knows it! You'd better tell me honestly: do you understand yourself or not! You came in here as an honest man and insulted him so viciously that it nearly killed me; before, when you used to follow him like a shadow and interfered with his life, you were convinced that you were doing your duty, that you were being honest. You interfered in his private life, vilified him, and judged him; whenever possible you flooded me and everyone you knew with anonymous letters—and the whole time you thought you were an honest man. Thinking that it's honest, doctor, you didn't even spare his ailing wife, constantly bothering her with your suspicions. And no matter what low, cruel, or violent thing you did, you'd still imagine yourself an exceptionally honest and progressive person!

IVANOV [*Laughing*]: Not a wedding but a parliament! Bravo, bravo! . . .

SASHA [*To Lvov*]: Now you think about it: do you understand yourself or not? Stupid, heartless people! [*Takes Ivanov by the hand*] Nikolai, let's go! Father, let's go!

IVANOV: Go where? Wait, I'll end all this! Youth has awakened in me: this is the old Ivanov speaking! [*Takes out a revolver*]

SASHA [*Shrieks*]: I know what he wants to do! Nikolai, for God's sake!

IVANOV: I've been rolling downhill long enough, and now stop! Enough is enough! Move away! Thank you, Sasha!

SASHA [*Screams*]: Nikolai, for God's sake! Stop him!

IVANOV: Leave me alone! [*Runs to the side and shoots himself*]

Curtain.

THE SEAGULL

A Comedy in Four Acts

Characters

IRINA NIKOLAYEVNA ARKADINA, married name Trepleva, an actress

KONSTANTIN GAVRILOVICH TREPLEV, her son

PYOTR NIKOLAYEVICH SORIN, her brother

NINA MIKHAILOVNA ZARECHNAYA, a young woman, daughter of a rich landowner

ILYA AFANASIEVICH SHAMRAEV, retired lieutenant, Sorin's estate manager

POLINA ANDREYEVNA, his wife

MASHA, his daughter

BORIS ALEXEYEVICH TRIGORIN, a fiction writer

EVGENY SERGEYEVICH DORN, a doctor

SEMYON SEMYONOVICH MEDVEDENKO, a schoolteacher

YAKOV, a servant

COOK

MAIDSERVANT

The action takes place at Sorin's estate. Two years elapse between the third and fourth acts.

ACT ONE

A section of the park on Sorin's estate. A wide lane of trees leading to a lake in the background; the lake is obstructed by a stage, put together quickly for an amateur performance, completely hiding the lake from view. To the left and right of the stage—shrubbery.

Several chairs and a small table.

The sun has just set. On the stage, behind the curtain, Yakov and other workmen; coughing and hammering are heard. Masha and Medvedenko are walking on the left, coming back from taking a walk.

MEDVEDENKO: Why do you always wear black?

MASHA: I'm in mourning for my life. I'm unhappy.

MEDVEDENKO: Why? [*Reflecting*] I don't understand it . . . You're in good health, your father, while not exactly rich, is comfortably off. My life is much harder than yours. I make only twenty-three rubles a month, minus the pension fund deduction, and yet I'm not in mourning.

They sit down.

MASHA: It's not about money. A pauper can be happy.

MEDVEDENKO: That's in theory, but in real life: my mother, two sisters, my little brother, and myself, and the salary is just twenty-three rubles a month. We have to eat and drink, don't we? Buy tea and sugar? And tobacco? Try to make ends meet.

MASHA [*Looking back at the stage*]: The performance is about to begin.

MEDVEDENKO: Yes, Zarechnaya is acting, and the play is the work of Konstantin Gavrilovich. They're in love, and tonight their souls will unite in their yearning to express the same creative idea. But my soul and your soul have no points of tangency. I love you, can't sit home from this longing, walk four miles here every day and four miles back and find nothing but indifferentism on your part. That's understandable. I have no means, a large family . . . Who wants to marry someone who has nothing to eat himself?

MASHA: That's nonsense. [*Takes snuff*] I'm touched by your love, but I can't reciprocate, that's all. [*She offers him the snuff-box*] Feel free to borrow.

MEDVEDENKO: I don't feel like it.

A pause.

MASHA: The air is muggy; we'll have a thunderstorm tonight most likely. All you do is philosophize or talk about money. For you, there is nothing worse than poverty, but I think it's a thousand times easier to walk around in rags begging than . . . But you can't understand that . . .

Sorin and Treplev enter from the right.

SORIN [*Leaning on a cane*]: I am not quite myself living here in the country, my friend, and, obviously, I'll never get used to it. Last night I went to sleep at ten and this morning I woke up at nine feeling that from this perpetual sleeping my brain's gotten stuck to the skull and all that. [*Laughing*] And after lunch, I accidentally fell asleep again, and now I am a wreck, trapped in a nightmare, after all . . .

TREPLEV: It's true, you ought to live in town. [*Seeing Masha and Medvedenko*] Ladies and gentlemen, they'll call you right before it starts, but you can't stay here now. Please, go.

SORIN [*To Masha*]: Maria Ilinichna, would you kindly ask your Papasha to have them untie the dog; otherwise, it howls. My sister couldn't sleep again all night.

MASHA: Talk to my father yourself, I'm not going to. Spare me, please. [*To Medvedenko*] Come!

MEDVEDENKO: Then you will send someone to tell us before it starts.

Masha and Medvedenko leave.

SORIN: That means the dog will howl all night again. A pretty kettle of fish: I've never lived in the country the way I wanted to. I'd take a vacation, twenty-eight days, and come here to get some rest and all, but they bother you with all this nonsense to the point that from day one, all you want is to get out of here. [*Laughs*] I was always happy to leave this place . . . Well, but now I am retired, and I have no place to go, after all. Willy-nilly, I live here . . .

YAKOV [*To Treplev*]: We're going to go for a dip, Konstantin Gavrilych.

TREPLEV: All right, but be back in your places in ten minutes. [*Looking at the watch*] It's about to start.

YAKOV: Yes, sir. [*Goes out*]

TREPLEV [*Glancing at the stage*]: This is our little theatre. The curtain, the first and second wings, and the empty space beyond. No sets. A direct view of the lake and the horizon. We'll raise the curtain at half past eight sharp, when the moon is up.

SORIN: Splendid.

TREPLEV: If Zarechnaya is late, then the entire effect, of course, will be ruined. She should be here now. Her father and stepmother watch over her, and for her, getting away from home is as hard as escaping from jail. [*He straightens his uncle's tie*] Your hair and beard are all disheveled. You ought to get a haircut maybe . . .

SORIN [*Combing his beard*]: It's the tragedy of my life. Even in my youth, I always looked like a drunk—and all that. Women never loved me. [*Sits down*] Why is my sister in a bad mood?

TREPLEV: Why? She's bored. [*Sits down beside Sorin*] She's jealous. She's already set against me, and this performance, and against the play because she's not acting in it, and Zarechnaya is. She doesn't know the play but she hates it already.

SORIN [*Laughing*]: The things you make up, really . . .

TREPLEV: Yes, she's already upset because tonight on this tiny stage Zarechnaya will have success and not her. [*Glancing at his watch*] A psychological peculiarity—that's my mother. Unquestionably gifted and intelligent, capable of weeping over a book, she'll blurt out all of Nekrasov's[1] poetry by heart, nurses the sick like an angel, but just try praising Duse[2] in her presence. Whoa! You have to praise only her, write about her, rave about her extraordinary acting in *La dame aux camélias*[3] or in *The Daze of Life*,[4] but since there's none of this drug here in the country, she's bored and angry, and we are all her enemies, and it's all our fault. And then she's also superstitious: she dreads lighting three candles,[5] fears the thirteenth. She's stingy. I know for sure that she has seventy thousand rubles at a bank in Odessa.[6] But just try asking her for a loan, and she'll start crying.

SORIN: You got into your head that your mother doesn't like your play, and now you're getting all upset and all that. Calm down, your mother adores you.

TREPLEV [*Tears off the petals on a flower*]: She loves me—loves me not; loves me—loves me not; loves me—loves me not. [*Laughs*] You see, my mother doesn't love me. Of course! She wants to live, love, wear pastel blouses, but I'm twenty-five years old and a constant reminder that she's not young anymore. When I'm not around, she's only thirty-two; with me, she's forty-three, and she hates me for it. She also knows that I don't recognize theatre. She loves theatre, and thinks that she's serving humanity, a sacred art, but I think modern theatre is all routine and narrow-minded. When the curtain goes up and in the evening light, in a room with three walls, under artificial lights, these famously gifted people, these high priests of art portray how people eat, drink, love, walk, and wear their jackets; when from hackneyed scenes and phrases they try to drag out a moral—a small one, easily digestible, useful around the house; when in a thousand different variations I'm served same old, same old—then I run, I run away from it as Maupassant ran away from the Eiffel Tower that oppressed him with its vulgarity.

SORIN: You can't do without theatre.

TREPLEV: We need new forms. New forms are needed and if they're not there, then it's better not to have anything at all. [*Looking at his watch*] I love my mother, love her very much, but I think she leads a meaningless life: always running around with this fiction writer, her name is always being bandied about in newspapers—I find it all very tiring. Sometimes it's just the egoism of a mere mortal speaking in me, and sometimes I feel bad that my mother is a famous actress, and I think that were she an ordinary woman, I'd be happier. Uncle, can you imagine a situation more idiotic and hopeless: she has her guests over, all of them celebrities, actors and writers, and among them—I alone am a nobody, and they tolerate me only because I'm her son. Who am I? What am I? I parted from the university in my third year for circumstances beyond the editors' control, as they say, no talent, not a kopeck to my name, and, according to my passport, I'm a commoner from Kiev. My father was a commoner from Kiev although he, too, was a famous actor. And so, when in her drawing room, these actors and writers deigned to notice me, I thought that their glances were sizing up my nothingness; I read their thoughts, and suffered from the humiliation . . .

SORIN: By the way, tell me what this fiction writer is like? I can't figure him out. He keeps quiet.

TREPLEV: He's intelligent, without airs, a little, you know, melancholic. A very decent man. He's not even close to forty, but he's already famous and has had his fill . . . As far as his writing is concerned . . . how can I put it? He's a very nice and able writer . . . but . . . after Tolstoy or Zola you won't want to read Trigorin.

SORIN: You know, my friend, I love writers. Once I really wanted two things: to get married and to become a fiction writer, but I didn't manage to do either. Well. It must be nice to be even a small-time writer, after all.

TREPLEV [*Listening*]: I hear footsteps . . . [*Embraces his uncle*] I can't live without her . . . Even the sound of her footsteps is beautiful. . . . I'm incredibly happy. [*Hurries to greet Nina Zarechnaya, who enters*] My enchantress, my dream . . .

NINA [*Out of breath*]: I'm not late . . . Of course, I'm not late . . .

TREPLEV [*Kissing her hands*]: No, no, no!

NINA: I've been anxious all day, I was so scared! I was afraid that my father wouldn't let me go . . . But he's just left with my stepmother. The red sky, the moon's rising, and I kept urging, urging on the horse! [*Laughing*] But I'm so happy. [*Gives Sorin a firm handshake*]

SORIN [*Laughing*]: The eyes . . . look like they've been crying . . . Oh-oh! That won't do!

NINA: Yes, that's true . . . You see how hard it is for me to breathe. I'll go back in half an hour, we have to hurry. I can't, I can't, for God's sake, don't try to keep me. My father doesn't know that I'm here.

TREPLEV: Yes, really, it's time to get started. We have to go get everyone.

SORIN: I'll go and all that. Right away. [*He walks to the right singing*] "*To France two grenadiers . . .*" [*Looks back*] Once I started singing like this, and the assistant prosecutor says to me: "You have a strong voice, Your Excellency . . ." Then he thought a moment and added, "but . . . nasty." [*He laughs and goes out*]

NINA: My father and his wife don't let me come here. They say it's Bohemian . . . they're afraid I might take up acting . . . But I'm drawn to the lake like a seagull . . . My heart is filled with you. [*She looks about her*]

TREPLEV: We are alone.

NINA: I think someone's there . . .

TREPLEV: No one. [*A kiss*]

NINA: What kind of a tree is that?

TREPLEV: An elm.

NINA: Why is it so dark?

TREPLEV: It is evening already; all objects look darker. Don't leave early, I beg you.

NINA: I can't.

TREPLEV: And, Nina, what if I come to your house? I'll stand in the garden all night looking at your window.

NINA: You can't, the watchman will see you. The dog's[7] not used to you yet and will bark.

TREPLEV: I love you.

NINA: Shhh . . .

TREPLEV [*Hearing footsteps*]: Who is there? Yakov, is that you?

YAKOV [*Behind the stage*]: Yes, sir.

TREPLEV: Take your places then. It's time. Is the moon rising?

YAKOV: Yes, sir.

TREPLEV: Do we have alcohol? And the sulfur? When the red eyes appear, it has to smell of sulfur. [*To Nina*] Go, everything's ready. Are you nervous? . . .

NINA: Yes, very much so. Your mother—that's all right, I'm not afraid of her, but Trigorin is here . . . and acting in front of him is scary and embarrassing . . . A famous writer . . . Is he young?

TREPLEV: Yes.

NINA: What wonderful stories he writes!

TREPLEV [*Coldly*]: I don't know, never read them.

NINA: It's hard to act in your play. There are no live characters.

TREPLEV: Live characters! We must represent life not the way it is, and not the way it should be, but as we see it in our dreams.

NINA: There is little action in your play; just reciting. And I think a play must always have love in it.

Both walk behind the stage. Enter Polina Andreyevna and Dorn.

POLINA: It's getting damp. Go back and put on your galoshes.

DORN: I'm hot.

POLINA: You're not taking care of yourself. It's sheer stubbornness. You're a doctor and you know quite well that damp air is bad for you, but you feel like torturing me; yesterday, on purpose, you sat out on the terrace all night . . .

DORN [*Sings*]: "Oh, say not that youth has ruined . . ."[8]

POLINA: You were so captivated by your conversation with Irina Nikolayevna . . . you weren't even noticing the cold. Admit it, you are attracted to her . . .

DORN: I'm fifty-five years old.

POLINA: That's nonsense. For a man that's not old. You've kept your good looks, and women still find you attractive.

DORN: Then what is it you wish?

POLINA: You're all ready to kiss the ground before an actress. Every one of you!

DORN [*Sings*]: "Once more I stand before you . . ."[9] If people love actors and treat them differently from, say, merchants, then that's to be expected. It's called idealism.

POLINA: Women were always falling in love with you and throwing themselves at you. Is that idealism, too?

DORN [*Shrugging his shoulders*]: Well? Women treated me very well. They loved in me, above all, an excellent doctor. You remember, ten or fifteen years ago, I was the only decent obstetrician in the province. Plus, I've always been honest.

POLINA [*Seizes his hand*]: My darling!

DORN: Quiet! They're coming.

> *Arkadina and Sorin walk in arm in arm; also Trigorin, Shamraev, Medvedenko, and Masha.*

SHAMRAEV: In 1873, at the Poltava Fair, her acting was exquisite.[10] A sheer delight! She acted marvelously! Would you, also, by any chance, happen to know the whereabouts of the comedian Chadin—Pavel Semyonovich Chadin? He was inimitable as Raspluev,[11] better than Sadovsky, my dearest lady, take my word for it. Whatever happened to him?

ARKADINA: You keep asking me about these antediluvians. How should I know! [*She sits down*]

SHAMRAEV [*Sighing*]: Pashka Chadin! There's no one like him today. The stage has fallen, Irina Nikolayevna! There used to be giant oaks, but now only the stumps remain.

DORN: True, there are few truly gifted ones these days, but the average actor has risen considerably.

SHAMRAEV: I can't agree with you. However, it's a matter of taste, *De gustibus aut bene, aut nihil.*[12]

> *Treplev comes in from behind the stage.*

ARKADINA [*To her son*]: My dearest son, when does it all begin?[13]

TREPLEV: A minute longer. A little patience.

ARKADINA [*Reciting from* Hamlet]:

> My son!

Thou turn'st mine eyes into my very soul;

And there I see such black grained spots

As will not leave their tinct.[14]

TREPLEV [*Reciting from* Hamlet]:

Nay, but to live

In the rank sweat of an enseamed bed,

Stew'd in corruption . . .[15]

A horn sounds from behind the stage.

TREPLEV: Ladies and gentlemen, we are starting! May I have your attention, please!

A pause.

I'm starting. [*He taps with a stick and speaks in a loud voice*] O, ye honorable, ancient shadows roaming at night above this lake, make us sleep and let us dream about what will be in two hundred thousand years!

SORIN: In two hundred thousand years there will be nothing.

TREPLEV: Then let them show us that nothing.

ARKADINA: Let them. We are asleep.

The curtain rises opening the view to the lake; the moon is above the horizon, its reflection is on the water; on a big rock sits Nina Zarechnaya all dressed in white.

NINA: People, lions, eagles and quails, horned stags, geese, spiders, silent fish that used to inhabit the water, starfish, and those invisible to the eye—in short, all lives, all lives, all lives, having completed their mournful cycle, have died out . . . It's been thousands of centuries since the earth has supported a single living creature, and the poor Moon in vain lights its lantern. Cranes no longer awaken with a cry in the meadows, and the beetles can no longer be heard amid the linden groves. It's cold, cold, cold. It's empty, empty, empty. It's scary, scary, scary.[16]

A pause.

The bodies of living creatures disappeared into dust, and the eternal matter has transformed them into rocks, water, and clouds, and their souls have all merged into one. I am, I am the collective world soul. Contained in me are the souls of Alexander the Great, Caesar, Shakespeare, Napoleon, and of the lowest leech. In me, the consciousness of humans has merged with animal instincts, and I remember everything, everything, everything, and every life form inside me I relive again.

The will-o-the-wisps appear.

ARKADINA [*Quietly*]: There's something from the Decadents in this.

TREPLEV [*Imploringly and with reproach*]: Mama!

NINA: I'm lonely. Once every one hundred years I open my mouth to speak, and my voice sounds dull in this void, and no one hears it . . . And you, pale flames, you do not hear me . . . In the early morning you are born out of putrid marsh and you wander around till dawn, but without a single thought, without will, without a quiver of life. The Demon, father of eternal matter, fearing that you might engender life, is constantly exchanging atoms in you, as in rocks and water, and you are continuously transforming. In the universe, only the spirit remains constant and unchanged.

A pause.

Like a captive cast into a deep and empty well, I don't know where I am or what awaits me. All that's revealed to me is that I'm destined to win in this fierce and persistent struggle with the Demon, the source of all material forces, I am destined to win, and after that, matter and spirit will merge in beautiful harmony, and the kingdom of peace will come. But this will come only after the moon and light-colored Sirius, and the earth, little by little, following a long succession of millennia, turn to dust . . . Until then, horror, horror . . .

A pause; two red points appear against the lake.

Here comes my mighty opponent, the Devil; I see his scary crimson eyes . . .

ARKADINA: I smell sulfur. Am I supposed to?

TREPLEV: Yes.

ARKADINA [*Laughs*]: Well, it's quite an effect.

TREPLEV: Mama!

NINA: He misses people . . .

POLINA [*To Dorn*]: You've taken off your hat. Put it on, or you'll catch a cold.

ARKADINA: The doctor took off his hat to the Devil, the father of eternal matter.

TREPLEV [*Loudly and losing his temper*]: The play is over! Enough! Curtain!

ARKADINA: Why are you getting so upset?

TREPLEV: Enough! Curtain! Bring down the curtain! [*Stamping his foot*] The curtain!

The curtain comes down.

I'm sorry! It escaped me that only the chosen few can write plays and act on stage. I broke the monopoly! I . . . me . . . [*He would like to say more, but waves his arm instead, and goes out to the left*]

ARKADINA: What's wrong with him?

SORIN: Irina, dearest, you should not be so harsh on young pride.

ARKADINA: What did I say to him?

SORIN: You offended him.

ARKADINA: But he told me himself that it was a joke, and so I treated his play as a joke.

SORIN: Still . . .

ARKADINA: Now it turns out that he'd written a great work! Please! So then he arranged the performance and fumigated us with sulfur not as a joke but as a demonstration . . . He wanted to teach us how to write and what to act in. This after all is getting much too boring. These constant sallies and taunts against me, as you like, will tire anyone out! He is a capricious and selfish boy.

SORIN: He wanted to please you.

ARKADINA: Really? However, he didn't choose an ordinary play, and forced us to listen to this Decadent raving. As long as it's a joke, I'm willing to listen to the ravings even, but he claims that he's introducing new art forms and a new era in art. I think there's no new forms here; just a bad temper.

TRIGORIN: Everyone writes the way he wants and as best he can.

ARKADINA: Let him write what he likes and as best he can as long as leaves me alone.

DORN: Jupiter, you are getting angry . . .

ARKADINA: I'm not Jupiter, I'm a woman. [*She lights a cigarette*] I'm not getting angry, it's just that I feel bad that a young man spends his time so tediously. I did not mean to offend him.

MEDVEDENKO: No one has a reason to separate soul from matter because the soul itself may be the aggregate of material atoms. [*Energetically, to*

Trigorin] You know, what if you were to write a play, and then act out on stage, about the way we live—the likes of us—schoolteachers. It's a hard, hard life!

ARKADINA: That's all very reasonable, but let's not talk anymore about plays or atoms. The evening is so lovely! Ladies and gentlemen, can you hear the singing? [*She listens attentively*] It's so beautiful!

POLINA: It's on the side of the lake.

A pause.

ARKADINA [*To Trigorin*]: Sit next to me. Ten or fifteen years ago, here on the lake, you heard music and singing always, almost every night. There are six country estates there around the lake. I remember laughter, noise, shooting, and romance, romance . . . In those days, the *jeune premier*[17] and the favorite of all six estates was this man here [*nods toward Dorn*], please allow me, Doctor Evgeny Sergeyich. He is still charming, but he was irresistible then. However, it's beginning to weigh heavily on my conscience. Why did I have to offend my poor boy? I'm feeling restless. [*Loudly*] Kostya! Son! Kostya!

MASHA: I'll go look for him.

ARKADINA: Thank you, my dear.

MASHA [*Goes off to the left*]: Haloo! Konstantin Gavrilovich! . . . Haloo! [*She leaves*]

NINA [*Coming out from behind the stage*]: It looks like we're not going to continue and I can come out. Hello! [*She kisses Arkadina and Polina*]

SORIN: Bravo! Bravo!

ARKADINA: Bravo! Bravo! We were feasting our eyes. With your looks and such a wonderful voice you shouldn't sit here in the country, it's a sin. You must have talent. Do you hear me? You must join the stage!

NINA: Oh, that's my dream! [*With a sigh*] But it will never materialize.

ARKADINA: Who knows? Here, allow me introduce to you Boris Alexeyevich Trigorin.

NINA: Oh, I am so glad . . . [*Embarrassed*] I always read you . . .

ARKADINA [*Seating Nina close to her*]: Don't be embarrassed, my dear. He's famous, but he has a simple soul. See, he's already embarrassed.

DORN: I imagine we can raise the curtain now; otherwise it looks sinister.

SHAMRAEV [*Loudly*]: Yakov, my friend, raise the curtain!

The curtain rises.

NINA [*To Trigorin*]: A strange play, isn't it?

TRIGORIN: I didn't understand anything. Although I watched with interest. You acted with such sincerity. And the set was beautiful.

A pause.

There must be a lot of fish in this lake.

NINA: Yes.

TRIGORIN: I love fishing. I can't think of anything more pleasurable than to sit by the lake in the late afternoon watching the float.

NINA: But I think that those who have experienced the pleasure of creative work, for them other pleasures just don't exist.

ARKADINA [*Laughing*]: Don't say that. When people say nice things to him, he sinks into the ground.

SHAMRAEV: I remember in Moscow, at the Opera House, the famous Silva sang the low C. By chance, just then, a bass chorister from our church was sitting in the balcony. Well, you can imagine our complete astonishment when suddenly we hear "Bravo, Silva!" from the gallery, a whole octave lower . . . Like this: [*In a deep bass voice*] "Bravo, Silva . . ." The entire theatre just froze.[18]

A pause.

DORN: A quiet angel flew by.

NINA: It's time for me to go. Good-bye.

ARKADINA: Where to? So early? We won't let you go.

NINA: My father is waiting for me.

ARKADINA: Oh, he is really so . . .

They kiss.

What can we do! We're very sorry to let you go.

NINA: If you only knew how much I don't want to leave!

ARKADINA: Someone ought to see you home, my pet.

NINA [*Frightened*]: Oh, no, no!

SORIN [*To her, imploringly*]: Stay!

NINA: I can't, Pyotr Nikolayevich.

SORIN [*Imploringly to Nina*]: Stay for an hour, that's all. Please, really . . .

NINA [*Hesitating and then through tears*]: I can't. [*Shakes hands with him and leaves quickly*]

ARKADINA: A poor girl, really! I heard that her mother had bequeathed all her immense fortune to her husband, everything to the last kopeck, and now the girl is left with nothing because her father has already bequeathed everything to his second wife. It's an outrage.

DORN: Yes, to give him his due, her dear old papa is a real swine.

SORIN [*Rubbing his cold hands*]: Ladies and gentlemen, let's go in, too; it's getting damp. My legs are aching.

ARKADINA: They look like they're made of wood; can barely move. Let's go, my ill-fated old man. [*Takes him by the arm*]

SHAMRAEV [*Offering his arm to his wife*]: Madame?

SORIN: I hear the dog's howling again. Have them untie the dog.

SHAMRAEV: I can't. I don't want thieves getting into the granary. I have millet there. [*To Medvedenko, who is walking next to him*] Yes, a whole octave lower: "Bravo, Silva!" and he is not even a singer, just your ordinary church chorister.

MEDVEDENKO: How much does a church chorister make?

Everybody goes out except Dorn.

DORN [*Alone*]: I don't know, maybe I don't understand anything, or I've lost my mind, but I liked the play. There was something there. When the girl talked about loneliness, and then when the Devil's red eyes appeared, my hands trembled with emotion. It was so fresh and naïve . . . I think that's him coming. I feel like saying a lot of nice things to him.

TREPLEV [*Coming in*]: Everybody's gone.

DORN: I'm here.

TREPLEV: Masha is looking for me all over the park. She's intolerable.

DORN: Konstantin Gavrilovich, I liked your play so much. It's a little strange, and I did not hear the end, but still, it made a deep impression on me. You're talented, and you have to continue.

Treplev shakes his hand hard and then impetuously embraces him.

Phew! How high strung you are! Tears in your eyes . . . What am I trying to say? You picked the subject from the realm of abstract ideas. You did the right thing because a work of art invariably must express some big idea. Only what's truly serious is beautiful. How pale you are!

TREPLEV: So you are telling me—to continue?

DORN: Yes . . . but show only what's important and eternal. You know, I've lived a varied life and I enjoyed it and I'm satisfied; but if I ever were to experience the inspiration that an artist doing creative work feels, I think I would despise the material shell and everything that comes with it, and I would take wing and soar from it high into the sky.

TREPLEV: I am sorry, where is Zarechnaya?

DORN: And one more thing. Every work should contain a clear and specific idea. You have to know why you're writing; because if not, if you take this scenic road without a well-defined goal, you will get lost and your talent will destroy you.

TREPLEV [*Impatiently*]: Where is Zarechnaya?

DORN: She went home.

TREPLEV [*In despair*]: What should I do? I want to see her . . . I absolutely must see her . . . I'm going . . .

Masha enters.

DORN [*To Treplev*]: Calm down, my friend.

TREPLEV: I'm going. I must go.

MASHA: Konstantin Gavrilovich, go inside. Your mother is waiting for you. She's restless.

TREPLEV: Tell her I've left. And I beg all of you to leave me alone! Leave me alone! Don't follow me around!

DORN: Come, come, my dear . . . you shouldn't . . . It's not good.

TREPLEV [*Through tears*]: Good-bye, doctor. Thank you very much . . . [*He leaves*]

DORN [*Sighing*]: Youth, youth!

MASHA: When people don't have anything else to say, they say: "Youth, youth!" . . . [*She takes snuff*]

DORN [*Takes the snuff-box from her and flings it into the bushes*]: It's ugly!

A pause.

I think I hear them playing inside. We should go.

MASHA: Wait.

DORN: What?

MASHA: I want to say this once again. I feel like talking . . . [*Nervously*] I don't love my father . . . but I like you. For some reason, I feel with all my soul this connection to you . . . Help me. Help me, or I'll do something foolish, make a mockery of my life, and ruin it . . . I can't take it anymore . . .

DORN: What? Help you how?

MASHA: I am suffering. No one knows of my suffering! [*She lays her head on his chest and speaks softly*] I love Konstantin.

DORN: Oh, how high strung you all are! And all this love . . . Oh, this enchanted lake! [*Tenderly*] But, my child, what can I do! What? What?

Curtain.

ACT TWO

A croquet lawn. To the right of it, in the back, stands a house with a large terrace. The lake is visible on the left, and the sun is reflected brightly in it. Flowerbeds. It's midday. It's hot. Arkadina, Masha, and Dorn are sitting on a bench in the shade of an old linden tree along the side of the lawn. Dorn holds an open book on his lap.

ARKADINA [*To Masha*]: Let's stand up both.

Both stand up.

Let's stand side by side. You're twenty-two years old and I'm almost twice that. Doctor, tell me which one of us is more youthful?

DORN: You are, of course.

ARKADINA: See . . . You know why? Because I work, I feel, and I'm always running around, and you always sit on the same spot, you don't live . . . And I have a rule: never look into the future. I never think about old age or death. You can't escape the inevitable.

MASHA: And I feel like I was born ages ago, and have been dragging my life behind me like an endless train . . . And often I have no desire to live at all. [*Takes a seat*] Of course, that's all nonsense. I must cheer up and shake it off.

DORN [*Sings softly*]: "Tell her, my flowers . . ."[19]

ARKADINA: And then I am as proper as an Englishman. My dear, I keep myself in hand, as they say. I am well-dressed and always coiffed *comme il faut*.[20] Would I ever allow myself to walk out of the house, even if only into the garden, in a smock or with my hair all messy? Never! I've kept my looks precisely because I have never been a ragbag and I have never let myself go like others . . . [*Puts her arms akimbo, and walks up and down the lawn*] Here, see—like a sparrow. Ready to play a fifteen-year-old girl.

DORN: Well, nonetheless, I'm continuing anyway. [*He picks up the book*] We've stopped at the grain-dealer and the rats . . .

ARKADINA: And the rats. Go on. [*Sits down*] Actually, no, give it to me, I will read it. It's my turn. [*Takes the book and looks for the place*] And the rats . . . Ah, here it is . . . [*Reads*] "Of course, it is as dangerous for high society to lavish attention on writers and draw them in as it would be for grain-dealers to raise rats in their granaries. And yet, they love them. And so, when a woman singles out a writer whom she wants to captivate, she plies him with compliments, kindness, and favors." Well, this may be true for the French, but we have nothing like that, there are no agendas here. Here, please, a woman is already head over heels in love with a writer before captivating him. You don't need to search far, just take me and Trigorin . . .

Sorin walks in leaning on a cane, with Nina beside him; Medvedenko follows him, pushing an empty wheelchair.

SORIN [*As if speaking tenderly to a child*]: Really? We have good news? We are cheerful today after all? [*To his sister*] We have good news! The father and stepmother went to Tver, and we are free for three whole days!

NINA [*Sits down beside Arkadina and embraces her*]: I am happy! I am all yours now.

SORIN [*Sits down in his armchair*]: She is pretty today.

ARKADINA: Well-dressed and pretty . . . That's a good girl. [*She kisses Nina*] But we shouldn't give her too much praise lest we put an evil eye on her. Where is Boris Alexeyevich?

NINA: He is in the swimming area, fishing.

ARKADINA: Amazing how he never gets tired of it! [*She wants to continue reading*]

NINA: What is it?

ARKADINA: "On the Water," by Maupassant, darling. [*She reads a few lines to herself*] But the rest is boring and not true. [*She closes the book*] My heart is restless. Tell me, what's the matter with my son? Why is he so humorless and stern? He spends days on the lake, and I hardly ever see him.

MASHA: He is heartsick. [*Timidly, to Nina*] Please, read something from his play!

NINA [*Shrugging her shoulders*]: You really want me to? It's not interesting!

MASHA [*Restraining her delight*]: When he recites something himself, his eyes burn and his face turns pale. He has a beautiful, sad voice, and the manner of a poet.

Sorin's snoring is heard.

DORN: Good night!

ARKADINA: Petrusha!

SORIN: Eh?

ARKADINA: Are you sleeping?

SORIN: Not in the least.

A pause.

ARKADINA: You aren't taking any cures, my dear brother, and that's not good.

SORIN: I would love to take the cure, but the doctor here doesn't want me to.

DORN: Taking cures at sixty!

SORIN: I want to live, even at sixty.

DORN [*Annoyed*]: Eh! Take sedative drops[21] then.

ARKADINA: I think it would be good for him to go to take the waters.

DORN: Well? He could go. Or he could not go.

ARKADINA: Go figure.

DORN: There's nothing to figure out. It's quite clear.

Pause.

MEDVEDENKO: Pyotr Nikolayevich ought to quit smoking.

SORIN: That's nothing.

DORN: No, not nothing. Wine and tobacco rob you of your personality. After a cigar or a shot of vodka you're no longer Mr. Sorin, but Mr. Sorin plus somebody else; your 'I' fades: you begin to treat yourself in the third person—'he.'

SORIN [*Laughing*]: It's easy for you to talk like that. You've lived a good life; and me? I served in the court system for twenty-eight years, but I haven't lived, I haven't experienced anything, after all; obviously, I want very much to live. You've had your fill and you don't care, and that's why you are bent on philosophy, whereas I want to live and that's why I drink sherry at dinner and smoke cigars—and all that. That's all.

DORN: You have to take life seriously but, forgive me, taking cures at sixty or regretting that you did not experience more pleasure in your youth, forgive me, that's foolish.

MASHA [*Getting up*]: It must be time for lunch. [*Walks with a languid, lazy step*] My foot's asleep . . . [*Goes out*]

DORN: She'll go and down a couple of shots before lunch.

SORIN: The poor girl is unhappy.

DORN: Oh, idle talk, Your Excellency.

SORIN: You talk like someone who has had his fill.

ARKADINA: What can be more boring than this endearing country boredom? It's hot, quiet, and nobody's doing anything; only philosophizing . . . It's nice sitting and listening to you here, my friends, but . . . sitting in a hotel room memorizing lines—is so much better!

NINA [*Ecstatically*]: Yes it is! I agree with you.

SORIN: Of course it's better in the city. You sit in your office, the footman doesn't let anyone in unannounced, a telephone . . . and outside is cabs and all . . .

DORN [*Sings*]: "Tell her, my flowers . . ."

Enter Shamraev followed by Polina.

SHAMRAEV: Here they are. Hello! [*He kisses Arkadina's hand and then Nina's*] I'm delighted to see you in fine form. [*To Arkadina*] My wife tells me that the two of you are going to go into town today. Is that true?

ARKADINA: Yes, we're planning to.

SHAMRAEV: Hmm . . . That's just splendid; but how are you getting there, my esteemed lady? They're hauling rye today, and all the laborers are busy. And what horses, may I ask?

ARKADINA: What horses? How would I know—what horses!

SORIN: We have carriage horses.

SHAMRAEV [*Nervously*]: Carriage horses! And where will I get the harnesses for them? Where will I get the harnesses? No, this is incredible! It's astonishing! My venerated lady! I have profound respect for your talent, and would give ten years of my life for you, but I can't give you the horses!

ARKADINA: But if I must go? This is very strange!

SHAMRAEV: My dearest lady! You don't know what it means to run a farmstead!

ARKADINA [*Flaring up*]: That's the same old story! In this case, I'm leaving for Moscow this very day. Hire the horses from the village for me, or I will walk to the station!

SHAMRAEV [*Flaring up*]: In this case I resign my position! Go look for another
       manager! [*Goes out*]

ARKADINA: Every summer, every summer they insult me here! I will not set
       foot here again! [*Goes out to the left, in the direction of the swimming
       area. In a few minutes she is seen entering the house, followed by Trigorin
       carrying fishing rods and a bucket.*]

SORIN [*Flaring up*]: Such insolence! This is God knows what! I'm fed up with
       it, after all. Bring all the horses here immediately!

NINA [*To Polina*]: To refuse Irina Nikolayevna, the famous actress! Isn't her
       every wish, every fancy more important than running your farmstead?
       It's unbelievable!

POLINA [*In despair*]: What can I do? Put yourself in my place: what I can do?

SORIN [*To Nina*]: Let's go see my sister . . . We'll all beg her not to leave. [*He
       looks in the direction in which Shamraev went out*] Won't we? He's insuf-
       ferable! A despot!

NINA [*Preventing him from getting up*]. Sit, sit . . . We'll wheel you . . . [*She and
       Medvedenko push the wheelchair before them*] Oh, that's just awful! . . .

SORIN: Yes, yes, that's just awful . . . But he won't leave, I'll have a word with
       him right now.

       They go out; only Dorn and Polina are left.

DORN: People are tedious. Essentially, they should have kicked your husband
       out of here, but it will all end with this old woman Sorin and his sister
       apologizing to him. You'll see!

POLINA: He has sent even carriage horses into the field. Every day mix-ups
       like that. If you only knew how it upsets me! I am taking ill; see! I am
       trembling all over . . . I cannot take his rudeness. [*Imploringly*] Evgeny,
       my dear, my darling, take me with you . . . Our time is slipping away;
       we are not young anymore; and, at least at the end of our lives, to stop
       hiding and lying . . .

       A pause.

DORN: I am fifty-five-years old, it's too late to change my life.

POLINA: I know, you say no to me because there are other women you're close
       to. You can't take them all in. I understand. Forgive me—you're tired
       of me.

       Nina appears near the house; she is picking flowers.

DORN: No, it's all right.

POLINA: I'm suffering from jealousy. Of course, you are a doctor and can't avoid women. I understand . . .

DORN [*To Nina, who is coming toward him*]: How's it there?

NINA: Irina Nikolayevna is crying, and Pyotr Nikolayevich is having an asthma attack.

DORN [*Getting up*]: Maybe I should give them both sedative drops . . .

NINA [*Hands him a bunch of flowers*]: Here you go!

DORN: *Merci bien.*[22] [*He goes toward the house*]

POLINA [*Walking next to Dorn*]: What sweet flowers! [*As they reach the house she says in a muffled voice*] Give me those flowers! Give them to me! [*After getting the flowers, she tears them up and throws them away; the two of them walk into the house*]

NINA [*Alone*]: It's so strange to see a famous actress cry, and over nothing! And isn't it strange, too, that a famous author, a celebrity, the newspapers all write about him, his portraits are for sale, he is translated into foreign languages, and he spends the entire day fishing and is happy when he's caught a couple of fish.[23] I used to think that famous people were proud and unapproachable, and that they loathed the crowd and used their fame and the glory of their name to get back at people for worshipping blue blood and wealth. But here they cry, fish, play cards, laugh, and get upset just like the rest of us . . .

TREPLEV [*Comes in without a hat on, carrying a gun and a dead seagull*] Are you alone here?

NINA: Yes.

> *Treplev lays a dead seagull at her feet.*

NINA: What does this mean?

TREPLEV: I had the dishonor today to kill this seagull. I lay it at your feet.

NINA: What's going on with you? [*She picks up the seagull and looks at it*]

TREPLEV [*After a pause*]: Soon I'll kill myself the same way.

NINA: I don't recognize you.

TREPLEV: Yes, but that's after I stopped recognizing you. You've changed toward me; your look is cold now; my presence makes you uncomfortable.

NINA: Lately, you've become irritable; you express yourself in a way that's impossible to understand, with symbols. And this seagull is probably a symbol, but I am sorry, I don't understand . . . [*She lays the seagull on the bench*] I am too ordinary to understand you.

TREPLEV: It all began the evening my play flopped so stupidly. Women don't forgive failure. I burnt it, to the last page. Oh, if you only knew how misterable I am! Your coldness toward me is terrifying beyond belief; it is as if I suddenly woke up to see this lake dried up or vanished into the ground. You just said that you were too ordinary to understand me. Oh, but what's there to understand?! They didn't like my play, you loathe my inspiration, you already think me a mediocrity, a nothing, one of many . . . [*Stamping his foot*] I understand it all too well! It's like a nail in my head; to hell with it and my pride, which is sucking my blood, sucking it out like a viper . . . [*Upon seeing Trigorin, who approaches reading a book*] Here comes a true talent; striding like Hamlet and with a book, too. [*Mockingly*] "Words, words, words . . ." This sun hasn't even come close to you, but you're smiling already; your gaze is melting in his rays. I don't want to disturb you. [*Leaves quickly*]

TRIGORIN [*Writing in the notebook*]: Takes snuff and drinks vodka . . . Always in black. A schoolteacher loves her . . .

NINA: Hello, Boris Alexeyevich!

TRIGORIN: Hello. Due to an unexpected turn of events, it seems that we're leaving today. You and I will probably never see each other again. That's too bad. It's not very often that I get to meet young women, young and pretty, I already forgot and have trouble imagining clearly what one feels at eighteen, nineteen, and that's why in my stories the young girls don't ring true. I'd like to be in your place for an hour to find out what you're thinking and what kind of a thingy you really are.

NINA: And I'd like to be in your place.

TRIGORIN: What for?

NINA: To understand how a famous and talented writer feels. How does fame feel? How does it feel to be famous?

TRIGORIN: How? Probably not at all. I've never thought about it. [*Thoughtfully*] It's one of two things: either you're exaggerating my fame, or it just doesn't feel like anything.

NINA: And if you're reading about yourself in the newspapers?

TRIGORIN: If they're praising me, it is nice; if they're chewing me out, I'm in a bad mood for two days.

NINA: A wonderful world! If you only knew how I envy you! People's lots are so different. Some can barely eke out their boring and imperceptible existence, all of them alike, all unhappy; the others, in turn, like you, for example—you're one in a million—are destined to live an interesting, bright life, full of meaning . . . You are happy . . .

TRIGORIN: Me? [*Shrugging his shoulders*] Hmm . . . You're talking about fame and happiness, about a bright and interesting life, but for me all these nice words, forgive me, are just like fruit jelly, which I don't eat. You are very young and very kind.

NINA: Your life's so beautiful!

TRIGORIN: What's so good about it? [*Looks at his watch*] I must go now and write. I'm sorry, I have to go . . . [*Laughs*] You've just stepped on my most sore spot, as they say, and I'm getting upset and a little angry. Well then, let's talk about it. Let's talk about my bright and beautiful life. Well, where should we start? [*After a moment's thought*] There are things like invasive notions, when a person day and night thinks about something; for instance, always about the moon; and I have such a moon, too. Day and night I'm obsessed by one recurring thought: I must write, I must write, I must write . . . The moment I finish a tale, I must, for some reason, write another one, then a third, and after the third, a fourth one . . . I'm writing nonstop, like a traveler switching horses midway, and I can't do otherwise. So, what's so bright and beautiful about it, I ask you? Oh, this wild life! I'm with you here, nervous, and yet, the whole time I remember that an unfinished tale is waiting for me. I see here a cloud shaped like a grand piano, and I'm thinking that I must mention somewhere in the story that a cloud floated by shaped like a grand piano. I smell lilac. Quickly I make a mental note of it: a cloying smell; a color worn by widows, to mention it when describing a summer evening. I clutch onto every word and phrase that you and I say and hurry to lock up all these words and phrases in my literary stockroom: may come in handy! When I finish work, I run to the theatre or go fishing—to relax supposedly, but no! a cast-iron cannonball—a new plot—is already rolling around in my head, and I long to get back to my desk, and I must hurry to write and write again. And it's always like this, always, and I can't leave myself alone, and I feel that I'm devouring my own life, and that for the honey, which I give away to someone out there, I'm collecting pollen from my own best flowers, pulling out the flowers themselves, and trampling on the roots. Don't you think I'm crazy? Would you say that my relatives and friends treat me like they would a sane person? "What are you writing nowadays?" "What will you present us with next?" It's always the same thing, always the same thing, and it seems that all this attention from friends, their praise and admiration—is all a lie; they lie to me like to a sick person, and sometimes I'm afraid that they're about to sneak up on me and grab me from behind, and take me, like Poprishchin,[24] to an insane asylum. And during those years, my best years, when I was young and just starting out, writing was sheer torture. A small-time writer, especially when it's not going well, sees himself as awkward and clumsy, superfluous, he is on edge and his nerves are strained; he's drawn to wander among the literary and artistic types, unrecognized and unnoticed, afraid to look them directly and boldly in the eyes, like a compulsive gambler who has no money. I didn't see my reader, but for some reason, I imagined him unfriendly, distrustful. I feared the public, it scared me, and whenever I had to stage my new play, it seemed to me each time that the dark-haired ones were hostile, and the fair-haired ones—coldly indifferent. Oh, how awful! What a torture it was!

NINA: But inspiration and the creative process itself, don't they offer sublime and happy moments?

TRIGORIN: Yes. When I'm writing, it's nice. Reading the proofs is nice, too, but . . . as soon as it gets published, I can't stand it and I already see that it's not it, a mistake, and that it shouldn't have been written at all, and I'm annoyed and feeling dreadful . . . [*Laughing*] Then the public reads it: "Yes, it's nice and well written . . . He's a nice and able writer . . . very nice, but a far cry from Tolstoy," or "It's a wonderful work, but Turgenev's *Fathers and Sons* is better." And until the day I die, I'll be a nice and able writer; nice and able—nothing more; and when I die, friends will say as they walk past my grave: "Here rests Trigorin. He was a good writer, but not as good as Turgenev."

NINA: I'm sorry, but I don't understand you. You've simply been spoiled by success.

TRIGORIN: What success? I never liked myself. I don't like myself as a writer. The worst thing is that I'm in this daze and I often don't know what I'm writing . . . I love this water, the trees, and the sky, I feel nature, it stirs passion in me, and an uncontrollable desire to write. But I'm not just a landscape painter, I'm a citizen, too, I love my homeland, my people, I feel that if I'm a writer, I must speak about the people, their suffering, about their future, about science, human rights, and so on and so forth, and I speak about everything, I hurry, and everybody is urging me on all sides, getting upset with me, and I dart from side to side like a fox exhausted by a pack of hounds, seeing that life and science are advancing farther and farther, and I keep falling more and more behind, like a peasant who has missed his train, and in the end I feel that I can only paint landscapes and that as far everything else is concerned, I'm a fraud, a fraud through and through.

NINA: You're overworked, and you don't have the time or desire to recognize your own significance. Even if you are not pleased with yourself, to others you are famous and brilliant! If I were a writer like you, I would give my life to the crowd, keeping in mind, though, that their happiness is in rising up to me, and they would pull me in a chariot.

TRIGORIN: Sure, a chariot . . . like Agamemnon or something?

They both smile.

NINA: For the joy of being a writer or an actress, I'd put up with a lack of sympathy from my family and friends, hardship, disappointment, I'd live on rye bread alone, in a garret, suffer from not liking myself, realize my imperfections, but in return, I would demand fame . . . real, dazzling fame . . . [*She covers her face with her hands*] My head is spinning . . . Phew!

Arkadina's voice coming from inside the house. "Boris! Boris Alexeyevich!"

TRIGORIN: Someone's calling me . . . To pack, most likely, but I don't feel like leaving. [*He looks back at the lake*] A heavenly sight, really! . . . Beautiful!

NINA: Do you see the house with an orchard across the lake?

TRIGORIN: Yes.

NINA: That's my late mother's estate. I was born there. I've spent my whole life by the lake and I know every islet on it.

TRIGORIN: It's so lovely here! [*Upon seeing the seagull*] What's this?

NINA: A seagull. Konstantin Gavrilych killed it.

TRIGORIN: A beautiful bird! No, I certainly don't feel like leaving. Why don't you talk Irina Nikolayevna into staying. [*Writes something in his notebook*]

NINA: What are you writing?

TRIGORIN: Just jotting a few things . . . I had an idea . . . [*He hides the book*] An idea for a short story: a young girl, like you, has lived by the lake since childhood; she loves the lake like a seagull, and is happy and free like a seagull. But a man happened to come by, saw her and, for lack of anything better to do, destroyed her, like this seagull here.

Arkadina appears in the window.

ARKADINA: Boris Alexeyevich, where are you?

TRIGORIN: Coming! [*Walks forward while looking back at Nina; by the window to Arkadina*] What is it?

ARKADINA: We're staying.

Trigorin walks into the house.

NINA [*walks towards the footlights and after a moment's reflection*]: I'm dreaming!

Curtain.

ACT THREE

A dining room in Sorin's house. To the left and right—doors. A sideboard. A medicine chest. In the center of the room, a table. Suitcase, boxes, and other signs of someone's leaving. Trigorin is having breakfast. Masha is standing by the table.

MASHA: I am telling you all this because you're a writer. Feel free to use it. In all honesty, if he had wounded himself seriously, I wouldn't have lived another minute. But still, I'm brave. I upped and made a decision: to pull this love out of my heart, pull it by the roots.

TRIGORIN: In what manner?

MASHA: I'm getting married. To Medvedenko.

TRIGORIN: To the schoolteacher?

MASHA: Yes.

TRIGORIN: I don't understand why you have to.

MASHA: To love hopelessly for years, spend years waiting for something . . . But as soon as I get married, there won't be time for love; new worries will drown out the old. After all, it's a change, you know. Why don't we have another round?

TRIGORIN: Won't it be too much?

MASHA: There! [*She fills both glasses*] Don't look at me like that. Women drink more often than you think. The minority drink openly, like me, but the majority do it in secret. They do. And it's always vodka or cognac. [*Clinks glasses*] I wish you the best! You're nice, without airs, and I'm sorry we have to part.

They drink.

TRIGORIN: I don't feel like leaving myself.

MASHA: Then ask her to stay.

TRIGORIN: No, she isn't going to stay now. Her son is being utterly tactless. First he shoots himself, and now, I hear, he's going to challenge me to a duel. And for what? He sulks, sneers at everything, and preaches new forms . . . But there's room for everybody, the old and the new—why jostle?

MASHA: Well, and jealousy, too. But that's none of my business.

A pause. Yakov crosses the room from left to right with a suitcase; Nina enters and stops by the window.

My schoolteacher may not be all that intelligent, but he's a good-hearted man and poor, and he loves me very much. I feel sorry for him. And I feel sorry for his old mother, too. Well, sir, allow me to wish you all the best. Don't think ill of me. [*She shakes his hand firmly*] Thank you very much for your kind disposition. Send me your books, of course, with an autograph. Only don't write "to the esteemed," but simply "to Maria, who knows not her origin nor reason for living in this world." Good-bye! [*Goes out*]

NINA [*Holding out her closed hand to Trigorin*]: Odd or even?

TRIGORIN: Even.

NINA [*With a sigh*]: No. I only have one piece in my hand. I wanted to find out if I should become an actress or not. If only someone would give me advice.

TRIGORIN: You can't give advice about that.

A pause.

NINA: We have to part . . . perhaps never see each other again. Please accept this little medallion as a keepsake. I had your initials engraved on it . . . and on this side the title of one of your books: *Days and Nights*.

TRIGORIN: How elegant! [*He kisses the medallion*] A delightful present!

NINA: Think of me sometimes.

TRIGORIN: I will think of you. I will think of you as I saw you on that clear day—remember?—a week ago, when you had that pastel dress on . . . We were talking . . . and on the bench there was a white seagull.

NINA [*Lost in thought*]: Yes, a seagull . . .

A pause.

We can't talk anymore, someone's coming here . . . Before you leave, give me two minutes, I entreat you . . . [*Goes out to the left*]

Simultaneously entering, Arkadina, Sorin dressed in tails with a star, then Yakov, who is preoccupied with packing up.

ARKADINA: Why don't you, old man, stay home. To pay visits with your rheumatism? [*To Trigorin*] Who walked out just now? Nina?

TRIGORIN: Yes.

ARKADINA: *Pardon* for disturbing you . . . [*She sits down*] I think I'm all packed. I am exhausted.

TRIGORIN [*Reading the inscription on the medallion*]: "*Days and Nights*, page 121, lines 11 and 12."

YAKOV [*Clearing the table*]: Would you like the fishing rods packed, too?

TRIGORIN: Yes, I'll need them. But the books you can give to someone.

YAKOV: Yes, sir.

TRIGORIN [*To himself*]: Page 121, lines 11 and 12. What's in those lines? [*To Arkadina*] Do we have any of my books here at the house?

ARKADINA: In my brother's study, in the corner bookcase.

TRIGORIN: Page 121 . . . [*Goes out*]

ARKADINA: Really, Petrusha, why don't you stay home . . .

SORIN: You're leaving and it'll be hard for me at home without you.

ARKADINA: And what's in town?

SORIN: Nothing special, but still. [*Laughs*] Breaking ground for a new county seat and all that . . . I want to cheer up, if only for an hour or two, from this backwater existence because I am feeling stale as an old cigarette holder. I told them to bring the horses at one; we'll all leave together.

ARKADINA [*After a pause*]: Well, stay well, don't be lonely, and don't catch a cold. Keep an eye on the son. Take care of him. Instruct him.

A pause.

I'm leaving without knowing why Konstantin tried to shoot himself. I think the main reason was jealousy, and the sooner I take Trigorin away from here, the better.

SORIN: Well, is that all? There were other reasons, too. Obviously, a young man, intelligent, living in the country, in the sticks, without money, without any position, without any prospects. He's not doing anything. He's afraid and ashamed of his idleness. I love him terribly, and he's attached to me, but still, after all, he thinks he's superfluous in the house, a sponger, a hanger-on. Obviously, his pride . . .

ARKADINA: He causes me a lot of worry! [*Pondering*] He ought to get a job, maybe . . .

SORIN [*Whistles, and then speaks hesitantly*]: I think that the best thing would be if you . . . gave him a little money. First of all, he needs to get some decent clothes and all that. Take a look, he's been wearing the same little old frock coat for three years, he doesn't have an overcoat. [*Laughing*] And it wouldn't hurt the youngster to have a little fun . . . Go abroad . . . maybe . . . It doesn't really cost that much.

ARKADINA: Still . . . Well, I could pay for a suit, but to go abroad . . . No, at the present time, I can't, even a suit. [*Resolutely*] I don't have any money!

Sorin laughs.

I don't!

SORIN [*Whistles*]: Well. Forgive me, my dear; don't get angry. I believe you . . . You are a kind and noble woman.

ARKADINA [*Through tears*]: I don't have any money!

SORIN: If I had the money, I would, obviously, give it to him, but I have nothing, zero. The manager takes my pension and spends it on farming, cattle, or beekeeping, and my money goes to waste. The bees croak, the cows croak, and they never give me horses . . .

ARKADINA: Yes, I have money, but I'm an actress, and my outfits alone have completely ruined me.

SORIN: My dear, you're very kind . . . I respect you . . . Well . . . But I'm again not quite . . . [*He staggers*] My head is spinning. [*He holds onto the table*] I feel faint and all that.

ARKADINA [*Frightened*]: Petrusha! [*Trying to support him*] Petrusha, my
    dear! . . . [*She yells*] Help me! Help! . . .

    Enter Treplev with a bandage around his head, and Medvedenko.

    He feels faint!

SORIN: It's all right, it's all right . . . [*He smiles and drinks water*] It's all
    gone . . . and all that . . .

TREPLEV [*To his mother*]: Don't be frightened, Mama, it's not dangerous. It
    happens quite often to Uncle now. [*To his uncle*] Uncle, you should go
    lie down for a bit.

SORIN: A little bit, yes . . . But I'm still going into town . . . I'll lie down for a bit
    and then I'll go, obviously . . . [*He goes out leaning on his cane*]

MEDVEDENKO [*Supporting him by the arm*]: Here's a riddle: on all fours in
    the morning, on two legs at noon, and on three legs in the evening . . .

SORIN [*Laughing*]: Indeed. And on his back at night. Thank you very much, I
    can walk by myself . . .

MEDVEDENKO: Oh, standing on ceremony! . . . [*He and Sorin go out*]

ARKADINA: How he frightened me!

TREPLEV: This country living is not good for him. He's sad. What if suddenly
    you became overly generous and lent him one or two thousand rubles,
    then he could spend a whole year living in town.

ARKADINA: I don't have the money. I'm an actress, not a banker.

    A pause.

TREPLEV: Mama, change the bandage for me. You do it well.

ARKADINA [*Goes to the medicine chest and takes out a box with bandages*]: The
    doctor's late.

TREPLEV: He said he'd be here by ten, and it's already noon.

ARKADINA: Have a seat. [*She takes the bandage off his head*] It's as if you're
    wearing a turban. Yesterday, someone in the kitchen asked what nation-
    ality you were. It's practically all healed. Just a little bit left. [*She kisses
    his head*] You won't try to do bang-bang again while I'm gone?

TREPLEV: No, Mama. That was a moment of overwhelming despair, when I
    lost control of myself. It won't happen again. [*He kisses her hand*] You
    have a magic touch. I remember a long time ago when you were still
    acting at the state theatre—I was little then, and one day there was a
    fistfight in our courtyard, and a tenant, a washerwoman, got beaten
    pretty badly. Do you remember? She was unconscious when they got

her ... and you kept going to see her, brought her medicine, washed her children in the washbasin. Don't you remember?

ARKADINA: I don't. [*She puts on a new bandage*]

TREPLEV: Two ballet dancers lived in the same building with us then ... They used to come over for coffee ...

ARKADINA: That I remember.

TREPLEV: They were very pious.

A pause.

Lately, these few days, I love you again just as tenderly and wholeheartedly like when I was a child. I don't have anyone but you now. Why, why do you fall under the influence of that man?

ARKADINA: You don't understand him, Konstantin. He is a most noble person ...

TREPLEV: However, when they informed him that I was going to challenge him to a duel, his nobleness didn't stop him from playing a coward. He's leaving. Shameful fleeing!

ARKADINA: What nonsense! I'm asking him to leave myself.

TREPLEV: A most noble individual, indeed! Here, we're practically quarreling over him, and he's probably somewhere in the drawing room or in the garden laughing at us now ... educating Nina, trying to convince her once and for all that he's a genius.

ARKADINA: You take pleasure in saying unpleasant things to me. I respect this person, and I ask you not to speak poorly of him in my presence.

TREPLEV: But I don't respect him. You want me to think of him as a genius, too, but, forgive me, I can't lie: his writing sickens me.

ARKADINA: It's jealousy. People who lack talent, not pretensions, can do nothing else but criticize those with real talent. That's some consolation!

TREPLEV [*With irony*]: Real talent! [*Angry*] I'm more talented than all of you if you care to know! [*Pulls the bandage off his head*] You've all lost yourselves to routine; you've seized the top place in the arts, and now you consider only what you do to be legitimate and real; you repress and choke the rest! I don't recognize you! I don't recognize either one of you!

ARKADINA: Decadent!

TREPLEV: Go back to your darling theatre and act there in those worthless, pathetic plays!

ARKADINA: I've never acted in a play like that in my life. Leave me alone! You
    couldn't write a pathetic vaudeville skit even if you wanted to. A com-
    moner from Kiev! A sponger!

TREPLEV: Miser!

ARKADINA: Ragamuffin!

    Treplev sits down and begins to cry softly.

    A nobody! [*After walking in agitation*] Don't cry! No need to cry!
    [*Crying*] Don't . . . [*She kisses him on the forehead, cheeks, head*] My
    darling child, forgive me . . . Forgive your sinful mother. Forgive a poor
    woman.

TREPLEV [*Embraces her*] Oh, if you only knew! I've lost everything. She doesn't
    love me, I can't write anymore . . . all my hopes are gone . . .

ARKADINA: Don't despair . . . It'll work out. He's leaving and she'll love you
    again. [*She wipes away his tears*] There, there. We have made up already.

TREPLEV [*Kissing her hand*]: Yes, Mama.

ARKADINA [*Tenderly*]: Make peace with him, too. There is no need for a
    duel . . . No need for it, right?

TREPLEV: All right . . . Only, please Mama, allow me not to see him. It's too
    hard for me . . . , more than I can bear . . .

    Trigorin comes in.

    Here . . . I'll go out . . . [*He quickly puts the medicine away in the
    cupboard*] The doctor will fix the bandage later . . .

TRIGORIN [*Looking through the pages of a book*]: Page 121, lines 11 and 12 . . .
    Here . . . [*He reads*] "Should you ever need my life, come and take it."

    Treplev picks up the dressing off the floor and leaves.

ARKADINA [*After looking at her watch*]: They'll bring the horses around soon.

TRIGORIN [*To himself*]: Should you ever need my life, come and take it.

ARKADINA: Your things, I hope, are all packed?

TRIGORIN [*Impatiently*]: Yes, yes . . . [*Musing*] Why did I hear a note of sad-
    ness in this call of a pure soul and why is my heart so painfully wrung?
    Should you ever need my life, come and take it. [*To Arkadina*] Let's stay
    here one more day!

    Arkadina shakes her head no.

    Let's stay!

ARKADINA: My dear, I know *what's* keeping you here. Control yourself. You're a little drunk; sober up.

TRIGORIN: You be sober, too, be intelligent and reasonable, I implore you, look at all this like a true friend . . . [*Squeezes her hand*] You're capable of sacrifice . . . Be my friend, let me go . . .

ARKADINA [*Anxiously*]: Are you so taken with her?

TRIGORIN: I'm drawn to her! Maybe it's exactly what I need.

ARKADINA: The love of a provincial girl? Oh, how little you know yourself!

TRIGORIN: Sometimes people dream while awake, and here I'm talking to you and it's as if I'm sleeping and dreaming of her . . . I'm overcome with sweet and wondrous dreams . . . Let me go . . .

ARKADINA [*Trembling*]: No, no . . . I'm an ordinary woman; you can't talk to me like this . . . Don't torture me, Boris . . . I'm frightened . . .

TRIGORIN: If you want to, you can be extraordinary. Only youthful, exquisite, poetic love transporting one to the realm of dreams—in this world, it alone can provide happiness! I haven't experienced this love yet . . . When I was young, there was no time, I was beating down doors of editors, besieged by poverty . . . And now here it is, it has finally come, and it beckons me . . . What is the point of running away from it?

ARKADINA [*Enraged*]: You've lost your mind!

TRIGORIN: So be it.

ARKADINA: You've all conspired today to torture me. [*She cries*]

TRIGORIN [*Clutching his head*]: She doesn't understand! She doesn't want to understand!

ARKADINA: Am I so old and hideous that you can, without shame, talk to me about other women? [*She embraces and kisses him*] Oh, you've lost your mind! My beautiful, my wondrous . . . You are the final page of my life! [*She kneels*] My joy, my pride, my bliss . . . [*She embraces his knees*] If you leave me even for an hour, I won't survive it; I'll lose my mind, my marvel, my splendor, my master . . .

TRIGORIN: Someone might come in here. [*He helps her get up*]

ARKADINA: Let them! I'm not ashamed of my love for you. [*She kisses his hands*] My treasure, my reckless boy; you want to behave like a madman, but I don't want to and I won't let go . . . [*She laughs*] You are mine, mine . . . This forehead's mine, and these eyes are mine, and this beautiful silken hair is mine, too . . . You're all mine. You are so talented, intelligent, the best of all writers nowadays; you're Russia's only hope . . . You have so much sincerity, ease, originality, and good humor . . . With a single stroke you can convey the essence of a face or a landscape; your characters all seem alive. One can't read you without admiration! Do you think it's adulation? I'm just flattering you? Look in my eyes . . . look . . . Do I look like a liar? So you see that I alone know how to appreciate you; I'm the only one telling you the truth, my dear, my darling . . . Will you come? You will? You won't leave me? . . .

TRIGORIN: I have no willpower . . . I never had my own will . . . Inert, doughy, always obedient—how can women like this? Take me, take me away, only don't let me out of your sight . . .

ARKADINA [*To herself*]: Now he's mine. [*Carelessly, as if nothing happened*] But you can stay if you wish. I'll go by myself, and you can come later, in a week. Really, what's the hurry?

TRIGORIN: No, let's go together then.

ARKADINA: Whatever you want. Together is fine . . .

A pause. Trigorin writes something in his notebook.

What is it?

TRIGORIN: This morning, I heard a good expression: "a virgin forest." It may come in handy. [*He stretches*] So we are going? Again, trains, train stations, refreshment bars, cutlets, conversations . . .

SHAMRAEV [*Comes in*]: I have the honor to announce with great regret that the horses are ready. It's time, my dear madame, to go to the station. The train arrives at five past two. And so, Irina Nikolayevna, do me a favor, don't forget to make an inquiry: where the actor Suzdaltzev is now? Is he around? Is he well? We used to go out drinking together. In *The Stage Coach Robbery* he was inimitable . . . I remember, in the same company with him in Elisavetgrad,[25] there was a tragedian, Izmailov, also a remarkable person . . . No need to rush, my dear madame, we have another five minutes. Once, the two of them were playing conspirators in a melodrama, and when they got nailed, the line was "We fell into a trap!" but instead Izmailov said: "We fell into a tap!" [*Shouts with laughter*] Into a tap! . . .

While he is talking, Yakov busies himself with the suitcases, a maid is bringing Arkadina her hat, coat, umbrella, and gloves; everybody helps Arkadina get dressed. From the door on the left, the cook looks in, and a little later hesitantly comes into the room. Enter Polina, then Sorin, and Medvedenko.

POLINA [*With a small basket*]: Here are some plums for the journey . . . They're very sweet. Maybe you'll want to treat yourself to a morsel . . .

ARKADINA: You are very kind, Polina Andreyevna.

POLINA: Good-bye, my dear! Forgive me if anything wasn't quite to your liking. [*She weeps*]

ARKADINA [*Embracing her*]: Everything was beautiful, just beautiful. Only there's no need to cry.

POLINA: Our time is slipping away!

ARKADINA: There's nothing we can do!

SORIN [*In a coat with a shoulder cape, hat, and with a cane comes out of the door on the left and crosses the room*]: Sister, it's time, we don't want to miss it, after all. I'll go sit in the carriage. [*He goes out*]

MEDVEDENKO: And I'll walk to the station . . . to see you off. I'll be quick . . . [*He goes out*]

ARKADINA: Good-bye, my dears . . . If everything goes well, we'll see each other again next summer . . .

The maid, Yakov, and the cook kiss her hand.

Think of me. [*She gives the cook a ruble*] Here's a ruble for the three of you.[26]

THE COOK: Thank you kindly, ma'am. Have a pleasant journey. Much thankful we are by you!

YAKOV: Good luck!

SHAMRAEV: Make us happy, send us a letter! [*To Trigorin*] Good-bye, Boris Alexeyevich.

ARKADINA: Where's Konstantin? Tell him I'm leaving. We have to say good-bye. Well, think kindly of us. [*To Yakov*] I gave the cook a ruble. That's for the three of them.

Everybody goes to the right. The stage is empty. From behind the stage sounds of good-byes and similar sounds associated with parting. The maid comes back to get the basket of plums from the table and goes out again.

TRIGORIN [*Coming back*]: I forgot my cane. I think it's on the terrace. [*He walks and by the door on the left he runs into Nina, who's coming in*] It's you? We're leaving . . .

NINA: I had a feeling that we'd see each other. [*Excitedly*] Boris Alexeyevich, I made an irrevocable decision, the die is cast, and I am joining the stage. As of tomorrow I won't be here; I'm leaving my father, abandoning everything, beginning a new life . . . I'm leaving just like you . . . for Moscow. We'll see each other there.

TRIGORIN [*After turning around*]: Stay at the Hotel Slavic Bazaar. Let me know right away . . . Grokholsky's house on Molchanovka²⁷ Street . . . I'm in a hurry . . .

A pause.

NINA: Just one more minute . . .

TRIGORIN [*In a whisper*]: You're so beautiful . . . Oh, it makes me so happy to know that we'll see each other soon!

She leans her head on his chest.

I'll see again these marvelous eyes, this beautiful, indescribably beautiful and tender smile . . . these gentle features, expression of angelic purity . . . My dear . . .

A prolonged kiss.

Curtain.

Two years pass between the third and fourth acts

ACT FOUR

One of the drawing rooms in Sorin's house, transformed by Konstantin Treplev into a study. On the right and on the left—doors leading into inner rooms, and in the center—a glass door opening to the terrace. In addition to the usual drawing room furniture, in the right corner there is a desk, a Turkish divan by the door on the left, and a bookcase; there are books on the window sills and chairs. It is evening. One lamp is lit; it is under a lampshade. It is dark. Trees are rustling and the wind is howling in the chimney. A night watchman taps.

Enter Medvedenko and Masha.

MASHA [*Calling out*]: Konstantin Gavrilych! Konstantin Gavrilych! [*Looking around her*] There's no one here. The old man is asking for him every

minute: where's Kostya? Where's Kostya? . . . He can't stand being without him . . .

MEDVEDENKO: He's afraid of loneliness. [*Listening*] What miserable weather!
It's the second day already.

MASHA [*Turning up the lamp*]: There are waves on the lake. They're huge.

MEDVEDENKO: It's dark in the garden. We ought to tell them to knock down
the theater in the garden. It stands there bare and hideous like a skel-
eton with the curtain flapping in the wind. Last night, when I walked
by, I thought I heard someone crying there.

MASHA: Please . . .

A pause.

MEDVEDENKO: Let's go home, Masha!

MASHA [*Shaking her head*]: I'm spending the night here.

MEDVEDENKO [*Imploringly*]: Masha, come! Our baby is surely hungry.

MASHA: That's nonsense. Matriona will feed him.

A pause.

MEDVEDENKO: I feel so sorry. It's a third night without his mother.

MASHA: You've become so boring. Before you used to philosophize now and
then, but now it's all baby this, come home, baby that, come home—
that's all I ever hear from you.

MEDVEDENKO: Masha, let's go!

MASHA: Go by yourself.

MEDVEDENKO: Your father won't give me a horse.

MASHA: He will. Ask him and he will.

MEDVEDENKO: Maybe I'll ask him. You'll come home tomorrow, then?

MASHA [*She takes snuff*]: Fine, tomorrow. Stop bothering me . . .

*Enter Treplev and Polina Andreyevna. Treplev brings pillows and a blanket,
and Polina Andreyevna is carrying bed linens; they put them on the Turkish
divan, then Treplev walks over to his desk and sits down.*

MASHA: What's this for, Mama?

POLINA: Pyotr Nikolayevich has asked to make his bed in Kostya's room.

MASHA: I'll do it . . . [*Makes the bed*]

POLINA [*With a sigh*]: Old folks are like children. [*She comes over to the desk
and leaning on her elbow, looks at a manuscript; a pause*]

MEDVEDENKO: So I'll go then. Good-bye, Masha. [*He kisses his wife's hand*] Good-bye, Mamasha. [*He wants to kiss his mother-in-law's hand*]

POLINA [*With annoyance*]: Well! God bless.

MEDVEDENKO: Good-bye, Konstantin Gavrilovich.

Treplev offers his hand in silence; Medvedenko walks out.

POLINA [*Looking at the manuscript*]: Kostya, no one saw it coming that one day you'd become a real writer. And now, thank God, you're getting money from magazines. [*She strokes his hair*] And you're handsome now . . . Kostya, dear, be a little sweeter with my Mashenka! . . .

MASHA [*Still making the bed*]: Leave him alone, Mama.

POLINA: She's nice.

A pause.

Kostya, a woman doesn't need much, just glance at her sweetly. I know from experience.

Treplev gets up from his desk and goes out without a word.

MASHA: There, now you upset him. You had to bother him!

POLINA: I feel sorry for you, Mashenka.

MASHA: I don't need it!

POLINA: My heart's aching for you. I see everything and understand everything.

MASHA: It's nothing. Hopeless love—it's only in novels. That's all nonsense. Just don't let yourself go and don't keep waiting for something, waiting by the sea for the wind to change . . . As soon as love creeps into your heart, get rid of it. They promised to transfer my husband to another district. And as soon as we move there—I'll forget it all . . . pull it out of my heart straight by the roots.

Sounds of a melancholy waltz are heard coming from two rooms away.

POLINA: Kostya's playing. He must be feeling sad.

MASHA [*Silently takes two or three waltz turns*]: The main thing, Mama, is not to see him. As soon as they give my husband a transfer, trust me, I will forget it all in a month or two. It's all nonsense.

The left door opens and Dorn and Medvedenko come in, wheeling Sorin in a wheelchair.

MEDVEDENKO: I now have six mouths to feed in my house. And the flour is seven hryvnas a bushel.[28]

DORN: Try to make ends meet.

MEDVEDENKO: It's easy for you to laugh. You've more money than you know what to do with.

DORN: Money? My friend, in thirty years of medical practice, busy practice, when I never belonged to myself, not during the day, not at night, I managed to save only two thousand, all of which I recently spent abroad. I have nothing left.

MASHA [*To her husband*]: You're still here?

MEDVEDENKO [*Apologetically*]: Well? What can I do? He won't give me a horse!

MASHA [*Under her breath, with bitter annoyance*]: I don't want to see you!

The wheelchair stops when it gets to the left side of the room; Polina, Masha, and Dorn sit down beside it. Medvedenko, offended, moves to the side.

DORN: All these changes, however! You turned a drawing room into a study.

MASHA: It's better for Konstantin Gavrilovich to work here. He can, whenever he wants to, walk out into the garden to think there.

The watchman taps.

SORIN: Where's my sister?

DORN: She went to the station to meet Trigorin. She'll be right back.

SORIN: If you thought it necessary to send for my sister, then I must be gravely ill. [*After a short silence*] A pretty kettle of fish: I'm gravely ill, and no one's giving me any medicine.

DORN: What do you want? Sedative drops? Sodium bicarbonate? Quinine?

SORIN: Oh, here you go with philosophy. I don't deserve this! [*He nods toward the couch*] Is the bed made for me?

POLINA: For you, Pyotr Nikolayevich.

SORIN: Much obliged.

DORN [*Sings*]: "The moon is sailing in the evening sky."[29]

SORIN: I want to give Konstantin an idea for a story. The title should be "A Man Who Wanted To," "*L'Homme qui a voulu.*" When I was young I wanted to become a fiction writer—I didn't; I wanted to speak eloquently— and I spoke dreadfully [*mocking himself*]: "and all that, and such, quite, not quite . . ." and I remember struggling, struggling to write a memo, even breaking out in a sweat. I wanted to get married—and I didn't; I always wanted to live in a town, and here I am, spending my last days in the country and all that.

DORN: You wanted to become state councilor—and you did!

SORIN [*Laughs*]: I didn't aspire to it. It happened by itself.

DORN: Admit it, expressing dissatisfaction with life at sixty-two is ungenerous.

SORIN: How stubborn you are. Don't you see, I feel like living!

DORN: That's foolish. It's the law of nature that every kind of life must come to an end.

SORIN: You sound like a man who's had his fill. You've had your fill and are therefore indifferent to life, you don't care. But you, too, will be afraid to die.

DORN: Fear of death—it's a blind fear . . . You have to suppress it. Only those who believe in eternal life consciously fear death and shudder at the thought of their sins. And you, first of all, you are a nonbeliever, and secondly, what sins? You served twenty-five years in the court system—that's all.

SORIN [*Laughs*]: Twenty-eight . . .

Treplev enters and sits down on a small bench by Sorin's feet. Masha does not take her eyes off him the whole time.

DORN: We're keeping Konstantin Gavrilovich from working.

TREPLEV: No, it's all right.

A pause.

MEDVEDENKO: Doctor, allow me to ask you, which city did you like the most abroad?

DORN: Genoa.

TREPLEV: Why Genoa?

DORN: There is a superb street crowd there. In the evening, when you leave the hotel, the entire street is jammed with people. You move about with the crowd this way and that way, without a goal, along a broken line, you live with it, you blend into it psychically, and you begin to believe that, yes, a single world soul like the one that Nina Zarechnaya portrayed in your play is possible. By the way, where's Zarechnaya now? Where and how is she?

TREPLEV: She must be fine.

DORN: I heard that she's had a rather peculiar life. What's the matter?

TREPLEV: It's a long story, Doctor.

DORN: Make it short.

A pause.

TREPLEV: She ran away from home and had an affair with Trigorin. Did you
　　know that?

DORN: Yes, I did.

TREPLEV: She had a child. The child died. Trigorin fell out of love with her and
　　went back to his former attachments, as you would expect. Or rather, he
　　never gave them up and, thanks to his spinelessness, he managed both
　　here and there. From what I understand, based on what I know, Nina's
　　personal life didn't turn out well at all.

DORN: And what about the stage?

TREPLEV: Even worse, I think. She made her debut at a summer theatre out-
　　side of Moscow; then she left for the provinces. I tried not to lose sight
　　of her and for some time wherever she went I followed. She took up big
　　roles mostly, but her acting was crude and tasteless, with wailing and
　　jerky gestures. There were moments when she showed talent: she would
　　shriek well, die well, but those were only moments.

DORN: So she does have talent?

TREPLEV: It was hard to tell. She must. I saw her, but she didn't want to see
　　me, and the servants wouldn't let me in her hotel room. I knew how she
　　felt and so didn't insist on meeting with her.

　　A pause.

　　What else can I tell you? Later, after I came home, I received letters
　　from her. Intelligent, warm, and always interesting letters; she never
　　complained, but I sensed that she was profoundly unhappy; every line
　　betrayed an aching and strained nerve. Her imagination was a little
　　disturbed, too. She signed her letters "A Seagull." In *The Water Nymph*[30]
　　a miller says that he's a raven, and just like him, she was always saying in
　　her letters that she was a seagull. She's here now.

DORN: What do you mean here?

TREPLEV: In town, at the inn. She's been staying there, in one of the rooms,
　　five days already. I almost went, and Maria Ilinichna went to see her as
　　well, but she refuses to see anyone. Semyon Semyonovich is convinced
　　that he saw her yesterday after dinner in a field a mile or so from here.

MEDVEDENKO: Yes, I saw her. She was walking in the direction of the town. I
　　bowed to her and asked her how come she hadn't come by to see us. She
　　said she would come by.

TREPLEV: She won't.

A pause.

Her father and stepmother don't want anything to do with her. They have placed watchmen all around not to let her even close to the house. [*He walks with the doctor toward the desk*] It's so easy, Doctor, to be a philosopher on paper, and so hard in real life!

SORIN: She was a lovely girl.

DORN: What was that?

SORIN: I said she was a lovely girl. State Councilor Sorin for some time was even in love with her.

DORN: The old Lovelace.

Shamraev's laughter is heard.

POLINA: I think they're back from the station . . .

TREPLEV: Yes, I hear Mama's voice.

Enter Arkadina, Trigorin, followed by Shamraev.

SHAMRAEV [*Entering*]: We all fade and grow old under the elements, while you, my dearest madam, are still young . . . Pastel blouse, lively . . . graceful . . .

ARKADINA: You want to put an evil eye on me again, you boring man!

TRIGORIN [*To Sorin*]: Hello, Pyotr Nikolayevich! Still ailing? That's not good! [*Upon seeing Masha, with joy*] How are you, Maria Ilinichna?

MASHA: You recognized me? [*She shakes his hand*]

TRIGORIN: Are you married?

MASHA: A long time.

TRIGORIN: Happy? [*He bows to Dorn and Medvedenko, and then walks hesitantly toward Treplev*] Irina Nikolayevna tells me that bygones are bygones and you are no longer furious with me.

Treplev offers him his hand.

ARKADINA [*To her son*]: Look, Boris Alexeyevich brought a magazine with your new story.

TREPLEV [*To Trigorin, as he takes the book*]: Thank you very much. You are very kind.

They sit down.

TRIGORIN: Your admirers send you their respects . . . In St. Petersburg and Moscow, they are generally interested in you, and always ask me about you. They ask: what's he like, how old, dark or fair-haired. The.y think for some reason that you are much older. And nobody knows your real name since you publish under a pseudonym. You're as mysterious as the Man in the Iron Mask.

TREPLEV: Staying long with us?

TRIGORIN: No, I'm planning to go back to Moscow tomorrow. I have to. I'm trying to finish a novella, and I also promised to produce something for the anthology. In short—it's the same old story.

While they are talking, Arkadina and Polina are opening a folding card table in the center of the room. Shamraev lights the candles and arranges the chairs. Then from the cupboard they bring out a game of bingo.

TRIGORIN: The weather has given me a rough welcome. The wind is brutal. Tomorrow morning, if it dies down, I'll go fishing by the lake. By the way, I need to look around the garden and that spot—do you remember?—where your play was. I've hatched a plot, and now I just need to refresh my memory on the place of action.

MASHA [*To her father*]: Papa, let my husband take a horse. He's got to go home.

SHAMRAEV [*Mockingly*]: A horse . . . go home . . . [*Sternly*] You saw it yourself: the horses have just got back from the station. You can't expect me to send them out again.

MASHA: But there are other horses . . . [*Seeing that her father remains silent, she makes a gesture of resignation with her hand*] No point in talking to you . . .

MEDVEDENKO: Masha, I'll walk. Really . . .

POLINA [*With a sigh*]: To walk, in this weather . . . [*Sits at the card table*] Come, ladies and gentlemen.

MEDVEDENKO: It's only four miles . . . Good-bye. [*He kisses his wife's hand*] Good-bye, Mamasha.

His mother-in-law reluctantly offers him her hand.

I wouldn't have troubled anyone, but the baby . . . [*He bows to everybody*] Good-bye . . . [*He leaves, walking apologetically*]

SHAMRAEV: He'll get there without. Who does he think he is.

POLINA [*Knocking on the table*]: Come, ladies and gentlemen. Let's not lose any time because supper will be served soon.

Shamraev, Masha, and Dorn sit down at the card table.

ARKADINA [*To Trigorin*]: When long evenings come in the fall, they play bingo here. Here, take a look: an antique bingo set that our mother used to play with us when we were still children. Won't you play a game with us before supper? [*She and Trigorin sit down at the table*] The game is boring, but if you get used to it, then it's not so bad. [*She deals three cards to each player*]

TREPLEV [*Flipping through the pages of the magazine*]: He's read his own story but didn't even cut open the pages of mine. [*He puts the magazine on his desk and then walks in the direction of the door on the left; as he passes by his mother, he kisses her on the head*]

ARKADINA: And you, Kostya?

TREPLEV: I am sorry, I just don't feel like it . . . I'll go take a walk. [*He goes out*]

ARKADINA: The ante—ten kopecks. Doctor, put in for me.

DORN: Yes, ma'am.

MASHA: Everybody is in? I'm starting . . . Twenty-two!

ARKADINA: Here.

MASHA: Three! . . .

DORN: So it is.

MASHA: Have you put down three? Eight! Eighty-one! Ten!

SHAMRAEV: Don't rush.

ARKADINA: What a reception they gave me in Kharkov,[31] my goodness, my head is still spinning!

MASHA: Thirty-four!

Someone is playing a melancholy waltz offstage.

ARKADINA: The students gave me a standing ovation . . . three baskets, two wreaths, and here . . . [*She takes off a brooch off her chest and throws it on the table*]

SHAMRAEV: That's really something . . .

MASHA: Fifty! . . .

DORN: Fifty even?

ARKADINA: I wore an amazing outfit . . . I am no slouch when it comes to dressing.

POLINA: Kostya's playing again. He's sad, poor boy.

SHAMRAEV: He's been criticized in the papers a lot.

MASHA: Seventy-seven!

ARKADINA: No need to pay attention.

TRIGORIN: He's out of luck. He can't seem to zero in on his true voice yet. It's all strange, vague, sometimes verging on delirium. Not a single live character.

MASHA: Eleven!

ARKADINA [*Looking back at Sorin*]: Petrusha, are you bored?

A pause.

He's asleep.

DORN: The state councilor is asleep.

MASHA: Seven! Ninety!

TRIGORIN: If I had an estate like this, by the lake, would I bother with writing? I would've gotten over that desire and all I'd do all day is fish.

MASHA: Twenty-eight!

TRIGORIN: To catch a ruff or a perch—that is bliss!

DORN: I believe in Konstantin Gavrilych. There is something there! There's something there! He thinks in images; his stories are vivid and striking, and they affect me deeply. It's a pity that he doesn't have a well-defined goal. He only makes an impression, and nothing else, but you can't get very far on impression alone. Irina Nikolayevna, are you glad that your son's a writer?

ARKADINA: Would you believe I haven't read him yet. I haven't had the time.

MASHA: Twenty-six!

Treplev comes in quietly and walks over to his desk.

SHAMRAEV [*To Trigorin*]: Boris Alexeyevich, we have one of your things here.

TRIGORIN: What is it?

SHAMRAEV: A while ago, Konstantin Gavrilych shot a seagull, and you asked me to have it stuffed.

TRIGORIN: I don't remember it. [*Pondering*] I don't remember!

MASHA: Sixty-six! One!

TREPLEV [*Throws open the window and stands listening*]: How dark it is! I don't understand why I'm feeling so restless.

ARKADINA: Kostya, close the window; it's drafty.

Treplev shuts the window.

MASHA: Eighty-eight!

TRIGORIN: I finished, ladies and gentlemen.

ARKADINA [*Happily*]: Bravo! Bravo!

SHAMRAEV: Bravo!

ARKADINA: This man is always lucky, no matter where he goes and what he does. [*She gets up*] And now, let's eat something. Our celebrity didn't have lunch today. After supper, we'll continue playing. [*To her son*] Come, Kostya, leave your manuscript, let's go eat.

TREPLEV: I don't want to, Mama; I am full.

ARKADINA: As you wish. [*She wakes up Sorin*] Let's have supper, Petrusha! [*She takes Shamraev by the arm*] I'll tell you about the reception they gave me in Kharkov . . .

Polina snuffs out the candles on the table, then she and Dorn roll the wheel-chair. Everybody goes out through the door on the left; Treplev is left alone on the stage sitting at his desk.

TREPLEV [*Getting ready to start writing; skims over what is already written*]: I talked so much about new forms, and now I feel myself that little by little I am sliding towards a routine. [*He reads*] "The poster on the fence announced . . . A pale face framed by dark hair." Announced . . . framed . . . It's worthless. [*He crosses it out*] I'll start with my hero waking up to the sound of the rain, and the rest must go. A description of a moonlit night is long and refined. Trigorin has worked out his techniques and it's easy for him. He has a neck of a broken bottle gleaming on the dam and the looming black shadows of the mill wheel—and there's your moonlit night, whereas I have a quivering light, quiet twinkling of stars, and the distant sounds of a piano fading into still and fragrant air . . . This is torture.

A pause.

Yes, I'm becoming more and more convinced that it's not the old or the new forms that are important, but that a person writes without thinking about forms at all, writes because it pours freely from his heart.

Someone knocks at the window nearest to the desk.

What's that? [*He looks out of the window*] I can't see anything . . . [*Opens the glass door and looks out into the garden*] Someone ran down the steps. [*He calls*] Who's there? [*He goes out, and is heard walking quickly along the terrace; after half a minute, he comes back with Nina Zarechnaya*] Nina! Nina!

Nina rests her head on Treplev's chest, and sobs quietly.

[*Deeply moved.*] Nina! Nina! It's you . . . you . . . It's as if I knew and in my soul agonized all day. [*Takes off her cape and hat*] Oh, my good girl, my precious, she came! We won't cry, we won't.

NINA: There's someone here.

TREPLEV: No one.

NINA: Lock the doors, so no one comes in.

TREPLEV: No one will come in.

NINA: I know Irina Nikolayevna is here. Lock the doors . . .

TREPLEV [*Locks the door on the right and walks over to the door on the left*]: There's no lock here. I'll block it with an armchair. [*Puts the armchair against the door*] Don't be afraid, no one will come in.

NINA [*Gazing intently at his face*]: Let me look at you. [*She looks about her*] It's nice and warm here . . . This used to be the drawing room then. Have I changed much?

TREPLEV: Yes . . . You've become thinner and your eyes are bigger now. Nina, it's so strange for me to see you. Why wouldn't you let me see you? Why hadn't you come sooner? I know you've been staying here almost a week . . . I went to your place several times a day and stood under your windows, like a beggar.

NINA: I was afraid that you hated me. I dream every night that you're looking at me and don't recognize me. If you only knew! Ever since I arrived here, I've been wandering around . . . by the lake. I walked by your house many times, but I didn't have the courage to come in. Let's sit down.

They sit down.

We'll sit down and we'll talk, talk. It's nice here, warm and homey . . . Do you hear—the wind? There is a passage in Turgenev: "It's good for someone on a night like this to have a roof over his head and a warm corner to sit in."[32] I'm—a seagull . . . No, that's not it. [*Rubs her forehead with her hand*] What was I saying? Yes . . . Turgenev . . . He says, "and may God help all the homeless wanderers . . ." [*Sobs*] It's all right. [*She sobs*]

TREPLEV: Nina, you are again . . . Nina!

NINA: It's all right and I feel better . . . I haven't cried for two years. Late last night I went to look in the garden, if our theatre was still there. And it's still there. I cried there for the first time in two years, and I felt a sense of relief, and it felt lighter in my soul. See, I'm not crying anymore. [*She takes his hand in hers*] So, you've already become a writer . . . You're a writer, and I'm an actress . . . Together we've fallen into this spinning circle . . . I lived a happy life, like a child—wake up in the morning and start singing; I loved you, I dreamed about fame, and now? Tomorrow, I take an early train to Yelets, in the third class . . . with the muzhiks,[33] and in Yelets, cultured merchants will bother me with their compliments. Life is vulgar!

TREPLEV: What's in Yelets?

NINA: I have a contract there for the winter. It's time to go.

TREPLEV: Nina, I cursed you, I hated you, tore up your letters and photographs, and yet every minute I knew that my soul is forever attached to yours. Nina, I can't stop loving you. Ever since I lost you and since I started getting published, my life has become unbearable—I suffer . . . It's as if my youth was suddenly torn away from me, and it feels like I've already been here for ninety years. I call out to you, kiss the ground you walked on; wherever I look, I see your face, this tender smile that brightened the best years of my life.

NINA [*Perplexed*]: Why is he saying that, why is he saying that?

TREPLEV: I'm alone, not warmed by anyone's affection, I'm cold as in a cave, and whatever I write comes out dry, callous, and dark. Stay here, Nina, I implore you, or else allow me go with you!

Nina quickly puts on her hat and cape.

TREPLEV: Nina, why? For God's sake, Nina . . . [*He watches her as she puts on her cape*]

A pause.

NINA: My horses are at the gate. Don't see me off, I'll go myself . . . [*Through tears*] Give me some water . . .

TREPLEV [*Hands her water*]: Where are you going now?

NINA: To town.

A pause.

Is Irina Nikolayevna here?

TREPLEV: Yes . . . My uncle fell ill on Thursday, and we sent a telegram for her to come.

NINA: Why do you say that you kissed the ground I walked on? Someone should kill me. [*She bends over the table*] I'm tired out! If only I could

rest . . . rest! [*She raises her head*] I'm—a seagull . . . That's not it. I'm—
an actress. Well, then! [*Upon hearing Arkadina and Trigorin laughing,
she listens, then she runs to the door on the left and looks through the key-
hole*] And he's here, too . . . [*Walking back to Treplev*] Well then . . . It's
all right . . . Yes . . . He didn't believe in theatre, made fun of my dreams,
and little by little I stopped believing in it, too, and lost heart . . . Then
all these worries of love, jealousy, and a constant fear for the baby . . . I
became petty, worthless, my acting was meaningless . . . I didn't know
what to do with my hands; I didn't know how to stand up on stage,
couldn't control my voice. You don't understand what that condition
is, when you know that your acting is awful. I'm—a seagull. No, that's
not it . . . Do you remember you shot a seagull? A man happened to
come by, saw, and for the lack of anything better to do, destroyed . . . An
idea for a short story. That's not it. [*Rubs her forehead*] What was I saying? . . . Oh, yes, I'm talking about the stage. I'm not like that . . . I'm a
real actress now and I act with joy and excitement; I get intoxicated on
stage and I feel beautiful. But now, while I'm here, I walk everywhere, I
walk and I think; I think and I feel that with every passing day my mental strength grows . . . Now I know, I understand, Kostya, that for our
work—it doesn't matter whether it's acting or writing—the important
thing is not fame or glory, not what I dreamed about, but the ability to
endure. Know how to bear your cross and have faith. I have faith and
it doesn't hurt as much, and when I think about my calling, I'm not
afraid of life.

TREPLEV [*Sadly*]: You have found your path and you know where you're
going, but I'm still rushing about in the chaos of dreams and images,
not knowing who needs it and what for. I don't believe in it and I don't
know what my calling is.

NINA [*Listening*]: Shhh! I'm going. Good-bye. When I become a famous actress, come have a look at me. You promise? But now . . . [*She shakes
his hand*] It's late. I can barely stand up on my feet . . . I'm completely
exhausted, I'd like something to eat . . .

TREPLEV: Stay, I'll bring you supper . . .

NINA: No, no . . . Don't see me off, I'll get there myself . . . The horses are
nearby . . . So she brought him with her? Well, it doesn't matter. When
you see Trigorin, don't tell him anything . . . I love him. I love him

even more than before . . . An idea for a short story . . . I love, love him passionately, I love him desperately. It was so nice before, Kostya! Do you remember? What a bright, warm, joyous, innocent life, and the feelings—feelings resembling tender and elegant flowers . . . Do you remember? . . . [*She recites*] "People, lions, eagles and quails, horned stags, geese, spiders, silent fish that used to inhabit the water, starfish, and creatures were invisible to the eye—in short, all lives, all lives, all lives, having completed their mournful cycle have died out. It has been thousands of centuries since the earth has supported a single live creature, and this poor Moon in vain lights its lantern. The cranes in the meadows no longer awaken with a call, and the beetles are not heard anymore in the linden groves. . . ." [*Abruptly embraces Treplev and runs out through the glass door*]

TREPLEV [*After a pause*]: It's bad if someone sees her in the garden and then tells Mama about it. It may upset Mama . . . [*For two minutes he tears up all his manuscripts and throws them under the desk, then he unlocks the door on the right and goes out*]

DORN [*Trying to open the door on the left*]: That's strange. The door seems locked . . . [*He comes in and puts the chair back*] An obstacle course.

Arkadina and Polina enter, behind them Yakov carrying the bottles; then Masha, then Shamraev and Trigorin.

ARKADINA: The red wine and the beer for Boris Alexeyevich goes right here on the table. We will play and drink. Let's take our seats, ladies and gentlemen.

POLINA [*To Yakov*]: Bring us tea at the same time, too. [*She lights the candles and sits down at the card table*]

SHAMRAEV [*Leads Trigorin to the bookcase*] Here's the thing I was just telling you about . . . [*He takes the stuffed seagull out of the bookcase*] Made to order.

TRIGORIN [*Looking at the seagull*]: I don't remember! [*After thinking a little*] I don't remember!

[*A shot is heard from offstage right; everyone jumps*]

ARKADINA [*Frightened*]: What was that?

DORN: It's nothing. Something must have exploded in my portable medicine case. Don't worry. [*He goes out through the door on the right, and comes back half a minute later*] Just as I thought. A jar of ether exploded. [*He sings*] "Spellbound once more I stand before you . . ."³⁴

ARKADINA [*Sitting down at the table*]: Phew! I got frightened. It reminded me when . . . [*She covers her face with her hands*] Everything went dark for a second even.

DORN [*Flipping through the pages of a magazine, to Trigorin*]: About two months ago, they published an article here . . . a letter from America, and I wanted to ask you by the way . . . [*Puts his arm around Trigorin's waist and takes him toward the footlights*] since I'm very interested in this subject . . . [*He lowers his voice to a half-whisper*] Take Irina Niko-layevna away from here. The thing is, Konstantin Gavrilovich has shot himself . . .

Curtain.

UNCLE VANYA

Scenes from Country Life in Four Acts

Characters

SEREBRIAKOV, ALEXANDER VLADIMIROVICH, a retired professor

ELENA ANDREYEVNA, his wife, 27 years old

SOFIA ALEXANDROVNA, his daughter from the first marriage

MME VOINITSKAYA, MARIA VASILYEVNA, a widow of a privy councilor
    and mother of Professor Serebriakov's first wife

VOINITSKY, IVAN PETROVICH, her son

ASTROV, MIKHAIL LVOVICH, a doctor

TELEGIN, ILYA ILYCH, an impoverished landowner

MARINA, AN OLD NANNY

LABORER

    The action takes place on Serebriakov's estate.

ACT ONE

A garden. A veranda and a part of the house are visible. In the path, under an old poplar tree, a table is set for tea. Benches and chairs; on one of the benches—a guitar. Not far from the table—a swing. It is past two in the afternoon. It is overcast.

Marina, a pudgy, slow-moving old peasant woman, sits by the samovar knitting a stocking and Astrov paces next to her.

MARINA [*Pours tea into a glass*]: Have some, my dear.

ASTROV [*Reluctantly accepts the glass*]: I don't feel like it.

MARINA: A little vodka, maybe?

ASTROV: No, I don't drink vodka every day. And it's stuffy today.

A pause.

Nanny, how long have we known each other?

MARINA [*Thinking*]: How long? Goodness, let me think . . . You first came here, to these parts—when was it? . . . Vera Petrovna, Sonia's mother, was still alive then. In her day, you came to see us two winters . . . Well, then, it's been eleven years. [*After a moment's thought*] And maybe even more . . .

ASTROV: Have I changed much since then?

MARINA: Very much. You were young and handsome then and you've grown old now. Your looks aren't what they used to be. And you drink vodka now, too.

ASTROV: Well . . . In ten years I've become a different person. And why is that? I'm overworked, Nanny. On my feet from morning till night, never resting; at night, I lie in bed afraid that they might drag me out to see a patient. The entire time we've known each other, I haven't had a single day off. How could I not grow old? But then, life itself is boring, stupid, and filthy . . . This life . . . it sucks you in. You're surrounded by oddballs, nothing but oddballs; and after living with them two or three years, you, too, unbeknownst to yourself, little by little, become an oddball yourself. It's your inescapable lot in life. [*Twisting his long moustache*] Look at this long moustache . . . A stupid moustache. I've become an oddball, Nanny . . . maybe I haven't grown stupid yet, thank God; still have my wits about me, but the feelings have somehow grown blunt. I don't want anything, I don't need anything, I don't love anybody . . .

Well, with the exception of you, of course. [*He kisses her on the head*] When I was little, I had a nanny like you.

MARINA: You want something to eat, maybe?

ASTROV: No. The third week of Lent, I went to Malitskoe where the epidemic was . . . spotted fever . . . In the huts, peasants are side-by-side, all in a row . . . The filth, the stench, the smoke, the calves are on the floor next to the sick . . . And the pigs are there, too . . . I plugged away all day without sitting down once, not a drop passed my lips, and when I got home—they won't let me rest either—they brought a switchman from the railroad; I put him on the table to operate, and he ups and dies under the chloroform. And when I need it least, pangs of conscience act up as if I had intentionally killed him . . . I sat down, closed my eyes—like this—and I'm thinking: those who'll live a hundred or two hundred years after us and for whom we're now paving the way, will they remember us kindly? No, Nanny, no they won't!

MARINA: People won't, but God will.

ASTROV: Thank you for that. Well said.

Enter Voinitsky.

VOINITSKY [*Walks out of the house; he took a nap after lunch and looks rumpled; sits down on the bench and straightens his stylish tie*]: Well . . .

A pause.

Well . . .

ASTROV: Did you sleep well?

VOINITSKY: Yes . . . Very. [*He yawns*] Ever since the professor and his spouse came here, our life has jumped the track . . . I sleep at the wrong time, eat spicy food at breakfast and lunch, drink wine . . . that's not good! Before, we didn't have a moment to spare; Sonya and I worked—my respects, but now Sonya works, and all I do is sleep, eat, drink . . . That's not good!

MARINA [*After shaking her head*] Some customs! The professor gets up at noon, and the samovar's been boiling all morning, just waiting for him. Before they got here, we used to sit down to eat at noon, like everybody, but now it's after six. At night, the professor reads and writes, and then, around one in the morning, out of the blue, there goes the bell . . . Heavens, what is it? Tea! Wake everyone up for him, start the samovar . . . Some customs!

ASTROV: How long are they going to stay here?

VOINITSKY [*Whistles*]: A hundred years! The professor has decided to settle
  down here.

MARINA: Same as now. The samovar's been on the table for two hours, and
  they go for a walk.

VOINITSKY: Here they come . . . Don't you worry.

  *Voices are heard; from the depths of the garden, returning from their walk,
  come Serebriakov, Elena, Sonya, and Telegin.*

SEREBRIAKOV: Fine, fine . . . Wonderful views.

TELEGIN: Yes, remarkable, Your Excellency.

SONYA: Tomorrow, we'll go to the forest preserve, Papa. Would you like to?

VOINITSKY: Ladies and gentlemen, tea is served!

SEREBRIAKOV: My dear friends, send the tea to my study, would you! I still
  have to finish a few things today.

SONYA: You'll definitely like it in the forest preserve . . .

  *Elena, Serebriakov, and Sonya go into the house; Telegin walks over to the
  table and sits down beside Marina.*

VOINITSKY: It's hot and stuffy, but our famous scholar is wearing a coat, galoshes, gloves, and carrying an umbrella.

ASTROV: That means he's taking care of himself.

VOINITSKY: How beautiful she is! So beautiful! Never in my life have I seen a
  more beautiful woman.

TELEGIN: You know, Marina Timofeyevna, riding through the fields, walking in the shade of the garden, or looking at this table here, I feel this
  inexpressible bliss! The weather is charming, the birds are singing, we
  all live in peace and harmony—what more do we need? [*Takes a glass of
  tea*] Much too much obliged.

VOINITSKY [*Dreaming*]: Her eyes . . . A marvelous woman!

ASTROV: Come, tell us something, Ivan Petrovich.

VOINITSKY [*Slowly*]: What can I tell you?

ASTROV: Is there anything new?

VOINITSKY: There's nothing new. Same old. I'm same as always, probably
  even worse because I've become lazy, I don't do anything, and grumble
  like an old fart. The old chatterbox, *Maman*, is still blathering about the
  emancipation of women; one eye looks into the grave, while the other
  still searches her learned books for the dawn of a new life.

ASTROV: And the professor?

VOINITSKY: The professor still sits in his study from morning till night writing.

> With straining brain and furrowed brow,
> We write heroic odes nights and days,
> But neither we nor they receive the praise.[1]

I feel pity for the paper he's writing on! He should do his autobiography instead. Now, that's an extraordinary story! Just think, a retired professor, this learned old fossil, this cold fish . . . Gout, rheumatism, migraine, his liver's swollen from jealousy and envy . . . This fossil is living on his first wife's estate, living here against his will because he can't afford to live in the city. He's always complaining about his misfortunes, although, in fact, he's unbelievably fortunate. [*Nervously*] Just think how lucky he is! A son of a simple deacon, a seminarian, attains academic degrees, lands a professor's chair, and becomes His Excellency, a son-in-law of a senator, etc. etc. Never mind that. But take this: the man's been writing about art for twenty-five years and he doesn't understand a thing about it. For twenty-five years, he's been chewing other people's thoughts on realism, naturalism, and other such nonsense; for twenty-five years, he's been reading and writing things that any intelligent person has known for ages, and the stupid ones couldn't care less about: it means that for twenty-five years he's been pouring water through a sieve. Yet, what conceit! What pretensions! He's retired, and not a single living person knows of him, he's utterly unknown; it means that for twenty-five years he occupied someone else's place. But look at him strutting there like a demigod!

ASTROV: Well, it seems you're jealous.

VOINITSKY: Yes, I'm jealous! His success with women! Not even Don Juan ever had this kind of success! His first wife, my sister, a beautiful and gentle creature, pure as this blue sky, honorable, generous soul, who had more suitors than he ever had students—she loved him as only the purest of angels can love others as pure and fine as themselves. My mother, his mother-in-law, still adores him and he still inspires sacred awe in her. His second wife, a beauty, very intelligent—you just saw her—she married him when he was already old; she gave him her youth, beauty, freedom, her radiance. For what? Why?

ASTROV: Is she faithful to the professor?

VOINITSKY: Unfortunately, she is.

ASTROV: Why unfortunately?

VOINITSKY: Because her faithfulness is a fraud through and through. It's all rhetoric and no logic. Cheating on an elderly husband whom you can't stand—that's immoral; trying, on the other hand, to repress in yourself your poor youth and natural feelings—that's not immoral.

TELEGIN [*In a tearful voice*]: Vanya, I don't like it when you say things like that. No, please . . . Those who cheat on their wives or husbands are by definition disloyal; they could betray a country as well!

VOINITSKY [*With annoyance*]: Waffles, turn off the tap!

TELEGIN: Allow me, Vanya. My wife ran away with her beloved the day after our wedding due to my uncomely appearance. After that, I always fulfilled my duty. I love her to this day, I'm still faithful to her, I help her as much as I can, I gave her all I had in order to raise the children that she had by her beloved. I gave up happiness but I kept my pride. And she? Her youth is gone, her beauty, in keeping with the laws of nature, has faded, and her beloved passed away . . . What is she left with now?

Enter Elena and Sonya; following them, but a few moments later, Mme Voinitskaya comes in carrying a book. She sits down and starts reading; she is handed a glass of tea, and she drinks it without looking up.

SONYA [*Hurriedly, to Nanny*]: Nanny, the peasants are here. Go talk to them, I'll do tea myself . . . [*Pours the tea*]

Nanny exits. Elena takes her tea and drinks it sitting on the swing.

ASTROV [*To Elena Andreyevna*]: I came here to see your husband. You wrote to me that he was very ill, rheumatism and something else, but, it turns out, he's in tip-top shape.

ELENA: He was under the weather yesterday evening, complained of leg pains, but today he seems all right . . .

ASTROV: And I raced twenty miles here at break-neck speed. Oh, well, it's not the first time. But I'm staying till tomorrow and I'll at least sleep *quantum satis.*[2]

SONYA: Fine, then. It's not often that you spend the night here. You probably haven't eaten?

ASTROV: No, ma'am, I haven't.

SONYA: Then you'll eat with us, too. We eat around six now. [*Takes a sip*] The tea's cold!

TELEGIN: Yes, the temperature has dropped significantly in the samovar.

ELENA: It doesn't matter, Ivan Ivanych. We'll drink it cold.

TELEGIN: I'm sorry, ma'am . . . not Ivan Ivanych, but Ilya Ilych, ma'am—Ilya Ilych Telegin, or, as some call me on account of my pockmarked face, Waffles. A long time ago, I baptized Sonya, and His Excellency, your spouse, knows me very well. I'm now staying with you, at the same estate, ma'am . . . As you may have noticed, I dine with you every day.

SONYA: Ilya Ilych is our helper and our right hand. [*Tenderly*] Dear Godfather, let me pour you some more tea.

MME VOINITSKAYA: Ahh!

SONYA: What's the matter, Grandmother?

MME VOINITSKAYA: I forgot to tell Alexander that . . . I'm losing my mind . . . that I've received a letter from Kharkov[3] from Pavel Alexeyevich . . . He's sent me his new pamphlet . . .

ASTROV: Is it interesting?

MME VOINITSKAYA: Yes, interesting, but a little strange. He's refuting the very thing he defended seven years ago. It's awful!

VOINITSKY: There's nothing awful about it. *Maman*, drink your tea.

MME VOINITSKAYA: But I want to talk!

VOINITSKY: For fifty years we've been talking and talking and reading pamphlets. It's time to be done with it.

MME VOINITSKAYA: For some reason, you don't like listening when I'm speaking. Pardon me, *Jean*,[4] but in the last year you've changed so much that I don't recognize you at all . . . You used to be a man of convictions, an enlightened individual . . .

VOINITSKY: Oh, yes. I was an enlightened individual who shed light on no one . . .

A pause.

I was an enlightened individual . . . You could not have made a more spiteful joke! I'm forty-seven years old now. Until last year, I tried deliberately, just like you, to obscure my vision with all this pedantry of yours, so as not to see real life—and I thought I was doing the right thing. But now, if you only knew! I lie awake at night, frustrated and angry that I've so stupidly wasted the chance to enjoy all those things that my old age denies me now!

SONYA: Uncle Vanya, that's boring!

MME VOINITSKAYA [*To her son*]: It's as if you're accusing your former convictions of something . . . But they aren't the ones to blame—you are. You were forgetting that convictions alone are nothing, a dead letter . . . You had to commit to the cause.

VOINITSKY: The cause? Not everyone can be a writing *perpetuum mobile*[5] like your Herr Professor.

MME VOINITSKAYA: What are you trying to say?

SONYA [*Imploringly*]: Grandmother! Uncle Vanya! I entreat you!

VOINITSKY: I'll be quiet. I'll be quiet and I apologize.

   A pause.

ELENA: The weather is very good today . . . It's not hot . . .

   A pause.

VOINITSKY: It's good weather to hang yourself . . .

   Telegin tunes the guitar. Marina walks around the house, calling the chickens.

MARINA: Chicka, chicka, chicka . . .

SONYA: Nanny, what did the peasants want?

MARINA: It's the same old, same old thing, still about that empty field. Chicka, chicka, chicka . . .

SONYA: Who are you calling, then?

MARINA: The speckled hen took off with her little ones . . . I worry the crows might snatch them . . .

   Telegin plays a polka. All listen in silence. Enter Laborer.

LABORER: Is the doctor here? [*To Astrov*] This way, Mikhail Lvovich; they've sent for you.

ASTROV: From where?

LABORER: From the factory.

ASTROV [*Annoyed*]: Much obliged. Well, I have to go . . . [*Looking around him for his cap*] Damn, what a shame . . .

SONYA: Yes, it's so unfortunate, really . . . After the factory, come eat with us.

ASTROV: I'm afraid it'll be too late then. Not likely . . . Not possible . . . [*To the Laborer*] Look here, go get me, would you, a shot of vodka. [*The Laborer goes out*] Not likely . . . Not possible . . . [*Finds his cap*] There's a character in a play by Ostrovsky,[6] a man with a long moustache and short wits . . . That's me. Good-bye, ladies and gentlemen . . . [*To Elena Andreyevna*] Should you decide to drop by my place, with Sofia Alexandrovna here, I'll be most glad to see you. I have a puny little estate, less than eighty acres in all, but if you're interested, there's an excellent orchard, and a forest nursery the likes of which you couldn't find for a thousand miles around. Right next to me, there's a national forest preserve . . . The forester there is old and always sick, so I essentially take care of everything there.

ELENA: I've already been told about your love of forests. You can, of course, do a great deal of good, but doesn't it get in the way of your true calling? After all, you're a doctor.

ASTROV: God alone knows what our true calling is.

ELENA: Is it interesting?

ASTROV: Yes, it's very interesting.

VOINITSKY [*Sarcastically*]: Very!

ELENA [*To Astrov*]: You're still young, just looking at you . . . you're thirty-six or thirty-seven . . . and it probably isn't as interesting as you claim. Forest and more forest. I think it's monotonous.

SONYA: Oh, no, it's extraordinarily interesting. Every year, Mikhail Lvovich plants new forests, and he's already received a bronze medal and a diploma. He advocates the preservation of the old ones. If you only heard him speak, you'd agree with him entirely. He says that trees adorn the earth, and that they teach people to understand beauty and instill a sense of pride in them. Forests help temper harsh climates. In countries where climate is milder, people struggle with nature less, and that's why man is milder and gentler there; there, the people are beautiful, adaptable, passionate, their speech is elegant and their gestures are graceful. The arts and sciences flourish there, their philosophy isn't dark, and women are treated there with elegant dignity . . .

VOINITSKY [*Laughing*]: Bravo! Bravo! All that's very nice, but unconvincing, and so allow me [*to Astrov*], my friend, to continue to use firewood in the stove and build sheds out of wood.

ASTROV: You can burn peat in the stoves and build your sheds out of stone. Well, I accept cutting down trees out of necessity, but why decimate them? Russia's forests are shattering under the axe; billions of trees die, bird and other animal habitats lie barren, rivers are becoming shallow and drying up, beautiful landscapes vanish irretrievably, and all this because a lazy person doesn't have enough sense to bend down and pick up fuel from the ground. [*To Elena*] Wouldn't you agree, Madam? You have to be a blind barbarian to burn in the stove all that beauty, to destroy what we cannot create. Man is given reason and creative power to increase manifold what's been handed down to him, but to this day, he has not created but only destroyed. There are fewer and fewer forests, rivers are running dry, wildlife has disappeared, the climate is ruined, and each day, the earth is becoming poorer and more hideous still. [*To Voinitsky*] Here, you're giving me this ironic look, and you're not taking seriously any of what I'm saying, and . . . and maybe it really is odd, but when I walk by the peasant forests that I've saved from the axe, or when I hear the rustling of my young forest, planted with my own hands, I realize that I have a little power over the climate too, and if a thousand years from now people are happy, then it's partially my doing, too. When I plant a small birch tree and then watch it turn green and sway in the wind, my heart fills with pride and I . . . [*Seeing the Laborer, who has brought him a glass of vodka on a tray*] However . . . [*He drinks*] it's time to go. But all this may just be too odd after all. Good day, ladies and gentlemen! [*He walks toward the house*]

SONYA [*Takes him by the arm and walks with him*]: When will you then come see us?

ASTROV: I don't know . . .

SONYA: Again in a month? . . .

> *Astrov and Sonya go into the house; Mme Voinitskaya and Telegin remain at the table; Elena and Voinitsky walk toward the terrace.*

ELENA: Ivan Petrovich, you behaved absolutely impossibly again today. Why did you have to upset your mother and talk about *perpetuum mobile*! And today at breakfast you argued with Alexander again. This is all so petty!

VOINITSKY: But what if I hate him?

ELENA: You have no reason to hate Alexander; he's just like everyone else. No worse than you.

VOINITSKY: If you could only see your face, your movements . . . You're too lazy to live! Oh, this laziness!

ELENA: Ah, I'm lazy and bored, too! Everybody criticizes my husband and looks at me with pity: poor thing, her husband is old! This concern for me—oh, I understand it too well! It's what Astrov just said: you all are blindly destroying the forests, and soon there'll be nothing left on earth. The same way you are blindly destroying people, and soon, thanks to you, there will be no loyalty, no purity, no capacity for self-sacrifice. Why can't you look with equanimity at a woman who is not yours? Because—and the doctor's right there—the demon of destruction is inside all of you. You've no pity for forests, or birds, or women, or one another.

VOINITSKY: I don't like this philosophy!

A pause.

ELENA: This doctor has a weary and anxious face. An interesting face. Sonya must like him; she's in love with him, and I understand her. He's been here three times already since I arrived, but I'm a little shy and I haven't yet had a proper conversation with him, have not been nice to him. He must think that I'm mean. Most likely, Ivan Petrovich, the reason you and I are such good friends is that we're both tedious and boring people! Tedious! Don't look at me like that, I don't like it.

VOINITSKY: How can I look at you any other way if I love you? You're my happiness, my life, and my youth! I know, my chances for reciprocity are measly, equal to zero, but I don't need anything, just let me look at you, hear your voice . . .

ELENA: Shhh, they might overhear you!

They walk toward the house.

VOINITSKY [*Following her*]: Just let me speak of my love for you, don't shoo me away, and this alone will be the greatest happiness for me . . .

ELENA: This is unbearable . . .

They walk into the house.

Telegin is strumming the guitar and playing a polka. Mme Voinitskaya is writing something in the margin of the pamphlet.

Curtain.

ACT TWO

The dining room in Serebriakov's house. It's nighttime. The Watchman's tapping is heard coming from the garden.[7]

Serebriakov, sitting in an armchair by the open window, dozing, and Elena Andreyevna, sitting beside him, also dozing.

SEREBRIAKOV [*Opening his eyes*]; Who is that? Sonya, is that you?

ELENA: It's me.

SEREBRIAKOV: Oh, it's you, Lenochka . . . This excruciating pain!

ELENA: The blanket fell on the floor. [*She covers his legs with the blanket*] Alexander, I'll close the window.

SEREBRIAKOV: Don't, it's stifling here . . . I just dozed off and I had a dream that my left leg belonged to someone else. I woke up in excruciating pain. No, this is not gout, it's more like rheumatism. What time is it now?

ELENA: Twenty minutes past midnight.

A pause.

SEREBRIAKOV: In the morning, look for Batiushkov[8] in the library. I think we have him.

ELENA: What?

SEREBRIAKOV: Look for Batiushkov tomorrow morning. I seem to remember seeing his book. But why is it so hard for me to breathe?

ELENA: You're tired. You haven't slept in two nights.

SEREBRIAKOV: I heard that Turgenev's[9] gout developed into crushing chest pain. I worry it might happen to me. This damn disgusting old age! To hell with it. Having gotten old, I find myself disgusting. And, all of you, most likely, find me disgusting, too.

ELENA: You speak about your old age as if we're to blame that you're old.

SEREBRIAKOV: Disgusting you must find me first.

Elena walks away from him and sits down at a distance.

Of course, you're right. I'm not stupid and I do understand. You're young, healthy, beautiful, you want to live, and I'm an old man, practically a corpse. Well then? Do you think I don't understand? And, of course, it's stupid that I'm still alive. But wait, I'll set you all free. I don't have much longer.

ELENA: I can't take this anymore . . . For God's sake, be quiet.

SEREBRIAKOV: It turns out that, thanks to me, nobody can take it anymore, they are all bored, wasting their youth, all thanks to me; and I'm the only one content and enjoying life. Sure, of course!

ELENA: Keep quiet! You've exhausted me!

SEREBRIAKOV: Oh, I've exhausted everyone. Of course.

ELENA [*Through tears*]: That's unbearable! Tell me, what is it you want from me?

SEREBRIAKOV: Nothing.

ELENA: Then keep quiet. Please.

SEREBRIAKOV: What's interesting is that whenever Ivan Petrovich or that old idiot Maria Vasilyevna open their mouths—it's all right, everybody listens, but if I utter a word, everybody starts feeling miserable. Even my voice is disgusting. Well, let's suppose I'm disgusting, an egoist, a despot, but don't I, in my old age, have a certain right to be an egoist? Haven't I earned it? I'm asking you—don't you think that I have a right to a peaceful old age, some consideration from others?

ELENA: No one's impugning your rights.

The window slams in the wind.

The wind's picking up, I'll close the window. [*She shuts it*] It's going to rain. No one's impugning your rights.

A pause; the Watchman in the garden taps and sings a song.

SEREBRIAKOV: To devote my whole life to scholarship, get used to my study, an audience, my venerable colleagues—and, suddenly, to find myself in this crypt, look at stupid people here every day and listen to their inane conversations . . . I want to live, I love success, I love fame, excitement, but here—I'm in exile. To long every minute for the past, follow the success of others, and fear death . . . I can't! I do not have the strength! And now they don't want to forgive me my old age!

ELENA: Wait, have patience: in five or six years I'll be old, too.

Enter Sonya.

SONYA: Papa, you asked to send for Dr. Astrov, and when he came here, you refused to see him. It's impolite. We've troubled him for nothing . . .

SEREBRIAKOV: What do I need your Astrov for? He knows as much about medicine as I do about astronomy.

SONYA: We're not going to summon the entire Department of Medicine for your gout.

SEREBRIAKOV: I won't even talk to that holy fool!

SONYA: As you wish. [*She sits down*] I don't care.

SEREBRIAKOV: What time is it?

ELENA: It's after midnight.

SEREBRIAKOV: It's stifling . . . Sonya, hand me my drops from the table!

SONYA: Here. [*She hands him the drops*]

SEREBRIAKOV [*Irritably*]: Oh, not these! I can't ask her to do anything!

SONYA: Please, don't act up! Maybe there are those who like it, but spare me, please! I do not like it. And I don't have time, I have to get up early tomorrow for haymaking.

Enter Voinitsky in a housecoat and with a candle.

VOINITSKY: A thunderstorm is brewing.

Lightning.

There she goes! *Hélène* and Sonya, go to bed, I've come to relieve you.

SEREBRIAKOV [*Frightened*]: No, no! Don't leave me with him! Don't. He'll talk my head off!

VOINITSKY: But you have to let them rest! They haven't slept for two nights.

SEREBRIAKOV: Let them go to bed, but you go, too! Thank you very much. I beg you. For the sake of our former friendship, don't object. We'll talk later.

VOINITSKY [*With a smirk*]: Our former friendship . . . Former . . .

SONYA: Be quiet, Uncle Vanya!

SEREBRIAKOV [*To his wife*]: My dear, don't leave me with him! He'll talk my head off.

VOINITSKY: This is becoming ridiculous.

Enter Marina with a candle.

SONYA: Nanny, you should go to bed. It's late.

MARINA: The samovar hasn't been cleared off the table. Can't exactly go to bed.

SEREBRIAKOV: No one can sleep, everyone's exhausted, and I alone am in a state of bliss.

MARINA [*Goes up to Serebriakov and speaks tenderly*]: What's the matter, dear? Is it hurting? Oh, my legs are throbbing, oh, so throbbing. [*Arranges his blanket*] It's an old illness of yours. The late Vera Petrovna, Sonechka's mother, may she rest in peace, used to stay up nights crying her eyes out with you . . . Oh, she loved you so . . .

A pause.

The old are just like children, they so want someone to feel for them, but there's no one to feel sorry for us old people. [*She kisses Serebriakov on the shoulder*] Let's go to bed, sunshine, I'll make you linden tea[10] and warm your feet for you . . . I'll pray to God for you . . .

SEREBRIAKOV [*Touched*]: Let's go, Marina.

MARINA: My own legs are throbbing so bad, oh, so bad! [*She and Sonya lead him out*] Vera Petrovna used to cry her eyes out, cry and cry . . . You, Sonya, dear, were still too young then, too young to know . . . Come, come, my dear . . .

Serebriakov, Sonya, and Marina go out.

ELENA: I am utterly exhausted with him. I can barely stand up.

VOINITSKY: You are with him, and I am with myself. I haven't slept for three nights.

ELENA: Things are not well in this house. Your mother hates everything save her pamphlets and the professor; the professor is exasperated, afraid of you, and doesn't trust me; Sonia's angry with her father and me, and hasn't spoken to me for almost two weeks; you hate my husband and openly despise your mother; I'm exasperated and I must have been on the verge of tears twenty times today . . . Things are not well in this house.

VOINITSKY: Let's leave philosophy out!

ELENA: Ivan Petrovich, you're intelligent and educated, and it seems you should understand that the world is perishing not because of some thieves or fires but because of hate, rivalry, and all these petty squabbles . . . Instead of grumbling, you ought to help everyone make peace.

VOINITSKY: First, help me make peace with myself. My dear . . . [*Lunging to kiss her hand*]

ELENA: Stop it! [*She pulls her hand away*] Go away!

VOINITSKY: It will stop raining, and everything in nature will be refreshed and will breathe easier. I alone won't be refreshed by the thunderstorm. Day and night I'm haunted by the thought that my life is lost irretrievably. There is no past; it was wasted stupidly on trifles, and the present is hideous in its absurdity. Here's my life and my love: how and what am I going to do with them? My feeling is perishing in vain, like a ray of sunlight caught in a pit, and I'm perishing, too.

ELENA: When you talk to me about your love, I become stupid somehow and I don't know what to say. I'm sorry, I can't say anything to you. [*She wants to go*] Good night!

VOINITSKY [*Blocking her way*]: If you only knew how much I suffer knowing that next to me, in the same house, another life is perishing—yours! What are you waiting for? What damned philosophy stands in your way? Oh, can't you understand . . .

ELENA [*Looking at him intently*]: Ivan Petrovich, you're drunk!

VOINITSKY: Maybe, maybe . . .

ELENA: Where's the doctor?

VOINITSKY: He's there . . . spending the night in my room . . . Maybe, maybe . . . Anything may be!

ELENA: You were drinking again tonight? What for?

VOINITSKY: At least it feels like life . . . Don't try to stand in my way, *Hélène!*

ELENA: You didn't use to drink before, and you didn't use to talk so much . . . Go to bed! You bore me.

VOINITSKY [*Lunging to kiss her hand*]: My dear . . . marvelous!

ELENA [*Annoyed*]: Leave me alone. It's disgusting, after all. [*She goes out*]

VOINITSKY [*Alone*]: She's gone . . .

A pause.

Ten years ago, or so, I used to see her at my sister's. She was seventeen and I was thirty-seven then. Why didn't I fall in love with her and propose to her then? It was so possible then! She would've been my wife now . . . And . . . the thunderstorm would wake us up; she would be frightened by the thunder, and I would hold her in my arms and whisper: "Don't be afraid! I'm right here." Oh, such delightful thoughts, so nice that I'm laughing . . . but oh, my God, I'm getting all confused . . . Why am I old? Why doesn't she understand me? Her rhetoric, her lazy moralizing, ridiculous and lazy thoughts about the demise of the world—it's thoroughly hateful.

A pause.

Oh, how I've been deceived! I worshiped the professor, this pathetic, gouty man, worked like an ox for him! Sonya and I squeezed every drop from this estate for his sake; like kulaks, like rich peasants, we sold vegetable oil, beans, and farmer's cheese; we went short ourselves to scrape together enough change to send thousands to him. I was proud of him and his scholarship; I lived and breathed him! Everything he wrote or uttered seemed to me a work of genius . . . My God, and now? He's retired, and his life's work is now for all to see: not a single page of his labor will survive him, he's completely unknown, he's a nonentity! A soap bubble! And I've been deceived . . . I see . . . stupidly deceived . . .

Astrov comes in wearing a jacket, but without his waistcoat or tie; he is tipsy. Telegin follows him with a guitar.

ASTROV: Play!

TELEGIN: Everyone's asleep, sir.

ASTROV: Play!

Telegin strums softly.

ASTROV [*To Voinitsky*]: Are you here by yourself? No ladies? [*Sings quietly with his arms akimbo*] "Hut move here, stove move there, master can't sleep anywhere . . ."[11] The thunderstorm woke me up. Quite a rain. What time is it now?

VOINITSKY: Who the hell knows.

ASTROV: I thought I heard Elena Andreyevna's voice.

VOINITSKY: She was just here.

ASTROV: A gorgeous woman! [*Looking at the jars on the table*] Medicine. All sorts of prescriptions! From Kharkov, and Moscow, and Tula . . . Every town in Russia is fed up with his gout. Is he ill, or just pretending?

VOINITSKY: He is ill.

ASTROV: Why are you so sad tonight? Feeling sorry for the professor?

VOINITSKY: Leave me alone.

ASTROV: Or, maybe, you're in love with the professor's wife?

VOINITSKY: She's my friend.

ASTROV: Already?

VOINITSKY: What do you mean *already*?

ASTROV: A woman can be a friend to a man only after being first his acquaintance, then his lover, and only afterwards his friend.

VOINITSKY: A vulgar philosophy.

ASTROV: Really? Well . . . To tell you the truth, I'm turning into a vulgarian. See, I'm drunk, too. Usually I get drunk like this once a month. And when I'm in this state, I become impudent and insolent in the extreme. Everything's a breeze then! I take on the most complex surgeries and I do them flawlessly; I draw the most sweeping plans for the future, and I don't think of myself as an oddball then, and I believe that I am bringing enormous benefit to humanity . . . enormous! And I have my own philosophy then, and all of you, my buddies, appear to me the tiniest of bugs . . . mere microbes. [*To Telegin*] Waffles, play!

TELEGIN: My friend, for you, I would gladly, with all my heart, but don't you understand—everyone's asleep in the house!

ASTROV: Play!

Telegin strums softly.

A drink's in order. Come, I think there's still some cognac left. And as soon as it gets light out, we'll go to my place. Tsright? I have an assistant who never says "that's right." It's always "*tsright.*" A real cheat. So *tsright?* [*Upon seeing Sonya as she enters the room*] Sorry, no tie. [*Goes out quickly, Telegin follows him*]

SONYA: Uncle Vanya, you got drunk with the doctor again. Birds of a feather. Well, him, he's always like that, but what's gotten into you? It doesn't suit you at your age.

VOINITSKY: Age has nothing to do with it. When you don't have a real life, you make do with mirages. At least it's better than nothing.

SONYA: The hay's all cut, it's been raining every day, everything's rotting, and you're busy with mirages! You've completely neglected the estate . . . I've been working by myself, and I'm worn out . . . [*Frightened*] Uncle, you have tears in your eyes!

VOINITSKY: What tears? There's nothing . . . it's nonsense. You just looked at me now exactly like your late mother. My darling . . . [*He fervently kisses her face and hands*] My sister—my dearest sister—where is she now? If only she knew! Oh, if only she knew!

SONYA: What? Uncle, knew what?

VOINITSKY: It's painful, not good . . . Never mind . . . Later . . . Never mind . . . I'll go . . . [*Goes out*]

SONYA [*Knocks on the door*]: Mikhail Lvovich! Are you awake? May I see you a minute!

ASTROV [*Behind the door*]: Coming! [*A little later he comes in wearing a waist-coat and a tie*] What can I do for you?

SONYA: You can drink if you don't think it's disgusting, but I entreat you, don't let my uncle drink. It's bad for him.

ASTROV: All right. We won't drink any more.

A pause.

I'll go home now. It's signed and sealed. By the time they harness the horses, it'll be light out.

SONYA: It's still raining. Wait till morning.

ASTROV: The thunderstorm is passing over, and I'll avoid most of it. I should go. And, please, don't ask me to see your father again. I tell him—it's gout, and he says—it's rheumatism; I ask him to lie down, he's sitting up. And today he altogether refused to talk to me.

SONYA: He's spoiled. [*Looking in the sideboard*] Would you like something to eat?

ASTROV: Why not, sure.

SONYA: I love having something to eat at night. I think there's something in the sideboard. He had, I heard, great success with women, and the ladies spoiled him. Here, take some cheese.

The two of them eat standing by the sideboard.

ASTROV: I didn't have anything to eat today, I only drank. Your father's very difficult. [*He takes a bottle out of the sideboard*] May I? [*He pours himself a shot*] There's no one here and I can speak frankly. You know, I think I wouldn't last even a month in your house, I would suffocate in its air . . . Your father, who's consumed entirely by his gout and books, Uncle Vanya with his doldrums, your grandmother, and finally, your stepmother . . .

SONYA: What about my stepmother?

ASTROV: Everything must be beautiful in a person: face, clothes, soul, thoughts. *Beautiful she is, no doubt*[12] . . . but all she does is sleep, eat, walk, enchant us with her beauty—and nothing else. She has no responsibilities, others do the work for her . . . Isn't that right? But an idle life can't be pure.

A pause.

However, maybe I'm being too harsh. Like your Uncle Vanya, I'm not particularly satisfied with life, and we're both turning into grouches.

SONYA: You are unhappy with life?

ASTROV: I love life, in general, but I can't stand our Russian provincial, narrow-minded life and despise it with every fiber of my soul. As far as my own personal life is concerned, really and truly, there's nothing good about it at all. You know, when you're walking through the woods in the middle of the night and if there's a light there in the distance, then you forget about your fatigue and the darkness, and you don't notice the thorny branches beating you in the face . . . I work—and you know it—

harder than anyone in the district, life is constantly knocking me down, I suffer unbearably sometimes, but I have no light in the distance. I don't expect anything for myself, I don't love people . . . I haven't loved anyone in a long time.

SONYA: No one?

ASTROV: No one. I do have a soft spot for your Nanny—for old-times' sake. The peasants are all alike; backward, living in filth, but the intelligentsia is hard to get along with. It fatigues you. All our good friends think shallow, feel shallow, and can't see beyond the tip of their nose—simply put, they're stupid. And those who are wiser and weightier are prone to hysteria, suffering from analysis and reflection . . . They whine, hate, vilify each other morbidly, approach a person with dislike, look at him askance and pronounce: "Oh, he's a psychopath!" or "He's a phrase-monger!" And when they don't know which label to affix to my fore-head, they just say: "He's a strange man, strange!" I love forests—that's strange; I don't eat meat—that, too, is strange. People no longer relate to nature directly in a pure and free way, and to other people, either. No, they don't! . . . [Tries to have a drink]

SONYA [Preventing him]: No, please, I entreat you, don't drink any more.

ASTROV: Why not?

SONYA: It really doesn't suit you! You're so fine, your voice is so tender . . . More than that, you are, unlike anyone else I know—beautiful. Why would you ever want to be like ordinary people who drink and play cards? Oh, I entreat you, don't do it! You always say that people don't create and only destroy what's been handed to them from above. Why, why do you then destroy yourself? Don't, I entreat you, I implore you, don't!

ASTROV [Holds out his hand to her]: I won't drink any more.

SONYA: Give me your word.

ASTROV: My word of honor.

SONYA [Firmly shaking his hand]: Thank you!

ASTROV: Basta! I've sobered up. See, I'm completely sober, and I'll stay sober for the rest of my life. [He looks at his watch] So, let's continue. I'm say-ing: my time is over, it's too late for me . . . I've aged, I'm overworked, I've gotten vulgar, all my feelings have grown blunt, and I don't think I could ever become attached to someone. I don't love anyone . . . and I never will. The only thing that still fascinates me is beauty. I'm partial to that. I think that if Elena Andreyevna only wanted to, she could turn my head in a day . . . But that's not love, it's not attachment . . . [*He covers his eyes with his hand and shudders*]

SONYA: What's wrong with you?

ASTROV: Never mind . . . During Lent, a patient died under the chloroform.

SONYA: It's time to forget that.

A pause.

Tell me, Mikhail Lvovich . . . if I had a friend or a younger sister, and if you found out that she . . . well, let's say, loved you, how would you react to it?

ASTROV [*Shrugging his shoulders*]: I don't know. Most likely I wouldn't. I'd let her know that I wouldn't be able love her . . . and that I have other things on my mind. Anyway, if I'm going, then it's time. Good-bye, my dear; otherwise, we won't finish till dawn. [*Shaking her hand*] I'll go out through the drawing room, if I may; otherwise, I'm afraid your uncle might make me stay. [*He goes out*]

SONYA [*Alone*]: He didn't say anything to me . . . His heart and soul are still hidden from me, but why do I then feel so happy? [*Laughing with joy*] I told him: You are fine, noble, your voice is so tender . . . Was it out of place? His voice quivers, caresses . . . I feel it in the air. And when I told him about a younger sister, he didn't understand . . . [*Wringing her hands*] Oh, it's so awful that I am not pretty! So awful! I know that I'm not pretty, I know, I know . . . Last Sunday, when walking out of church, I overheard them talking about me and one woman said: "She's good-hearted, generous, but it's a pity that she's so plain" . . . So plain . . .

Enter Elena Andreyevna.

ELENA [*Opens the windows*]: The thunderstorm's passed. The air's so nice!

A pause.

Where is the doctor?

SONYA: He's gone.

A pause.

ELENA: *Sophie*[13]!

SONYA: What?

ELENA: How much longer are you going to pout at me? We haven't done each other any harm. Why should we be enemies then? Enough . . .

SONYA: I wanted to myself . . . [*Embraces her*] Enough pouting.

ELENA: Wonderful then.

> *They are both excited.*

SONYA: Did Papa go to bed?

ELENA: No, he's sitting in the drawing room . . . We don't talk to each other for weeks and God knows why . . . [*Seeing the open sideboard*] What's this?

SONYA: Mikhail Lvovich had supper.

ELENA: And there's wine, too . . . Let's drink to our friendship.

SONYA: Let's.

ELENA: From the same glass . . . [*Fills a shot glass*] That's much better. So we drop the formality,[14] right?

SONYA: Yes.

> *They drink and kiss.*

I've wanted to make peace for a long time, but I was a little embarrassed to . . . [*Crying*]

ELENA: So why are you crying?

SONYA: Oh, nothing, never mind.

ELENA: There, there . . . [*Crying*] Silly girl, now I'm crying, too.

> *A pause.*

You're angry with me because you think that it was a marriage of convenience . . . But if vows mean anything to you, I swear to you, I married your father for love. I fell for him as a scholar and someone famous. It wasn't true love; it was artificial, but I thought then that it was true. It's not my fault. And you, ever since our wedding, have looked at me accusingly with your intelligent and suspicious eyes.

SONYA: Well, peace, peace! Let's forget it.

ELENA: Don't look like that—it doesn't suit you. You have to trust everyone, you can't live your life otherwise.

> *A pause.*

SONYA: Tell me honestly, as a friend . . . Are you happy?

ELENA: No.

SONYA: I knew it. One more question. Tell me honestly—would you prefer to have a young husband?

ELENA: You're still a little girl. Of course, I would. [*She laughs*] Go ahead, ask me something else, ask me . . .

SONYA: Do you like the doctor?

ELENA: Yes, very much.

SONYA [*Laughing*]: I look silly . . . don't I? See, he's left, but I still hear his voice and his footsteps; and if I look at a dark window, I see his face. Let me finish . . . But I can't speak so loud, I'm ashamed. Let's go in my room, we'll talk there. Do I seem silly to you? Admit it . . . Tell me something about him . . .

ELENA: But what?

SONYA: He's intelligent . . . He's very capable, can do anything . . . He heals and he plants forests . . .

ELENA: It's not about medicine or forest . . . My dear, don't you see, he has a gift! Do you know what it means to have a gift? He's daring, a freethinker, he has a vision . . . He plants a tree and he thinks ahead to what it will mean a thousand years from now, and he's imagining happiness for all mankind. People like him are rare and we have to love them . . . He drinks, acts a little coarse sometimes—but so what? In Russia, a man of talent can't be squeaky clean. Just think about the kind of life he has! Muddy and impassable roads, freezing cold, snow storms, huge distances, and the people are coarse, uncivilized, illness and destitution are all around him, and under these circumstances, it's hard for someone working and struggling day in and day out to remain squeaky clean and sober by the time he's forty. [*Kisses her*] I wish you the best from the bottom of my heart, you deserve happiness . . . [*She gets up*] Me, I'm a tedious, minor character . . . In music, in my husband's house, in love—everywhere, I was always only a minor character. To tell you the truth, Sonya, come to think of it, I'm very, very unhappy! [*She paces restlessly on stage*] There's no happiness for me in this world. No! Why are you laughing?

SONYA [*Laughing and covering her face with her hands*] I'm happy . . . so happy!

ELENA: I'd play something . . . I'd play something now.

SONYA: Do play. [*She embraces Elena*] I can't sleep . . . Do play!

ELENA: I will. Your father's not asleep. When he's ill, music irritates him. Go ask him. If he's all right, I'll play something. Go ask him.

SONYA: I will. [*Goes out*]

The Watchman taps in the garden.

ELENA: I haven't played in a long time. I will play and cry, cry like a fool. [*Speaking out of the window*] Efim, is that you tapping?

> *The Watchman's voice: "Me!"*

ELENA: Don't, the master isn't well.

> *The voice of the Watchman: "I'm leaving." [Whistles to his dogs] "Come here, girl, come here, boy!"*

> *A pause.*

SONYA [*Returning*]: You can't.

> *Curtain.*

ACT THREE

> *The drawing room in the Serebriakovs' house. There are three doors: on the right, on the left, and in the middle.*

> *It's daytime.*

> *Voinitsky, Sonya (seated), and Elena Andreyevna (absorbed in thought and pacing the stage).*

VOINITSKY: Herr Professor has expressed a desire for all of us to gather in the drawing room at one o'clock. [*Looks at his watch*] It's now quarter to one. He wants to convey something to the world.

ELENA: Probably for a cause.

VOINITSKY: He has no causes. He writes rubbish, grumbles, and feels jealous—nothing else.

SONYA [*Reproachfully*]: Uncle!

VOINITSKY: All right, all right, forgive me. [*He points to Elena*] Just look at her: she walks and sways from laziness. Very nice! Very!

ELENA: You drone all day long—drone, drone—how you don't get fed up with it! [*With longing*] I'm bored to death and I don't know what to do.

SONYA [*Shrugging her shoulders*]: What to do? There's plenty to do if you only wanted to.

ELENA: For instance?

SONYA: You could help with the house, teach, treat the sick. What to do? Before you and father came here, Uncle Vanya and I used to go to the market to sell the flour ourselves.

ELENA: I don't know how. And it doesn't interest me. It's only in the novels of ideas that they teach and treat the peasants, but how am I all of a sudden supposed to just start treating or teaching them?

SONYA: But I can't understand how you can not go and teach. Just wait, and you'll get used to it, too. [*Embraces her*] Don't be so bored, my dear. [*Laughing*] You're bored, don't know what to do with yourself, but being bored and idle is contagious. Look: Uncle Vanya doesn't do anything, and only trails you like a shadow, I've left my work and run over here to talk to you. I've become so lazy, I can't tell you! The Doctor, Mikhail Lvovich, used to come see us rarely, once a month maybe, it was impossible to get him to come over, and now he comes over every day, he's abandoned his forests and medicine. You must be a sorceress.

VOINITSKY: Why languish? [*Lively*] Come on, my dear, my gorgeous, be a good girl! The blood of a water nymph flows in your veins, so then be a nymph![15] Let yourself go at least once in your life; quickly fall head over heels in love with a water sprite, and plunge head-first straight into a deep, still water, leaving Herr Professor and all of us at a loss for words!

ELENA [*Enraged*]: Leave me alone! This is so cruel! [*She tries to leave the room*]

VOINITSKY [*Doesn't let her go*]: There, there, my joy, forgive me . . . I'm sorry. [*He kisses her hand*] Peace.

ELENA: You would try the patience of a saint.

VOINITSKY: As a symbol of peace and harmony, I'm going to bring you a bouquet of roses; I made it for you this morning . . . Autumn roses— delightful, mournful roses . . . [*Goes out*]

SONYA: Autumn roses—delightful, mournful roses . . .

Both are looking out of the window.

ELENA: It's September already! How are we going to make it through the winter here!

A pause.

Where is the doctor?

SONYA: He's in Uncle Vanya's room. He's writing something. I'm glad that Uncle Vanya went out, I need to talk to you.

ELENA: About what?

SONYA: About what? [*Puts her head on Elena's chest*]

ELENA [*Stroking Sonya's hair*]: Well, there, there . . . [*Stroking her hair*] There.

SONYA: I am so plain.

ELENA: You have beautiful hair.

SONYA: No! [*Turns around to look at herself in the mirror*] No! When a woman is plain, they always tell her: "You have beautiful eyes or beautiful hair" . . . I've loved him for six years; I love him more than my own mother, and I hear him every waking moment, I feel his handshake, and I look at the door, waiting, and thinking that he might just walk in. And see, I keep coming to you to talk about him. Now he comes here every day, but he doesn't look at me, he doesn't see me . . . I'm suffering! I have no hope, none, none at all! [*Desperately*] Oh, God, give me strength . . . I was praying all night . . . I often walk up to him, myself start the conversation with him, I look into his eyes . . . I don't have any pride left, and can't control myself . . . I couldn't help it and confessed to Uncle Vanya yesterday that I love him . . . And all the servants know that I love him. Everybody knows.

ELENA: Does he?

SONYA: No, he doesn't notice me.

ELENA [*Thinking*]: He's a strange person . . . You know what? Allow me to speak with him . . . I'll be discreet and only drop a hint . . .

A pause.

After all, how much longer can you possibly remain in uncertainty . . . Allow me!

Sonya nods affirmatively.

Fine, then. Whether he loves you or doesn't love you—it's not difficult to find out. Don't be embarrassed, my dear girl, and don't worry—I'll question him discreetly, he won't even notice. All we need to find out is: yes or no?

A pause.

If it's no, then he shouldn't come here anymore. Yes?

Sonya nods affirmatively.

It's easier when you don't see him. We won't put it off and will interrogate him right now. He was going to show me some blueprints . . . Go tell him that I wish to see him.

SONYA [*In great agitation*]: Will you tell me the whole truth?

ELENA: Yes, of course. I think that truth, no matter how bad, can't be worse than uncertainty. Trust me, my dear girl.

SONYA: Yes . . . yes . . . I'll say that you want to see his drawings. [*She walks and stops by the door*] No, uncertainty is better . . . There's hope at least . . .

ELENA: What's wrong?

SONYA: Nothing. [*Goes out*]

ELENA [*Alone*]: There's nothing worse than when you know someone's secret and are unable to help. [*Pondering*] He's not in love with her—that much is clear, but why shouldn't he marry her? She isn't pretty, but for a country doctor, at his age, she would make a wonderful wife. She's such a good girl, generous, pure . . . No, no, but that's not it . . .

A pause.

I understand this poor girl. In the midst of this excruciating boredom, when instead of people, grey smudges surround you, and when you hear nothing but vulgar things, when all they do is eat, drink, sleep, sometimes he shows up, so unlike the rest—handsome, interesting, captivating, like a bright moon rising in the dark . . . Give in to his charm, forget yourself . . . I think I'm taken with him a little myself. Yes, I'm bored without him, and here I'm smiling just thinking about him . . . That Uncle Vanya says that a water nymph's blood flows in my veins: "Let yourself go at least once in your life" . . . Well? Maybe I should . . . Oh, if only I could fly as a free bird away from all of you, from your sleepy faces and conversations, forget that you even exist in this world . . . But I'm timid and a little shy . . . My conscience would bother me . . . He comes here every day now, I can guess why he's here, and I already feel guilty and ready to fall to my knees before Sonya to apologize, cry . . .

ASTROV [*Comes in with a cartogram*]: Good day! [*Shakes hands with her*] You wanted to see my artwork?

ELENA: Yesterday you promised to show me your work . . . Is this a good time?

ASTROV: Oh, of course! [*He stretches the cartogram on the card table and pins it to the table with thumbtacks*] Where were you born?

ELENA [*Helping him*]: In St. Petersburg.

ASTROV: And you're educated where?

ELENA: At the Conservatory.[16]

ASTROV: You probably won't be interested in this.

ELENA: Why not? I may not know much about country life, but I've read a great deal.

ASTROV: Here at the house I have my own desk . . . In Ivan Petrovich's room. When I get utterly exhausted and sink into torpor, I drop everything and run over here and play around with this thing for an hour or two . . . Ivan Petrovich and Sofia Alexandrovna are clicking away on the abacus, and I sit at my desk next to them, daubing, and I feel warm, peaceful, a cricket is chirping. But I don't allow myself this pleasure very often, only once a month . . . [*Pointing to the cartogram*] Now look over here. A picture of our district as it was fifty years ago. Light and dark green represent forests; half of the area is forested. Where you see red crosshatching on the green, it means there were elk and wild goats there . . . I'm showing here the flora and the fauna. On this lake lived swans, geese, ducks, and, as the old folks say, there were endless kinds of birds, visible and invisible: they used to swarm like a dark cloud overhead. In addition to large and small villages, here and there you see various settlements, little hamlets and farmsteads, small monasteries, and watermills . . . There used to be plenty of cattle and horses. You can see it marked in blue. For instance, this administrative district is colored deep blue; here there used to be herds of them, and there were three horses per household.

A pause.

Now, let's look down below. This was twenty-five years ago. Here, only one-third of the area is forested. The goats are no longer there but the elk still are. The green and blue are not as intense. And so on and so on. Now we move over to the third section: a picture of our district at the present. There are still places with the green, but it's no longer solid, only in patches; gone are the elk, the swans, and the wood grouse . . . The old settlements, hamlets, farmsteads, and watermills are gone without a trace. In general, a picture of gradual but unmistakable extinction, which in another ten or fifteen years will become complete. You may say that it's cultural influences, that the old style of life must give way to the new one. I understand if the cut-down forests were being replaced by new roads, railways, plants, factories, and schools—the people would be healthier, richer, more intelligent—but there's nothing of the sort! The same swamps and mosquitoes exist in the district, the same impassable roads, abject poverty, typhus, diphtheria, fires . . . Here we're dealing with extinction as a result of a back-breaking struggle for survival; this extinction is due to laziness and ignorance and a total lack of awareness—when a cold, hungry, and sick person, in order to save his children and whatever is left of his life, instinctively, without thinking, clutches at anything that can provide warmth and satisfy his hunger and destroys everything, not thinking about tomorrow . . . Almost everything has already been destroyed, yet nothing has yet been created in its place. [*Coldly*] I can tell by looking at you that you are not interested.

ELENA: But I understand so little about these things . . .

ASTROV: There is nothing to understand here really; you are just not interested.

ELENA: In all honesty, my thoughts are occupied with something else. Forgive me. I have to subject you to a little interrogation, and I'm a little embarrassed, I don't know quite how to begin.

ASTROV: An interrogation?

ELENA: Yes, a little interrogation, but . . . it's fairly innocent. Let's sit down!

They sit down.

It concerns a certain young person. We'll talk honestly as friends, in plain terms. We'll talk and then we'll forget what we were talking about. Yes?

ASTROV: Yes.

ELENA: It's about my stepdaughter, Sonya. Do you like her?

ASTROV: Yes, I respect her.

ELENA: Do you like her as a woman?

ASTROV [*Not right away*]: No.

ELENA: Just a couple of words before we finish. Have you noticed anything?

ASTROV: No, I haven't.

ELENA [*Takes him by the hand*]: You don't love her; I see it in your eyes . . . She's suffering . . . Try to understand that and . . . don't come here anymore.

ASTROV [*Gets up*]: My time has passed . . . And I have no time . . . [*Shrugging his shoulders*] When could I? [*He is embarrassed*]

ELENA: Phew! What an unpleasant conversation! I'm so uncommfortable as if I'd hauled a thousand pounds on my back. Well, thank God we are finished! Let's forget about it, as if we've never even had this conversation, and . . . and leave. You're an intelligent man, you'll understand . . .

A pause.

I'm all blushing even.

ASTROV: If you had told me a month or two ago, I might have considered it, but now . . . [*Shrugs his shoulders*] If she's suffering, then, of course . . . Only I don't understand one thing: why did you need this interrogation? [*Looks her straight in the eye and wags his finger at her*] You are very cunning!

ELENA: What do you mean?

ASTROV [*Laughing*]: Very cunning! Suppose Sonya is suffering, I'm willing to accept that, but why this interrogation of yours? [*Preventing her from speaking, and continuing quickly*] Please don't give me that surprised look; you know perfectly well why I come here every day. Why and for whose sake, you know perfectly well. My sweet vixen, don't look at me like that, I'm a wise old bird . . .

ELENA [*Perplexed*]: A vixen? I don't understand anything.

ASTROV: A beautiful, bushy polecat . . . You need new victims! I haven't done anything in a month, abandoned everything, all I do is seek you out greedily—and you like it terribly . . . terribly. Well, then? I've been con-quered; you knew that even without the interrogation. [*Crossing his arms and lowering his head*] I submit to you. Here, have me!

ELENA: You've lost your mind!

ASTROV [*Laughing through clenched teeth*]: A little shy . . .

ELENA: Oh, I'm higher and better than you think. I swear to you! [*She wants to leave*]

ASTROV [*Blocking her way*]: I will leave here today and won't come back, but . . . [*Takes her by the hand and looks around*] Where are we going to see each other? Tell me quickly, where? At any moment someone could walk in here, tell me quickly. [*With passion*] So beautiful, gorgeous . . . One kiss . . . Just to kiss your sweet-smelling hair . . .

ELENA: I swear to you . . .

ASTROV [*Not letting her speak*]: Why swear anything? No need to swear any-thing. No need for extra words . . . Oh, how beautiful you are! What beautiful hands! [*Kisses her hands*]

ELENA: But enough, enough of this . . . go . . . [*Pulls back her hands*] You're forgetting yourself.

ASTROV: Then tell me, tell me where are we going to meet tomorrow? [*Puts his arm around her waist*] You[17] see, it's inevitable, we have to see each other. [*Kisses her; at the same time Voinitsky enters with a bouquet of roses and stops by the door*]

ELENA [*Not seeing Voinitsky*]: Have pity . . . leave me alone . . . [*Puts her head on Astrov's chest*] No! [*Wants to leave*]

ASTROV [*Holding onto her waist*] Come to the forest preserve tomorrow . . . around two o'clock. Will you? Will you? Will you come?

ELENA [*Upon seeing Voinitsky*]: Let go of me! [*Deeply embarrassed walks over to the window*] That's terrible.

VOINITSKY [*Puts the bouquet on a chair, and uneasy, wipes his face and neck with a handkerchief*] It's all right . . . Well . . . It's all right . . .

ASTROV [*Needling*]: The weather is rather pleasant today, my most esteemed Ivan Petrovich. The morning was overcast, it looked as if it might rain, but now the sun is out. In all fairness, it's a beautiful autumn we are having . . . and the winter crops are not looking too bad. [*Rolls up the cartogram*] The only thing is: the days are getting shorter . . . [*Exits*]

ELENA [*Quickly comes up to Voinitsky*]: You'll do your best, you'll use all your influence to see to it that my husband and I leave this place today! Do you hear me? This very day!

VOINITSKY [*Wiping his face*]: Huh? Well, yes . . . all right . . . *Hélène*, I saw everything, everything . . .

ELENA [*Agitated*]: Do you hear me? I must leave this place this very day!

Enter Serebriakov, Sonya, Telegin, and Marina.

TELEGIN: Your Excellency, I'm a little under the weather myself. I've been sick for two days. My head is a little . . .

SEREBRIAKOV: Where are the others? I don't like this house. It's a labyrinth. Twenty-six enormous rooms, everyone wanders off, and you can never find anyone. [*He rings*] Invite Maria Vasilyevna and Elena Andreyevna to come here!

ELENA: I'm here.

SEREBRIAKOV: Ladies and gentlemen, please, have a seat.

SONYA [*Comes over to Elena and asks impatiently*]: What did he say?

ELENA: Later.

SONYA: You're trembling? Are you upset? [*Searches intently Elena's face with her eyes*] I understand . . . he said he's not going to come here any more . . . right?

A pause.

Tell me: yes?

Elena nods affirmatively.

SEREBRIAKOV [*To Telegin*]: I can put up with illness, but what I can't stomach is this rural way of life. I have a feeling as if I fell off the face of the earth and landed on another planet. Have a seat, ladies and gentlemen, please. Sonya!

Sonya does not hear him. She stands hanging her head low.

Sonya!

A pause.

She doesn't hear me. [*To Marina*] You too, Nanny, sit down.

Marina sits down and starts knitting her stocking.

Ladies and gentlemen, point your ears, so to speak, to the center of attention. [*He laughs*]

VOINITSKY [*Uneasy*]: Maybe you don't need me. Can I go?

SEREBRIAKOV: No, we need you here more than anyone.

VOINITSKY: What is it you wish from me, sir?[18]

SEREBRIAKOV: So formal . . . Why are you getting upset?

A pause.

If I've done you wrong, please, forgive me.

VOINITSKY: Drop that tone. Let us get down to the cause . . . What do you need?

Enter Maria Vasilyevna.

SEREBRIAKOV: Here's *Maman*. I'm starting, ladies and gentlemen.

A pause.

I've called you here, ladies and gentlemen, to tell you that the Inspector General is coming.[19] All right, joking aside. This is serious. I've gathered you here to ask for your help and advice, and knowing your ever-present kindness, I hope to receive them. I am a scholar, a man of books, and practical matters in life are alien to me. I cannot make do without the guidance of knowledgeable people, and so I ask you, Ivan Petrovich, and you, Ilya Ilych, and you, *Maman* . . . The thing is that *manet omnes una nox,*[20] that is to say, our lives are in God's hands, and since I'm old and ill, and for that reason I feel this to be an opportune time to make adjustments to my property matters, inasmuch as it concerns the interests of my family. My life is finished and I'm not thinking of myself, but I have a young wife and a daughter still a maiden.

A pause.

It is impossible for me to continue living in the country. We are not made for country living. To live in the city on the income that we receive from the estate is also impossible. If we were to sell, for example, the forest, then this would be an extraordinary measure, not something we could do every year. We need to procure such measures that would guarantee us a constant, more or less fixed amount of income. I have come up with one such measure and I have the honor of offering it to you for discussion. Skipping over the details, I'll cover it in broad terms. Our estate brings us, on average, no more than two percent. I propose we sell it. If we turn the proceeds into securities, then we'll receive anywhere from four to five percent, and I think we'll even have a few thousand left with which we would buy a summer house[21] in Finland.

VOINITSKY: Wait . . . I think my hearing is failing me. Repeat what you just said.

SEREBRIAKOV: Turn the money into securities, and with whatever money is left over buy a summer house in Finland.

VOINITSKY: No, not Finland . . . you said something else.

SEREBRIAKOV: I propose to sell the estate.

VOINITSKY: Yes, that's it. You'll sell the estate, fine, a brilliant idea . . . And where am I supposed to go, with my old mother and Sonya here?

SEREBRIAKOV: We'll talk about it in due time. We cannot do it all at once.

VOINITSKY: Wait. Up until now, obviously, I didn't have a drop of common sense. Up until now, I was stupid enough to believe that the estate belonged to Sonya. My late father bought the estate as a dowry for my sister. Up until now I was naïve and understood the law not the Turkish way,[22] and thought that the estate had passed from my sister to Sonya.

SEREBRIAKOV: Yes, the estate belongs to Sonya. Who's arguing? Without Sonya's consent, I would never try to sell it. Furthermore, I propose to sell it for Sonya's sake.

VOINITSKY: That's unbelievable, just unbelievable! Either I've lost my mind, or . . . or . . .

MME VOINITSKAYA: *Jean*, don't contradict Alexander. He does know better what's good and what isn't.

VOINITSKY: No, give me some water. [*Drinks the water*] Say whatever you want, whatever you want!

SEREBRIAKOV: I don't understand why you are so upset. I'm not saying that what I propose is ideal, and if everyone finds it unsuitable, I'm not going to insist.

A pause.

TELEGIN [*Embarrassed*]: Not only, Your Excellency, do I feel great admiration for scholarship, but kindred affinities as well. My brother Gregory Ilych's wife's brother, Konstantin Trofimovich Lakedemonov, you may know him, held a master's degree . . .

VOINITSKY: Wait, Waffles, this is serious . . . Wait, later . . . [*To Serebriakov*] Here, go and ask him. This estate was bought from his uncle.

SEREBRIAKOV: Oh, why should I ask? What for?

VOINITSKY: The estate was bought in those days for ninety-five thousand rubles. Father paid only seventy, leaving a debt of twenty-five. Now listen . . . The estate would not have been bought at all, had I not given up my share of the inheritance in favor of my sister, whom I loved dearly. And not only that, but for ten years, I worked like an ox and paid off the entire debt . . .

SEREBRIAKOV: I regret having started this conversation.

VOINITSKY: The estate's been paid off and is not in ruin thanks solely to my personal efforts. And now, when I am old, he wants to throw me the heck out!

SEREBRIAKOV: I don't understand what you're getting at!

VOINITSKY: Twenty-five years I managed this estate; I worked, sent you money like the most diligent of clerks, and during this whole time, you have not once thanked me for my work. This whole time—when I was young and now—you paid me a salary of five hundred rubles a year— a beggarly amount!—and it has never occurred to you to raise it even one ruble!

SEREBRIAKOV: Ivan Petrovich, how was I to know? I'm not a practical person and I don't understand any of this. You could've given yourself a raise as much as you wanted.

VOINITSKY: Yes, why didn't I steal? Why don't you despise me now for not stealing? It would've been fair, and I wouldn't be a pauper now!

MME VOINITSKAYA [*Sternly*]: Jean!

TELEGIN [*Agitated*]: Vanya, my dear friend, don't, don't . . . I'm trembling . . . Why destroy a good relationship? [*Kisses him*] Don't . . .

VOINITSKY: Twenty-five years, cooped up with this mother, like a mole, in these four walls ... All our thoughts and feelings were about you alone. During the day we talked about you, about your work, we were proud of you, uttered your name in awe; we wasted nights reading journals and books all of which I now despise!

TELEGIN: Don't, Vanya, don't ... I can't ...

SEREBRIAKOV [Enraged]: I do not understand, what do you want?

VOINITSKY: For us you were a higher being, and we knew your writing by heart ... But now my eyes are wide-open! I see everything! You write about art, but you understand nothing about art! All your work that I used to love is not worth a pin. You've been pulling the wool over our eyes!

SEREBRIAKOV: Ladies and gentlemen! Make him stop! I am leaving!

ELENA: Ivan Petrovich, I insist that you be quiet! Do you hear me?

VOINITSKY: I won't be quiet! [Blocking Serebriakov's way] Wait, I'm not finished! You ruined my life! I have not lived! I have not lived! Thanks to you, I destroyed and wasted the best years of my life! You are my worst enemy!

TELEGIN: I can't ... I can't ... I'm leaving. [In great agitation, he leaves]

SEREBRIAKOV: What do you want from me? And what right do you have to use this tone with me? A nonentity! If this estate is yours, then take it, I don't need it!

ELENA: I'm leaving this hellhole right this minute! [Shouts] I can't endure it any more!

VOINITSKY: I've wasted my life! I'm talented, clever, and brave ... If I lived a normal life, I could become another Schopenhauer or Dostoyevsky[23] ... I'm talking nonsense! I'm losing my mind ... Mama, I'm so miserable! Oh, Matushka![24]

MME VOINITSKAYA [Sternly]: Do what Alexander says!

SONYA [Falls to her knees beside the nurse, clinging to her]: Nanny, dear Nanny!

VOINITSKY: Mother, dear, what am I going to do? No, don't, don't tell me! I know what to do! [To Serebriakov] You will remember me! [Leaves through the middle door]

Mme Voinitskaya follows him.

SEREBRIAKOV Gentlemen, what in the world is going on? Get this madman away from me! I can't live under the same roof with him! He lives here

[*Points to the door in the middle*], practically next to me ... Make him move to the village or into the wing, or I'll move out, but I can't stay in the same house with him ...

ELENA [*To her husband*]: We're leaving today! We must make arrangenments right away.

SEREBRIAKOV: Worse than a nothing!

SONYA [*Kneeling, turns to her father and speaks to him nervously and through tears*]: You have to show mercy, Papa! Uncle Vanya and I are so unhappy! [*Controlling her despair*] You have to show mercy! Do you remember, when you were younger, Uncle Vanya and Grandmother at night would translate books for you and copy your papers ... every night, every night! Uncle Vanya and I worked without rest, were afraid to spend a kopeck on ourselves, and sent everything to you ... We earned our keep! That's not it, not it, but, Papa, you have got to understand us. You have to show mercy!

ELENA [*Agitated, to her husband*]: Alexander, for God's sake, talk to him ... I entreat you.

SEREBRIAKOV: Very well, I'll talk to him ... I'm not blaming him for anything, I'm not upset, but you have to admit, his behavior, to say the least, is very strange. As you wish, I'll go see him. [*He exits through the middle door*]

ELENA: Be gentle with him; calm him down ... [*Follows him out*]

SONYA [*Clinging to Marina*]: Nanny! Dear Nanny!

MARINA: It's all right, my child. The ganders will cackle awhile and then they'll stop ... Cackle and stop ...

SONYA: Nanny, dear!

MARINA [*Stroking her hair*]: Shivering like in winter! There, there, my orphan girl, God is gracious. A little linden tea, raspberry jam, and it'll go away ... No need to cry, my orphan ... [*Looking at the middle door, in anger*] How the ganders go at each other; damn them all!

A shot is heard offstage; Elena's scream is heard; Sonya shudders.

Oh, damn you!

SEREBRIAKOV [*Runs in, reeling with fright*]: Stop him! Stop him! He's lost his mind!

Elena and Voinitsky struggle in the doorway.

ELENA [*Trying to wrest the revolver from him*]: Give it to me! Give it to me, I said!

VOINITSKY: Let go, *Hélène!* Let go of me! [*Having freed himself, runs in searching with his eyes for Serebriakov*] Where is he? Ah, there he is! [*He shoots at him*] Bang!

A pause.

I missed? Another miss?! [*Enraged*] Oh, damn it, damn it . . . God damn it! [*He throws the revolver on the floor, and drops exhausted into a chair. Serebriakov is stunned. Elena Andreyevna is leaning against the wall, feeling faint.*]

ELENA: Take me away from here! Take me away; for the life of me, I can't stay here, I can't!

VOINITSKY [*Desperately*]: Oh, what am I doing! What am I doing?

SONYA: [*Softly*] Nanny! Dear Nanny!

Curtain.

ACT FOUR

Voinitsky's room; it is his bedroom and also the office for the estate. By the window, a large table with ledgers and all sorts of papers; a writing desk, cupboards, and a scale. A smaller desk for Astrov; on it are drawing materials, paints; a portfolio is next to them. A birdcage with a starling in it. A map of Africa is on the wall, most likely of no use to anybody here. A huge sofa covered in oilcloth. On the left—a door to the rest of the house, on the right—a door to the front hall; next to the door on the right is a doormat for the peasants to wipe off their muddy boots. It is an autumn evening. It is quiet.

Telegin and Marina sit facing one another, winding the wool for her stocking knitting.

TELEGIN: Hurry up, Marina Timofeyevna, they are about to call us to say good-bye. They already sent for the carriage.

MARINA [*Trying to wind more quickly*]: There's just a little more.

TELEGIN: They're going to Kharkov. They're going to live there.

MARINA: Even better.

TELEGIN: They had a scare . . . Elena Andreyevna said: "I don't want to spend another hour here, let's go, let's go . . . We'll stay in Kharkov, she says, looks around, and then we'll send for our things . . ." They're traveling light. It means, Marina Timofeyevna, that it wasn't in the cards for them to stay here. Wasn't in the cards . . . A fatal predestination.

MARINA: Even better. Raising a row like that just now, shooting—shame on them!

TELEGIN: Yes, a scene worthy of Aivazovsky's brush.[25]

MARINA: I wish I didn't have to see it.

A pause.

And we will go back to living like before: tea a little past seven, lunch at noon, and in the evening—we sit down to supper; everything same as before, like good Christians . . . [*Sighing*] It's been a long time since I oh, sinner that I am, had noodles.

TELEGIN: Yes, it has been a while since we've had noodles.

A pause.

Ages . . . This morning, I was walking through the village, Marina, and one of the shopkeepers yelled after me, "Hey, you, freeloader!" I felt so bitter!

MARINA: Pay no mind to that, dear. We are all freeloaders under God. Same as you, as Sonya, as Ivan Petrovich. No one sits around doing nothing, everybody's working hard! Everybody . . . Where is Sonya?

TELEGIN: In the garden. Still walking with the doctor, looking for Ivan Petrovich. Afraid he might lay hands on himself.

MARINA: Where's his pistol?

TELEGIN [*Whispers*]: I hid it in the cellar!

MARINA [*With a smirk*]: Oh, the sin!

Voinitsky and Astrov come in from outside.

VOINITSKY: Leave me alone! [*To Marina and Telegin*] Get out of here, leave me alone at least for an hour! I can't stand guardians.

TELEGIN: Sure, sure, Vanya. [*Tiptoes out*]

MARINA: The gander: cackle, cackle! [*Picks up the wool and goes out*]

VOINITSKY: Leave me alone!

ASTROV: I would with great pleasure, I should have left a while back, but I'm not leaving until you give back what you took from me.

VOINITSKY: I didn't take anything from you.

ASTROV: I'm serious—don't keep me waiting. I should have left by now.

VOINITSKY: I didn't take anything from you.

The two sit down.

ASTROV: Really? All right, I'll wait a little longer, but then, sorry, I'll have to resort to force. We'll tie you up and search you. I'm being very serious.

VOINITSKY: As you wish.

A pause.

Oh, what a fool I made of myself: to shoot at him twice and miss both times! I'll never forgive myself for this!

ASTROV: If you feel like shooting, shoot yourself in the head.

VOINITSKY [*Shrugging his shoulders*]: This is strange! I attempted murder but no one's arresting me, no one is taking me to court. Therefore, they must think that I'm crazy. [*With a bitter laugh*] I'm crazy, but those who, in the guise of professor, learned conjurer, hide their mediocrity, stupidity, and their blatant callousness—are not! Not crazy are those who marry old men and then deceive them in front of everybody. I saw it, I saw when you were embracing her!

ASTROV: Yes, sir, I was embracing her, and you get this. [*He thumbs his nose*]

VOINITSKY [*Looking at the door*]: No, crazy is the earth that still supports you!

ASTROV: Well, that's stupid.

VOINITSKY: Well then, I'm crazy, I'm beside myself, and I have a right to say stupid things.

ASTROV: The joke is stale. You are not crazy; you're just an oddball. A buffoon. Before, I used to think that all oddballs were either sick or crazy, but now I think that being an oddball is a normal state of being. You're quite normal.

VOINITSKY [*Covering his face with his hands*]: I'm so ashamed! If you only knew how ashamed I am! This sharp feeling of shame can't compare with any physical pain. [*With anguish*] It's unbearable! [*Leaning over the table*] What should I do? What should I do?

ASTROV: Nothing.

VOINITSKY: Give me something! Oh, my God . . . I'm forty-seven years old; suppose I make it till sixty, then I have another thirteen years left. Such a long time! How will I survive thirteen more years? What will I do, what will I fill them with? Oh, you see [*fitfully squeezing Astrov's hand*] . . . you see, if you could only spend the rest of your life in a new way. To wake up on a clear, quiet morning feeling that you have begun a new life, and that the past is all forgotten, diffused like smoke. [*Crying*] To begin a new life . . . Tell me how to begin . . . what to begin it with . . .

ASTROV [*With annoyance*]: Oh, come on, please! New life! Our situation, yours and mine, is hopeless.

VOINITSKY: Is it?

ASTROV: I'm convinced of it.

VOINITSKY: Give me something . . . [*He puts his hand to his heart*] It's burning right here.

ASTROV [*Shouts angrily*]: Stop it! [*Softening*] Those who will live a hundred or two hundred years after us, and who will despise us for having lived our lives so stupidly and tastelessly—they may find a way to be happy, but you and me . . . We have but one hope. The hope that when we're sleeping in our coffins, visions, maybe even pleasant ones, will visit us. [*After a sigh*] Oh, well, my friend. In the whole district there used to be only two decent intelligent people: you and me. But in a mere ten years, this narrow-minded, despicable life has sucked us in; it has poisoned our blood with its rotten fumes, and we've become vulgarians like everybody else. [*Quickly*] But don't try to smooth talk me, however. Give me back what you took from me.

VOINITSKY: I didn't take anything from you.

ASTROV: You took a jar of morphine from my medicine case.

A pause.

Listen, if you're so eager to kill yourself, then go off in the woods and shoot yourself there. But morphine, give it back to me; or people will start talking, speculating, and might think that I gave it to you . . . For me, it's enough that I'll be the one to do your autopsy . . . Do you think it's interesting?

Enter Sonya.

VOINITSKY: Leave me alone!

ASTROV [*To Sonya*]: Sofia Alexandrovna, your uncle has made off with a little jar of morphine from my medicine case, and won't give it back. Tell him that it's . . . not smart after all. I've no time. I have to go.

SONYA: Uncle Vanya, did you take the morphine?

A pause.

ASTROV: Yes, he did. I'm sure of it.

SONYA: Give it back. Why do you frighten us? [*Tenderly*] Give it back, Uncle Vanya! I may be just as unhappy as you, but I'm not giving in to despair. I endure and will endure until my life ends by itself . . . You, too, must endure it.

A pause.

Give it back! [*Kisses his hands*] My dear, good Uncle Vanya, give it back! [*Crying*] You're so kind-hearted, you'll have pity on us and give it back. You have to endure it, Uncle! Endure!

VOINITSKY [*Takes a jar from the desk drawer and hands it to Astrov*]: Here, take it! [*To Sonya*] But I must get to work quickly, do something quickly, otherwise, I can't . . . I just can't . . .

SONYA: Yes, yes, to work! As soon as we see our folks off, we'll sit down to work . . . [*Nervously straightening the papers on the table*] We've neglected everything!

ASTROV [*Puts the jar inside the medicine case and straps it together*]: Now I can go.

ELENA [*Entering*]: Ivan Petrovich, you are here? We're leaving . . . Go see Alexander, he wants to tell you something.

SONYA: Go, Uncle Vanya. [*Takes Voinitsky by the arm*] Let's go. You and papa have to make peace. It's important.

Sonya and Voinitsky leave.

ELENA: I'm leaving. [*Offers Astrov her hand*] Good-bye.

ASTROV: Already?

ELENA: The horses are here.

ASTROV: Good-bye.

ELENA: You promised me today that you would leave.

ASTROV: I remember. I'm leaving.

A pause.

Did I frighten you? [*Taking her hand*] Is it so scary?

ELENA: Yes.

ASTROV: Stay, why don't you! Well? Tomorrow in the forest preserve . . .

ELENA: No . . . It's done . . . And why I can look at you bravely now is because we're leaving . . . I ask you one thing: think better of me. I'd like you to respect me.

ASTROV: Ah! [*Making an impatient gesture*] Please stay! Admit it, there's nothing for you to do in this world; no goal in life, nothing to occupy your mind, and sooner or later you'll give in to feelings—it's inevitable. Then isn't it better if it doesn't happen somewhere in Kharkov or Kursk, but here, out in the country . . . At least it's poetic, even the autumn is beautiful . . . Here you have a forest preserve and rundown estates in the style of Turgenev . . .

ELENA: How funny you are . . . I'm a little upset at you and yet . . . I'll always remember you with fondness. You're interesting and unique. We'll never meet again, and so—why hide it? I was taken with you a little. Well, let's shake hands and part as friends. Don't think badly of me.

ASTROV [*Shook her hand*]: Yes, leave . . . [*Pondering*] You seem good and sensitive, and yet there's something strange about your whole being. You came here with your husband, and everyone who was working and pottering around here, who was creating something, suddenly had to drop whatever they were doing and spend the entire summer attending to your husband's gout and you. Both of you—you and he—have infected us all with your idleness. I was taken with you, I didn't do anything the whole month; and during this time people were ill, and the peasants were bringing their cattle to graze on the seedlings that I am planting . . . And so, no matter where you and your husband set foot, you bring destruction everywhere . . . I'm joking, of course, and yet . . . it's strange, and I'm convinced that if you stayed, the devastation would be enormous. I would perish, and you . . . wouldn't come out unscathed. So leave! *Finita la comedia!*[26]

ELENA [*Picks up a pencil off his table and hides it quickly*]: I'm taking this pencil as a keepsake.

ASTROV: It feels strange somehow . . . We knew each other, and suddenly, for some reason . . . we'll never see each other again. That's the way things are in life . . . While there's no one here, before Uncle Vanya walks in with his bouquet, allow me . . . to kiss you . . . In parting . . . Yes? [*Kisses her on the cheek*] Well . . . fine then.

ELENA: I wish you all the best. [*After glancing about her*] For once in my life, so be it! [*Embraces him impetuously, and the two quickly move away from each other*] I must go.

ASTROV: Go, go quickly. If the horses are ready, just go.

ELENA: I think someone's coming here.

They stand listening.

ASTROV: *Finita!*

Enter Serebriakov, Voinitsky, Maria Vasilyevna with a book, Telegin, and Sonya.

SEREBRIAKOV [*To Voinitsky*]: Let bygones be bygones. After what happened, in the last few hours I've thought so much about it that I could probably write a whole treatise for the edification of future generations on how to live one's life. I readily accept your apology and myself ask you to forgive me. Good-bye! [*Kisses Voinitsky three times*[27]]

VOINITSKY: You'll be receiving regularly the same amount as before. Everything will be the same as before.

Elena embraces Sonya.

SEREBRIAKOV [*Kisses Maria Vasilyevna's hand*]: Maman . . .

MARIA VASILYEVNA [*Kissing him*]: Alexander, have another photograph taken and send it to me. You know how dear you are to me.

TELEGIN: Good-bye, Your Excellency. Stay in touch!

SEREBRIAKOV [*After kissing his daughter*]: Good-bye . . . Good-bye everybody! [*Offering his hand to Astrov*] I want to thank you for the pleasure of your company . . . I respect your way of thinking, your passion and enthusiasm, but allow an old man to add one word of advice in his parting address: gentlemen, you have to commit to the cause! You have to! [*He bows to all*] All the best! [*He leaves; Maria Vasilyevna and Sonya follow him*]

VOINITSKY [*Affectionately kissing Elena's hand*]: Farewell . . . Forgive me . . . We'll never see each other again.

ELENA [*Moved*]: Good-bye, my dear. [*Kisses him on the head and goes out*]

ASTROV [*To Telegin*]: By the way, Waffles, go tell them to bring my horses too, at the same time.

TELEGIN: Yes, my friend. [*Goes out*]

Only Astrov and Voinitsky remain.

ASTROV [*Collects his paints off the table and hides them in the suitcase*]: Why aren't you going to see them off?

VOINITSKY: Let them leave, but I . . . I can't. It's hard for me. I need to occupy myself with something quick . . . Work, work! [*He rummages through the papers on the table*]

A pause; ringing of harness bells is heard.

ASTROV: They're gone. The professor is glad, I bet! Wild horses won't drag him here again.

MARINA [*Comes in*]: They're gone. [*Sits down in an armchair and knits her stocking*]

SONYA [*Comes in*]: They're gone. [*Wipes her eyes*] Hope to God they get there safely. [*To her uncle*] Well, Uncle Vanya, let's do something.

VOINITSKY: Work, work . . .

SONYA: We haven't sat at the table together for a long, long time. [*Lights the lamp on the table*] Looks like there's no ink . . . [*Takes the inkwell to the cupboard and fills it up with ink*] I'm sad that they're gone.

MARIA VASILYEVNA [*Comes in slowly*]: They're gone! [*She sits down and at once becomes absorbed in her book*]

SONYA [*Sits down at the table and leafs through the ledger*]: Uncle Vanya, we'll do the accounts first. We've neglected it terribly. Today again they sent to collect on it. Start writing. You write one account, and I do the other . . .

VOINITSKY [*Writing*]: "To the account . . . of Mr. . . ."

They both write in silence.

MARINA [*Yawns*]: Sleepyhead . . .

ASTROV: It's quiet. Pens are scratching and the cricket's chirping. It's warm and homey here . . . I don't want to leave.

Harness bells are heard.

Ah, they're bringing the horses around . . . All that's left is to say good-bye to you, my friends, say good-bye to my desk, and—go! [*Puts the cartograms in the folder*]

MARINA: What's all the fuss? Stay awhile.

ASTROV: I can't.

VOINITSKY [*Writing*]: "From the old debt, two seventy-five remaining . . ."

A Laborer comes in.

LABORER: Mikhail Lvovich, the horses are ready.

ASTROV: I heard. [*Hands him his medicine case, suitcase, and a folder*] Here, take this. Make sure you don't bend the folder.

LABORER: Yes, sir. [*Goes out*]

ASTROV: Well, then . . . [*Walks over to say good-bye*]

SONYA: When will we see each other?

ASTROV: Probably not before summer. In the winter—not likely . . . Needless to say, should anything happen, just let me know—and I'll come. [*Shakes hands with everybody*] Thank you for the bread and salt, and affection . . . in other words, for everything. [*He walks up to Marina and kisses her on the head*] Good-bye, old woman!

MARINA: Leaving before tea?

ASTROV: I don't want any, Nanny.

MARINA: A little vodka, maybe?

ASTROV [*Hesitantly*]: All right . . .

> Marina goes out.

> [*After a pause*] My trace horse[28] has started limping. I noticed it yesterday still when Petrushka[29] took it to water.

VOINITSKY: You have to reshoe.

ASTROV: I'll have to stop by at the blacksmith's in Rozhdestveny.[30] No getting around it. [*Walks to the map of Africa and looks at it*] It must be baking hot in this Africa now—something terrible!

VOINITSKY: It probably is.

MARINA [*Coming back carrying a tray with a shot glass of vodka and a small piece of bread*]: Have some.

> *Astrov drinks the vodka.*

> To your health, dear! [*Bows low to him*] You should have some bread with it.

ASTROV: No, I'm all right . . . Well, best wishes to all! [*To Marina*] Don't see me off, Nanny. Don't. [*He goes out; Sonya walks behind him with a candle to see him off; Marina sits down in her armchair*]

VOINITSKY [*Writing*]: "February 2nd, vegetable oil 20 pounds . . . February 16th, again, vegetable oil 20 pounds . . . Buckwheat . . ."

> *A pause. Harness bells are heard.*

MARINA: He's gone.

> *A pause.*

SONYA [*Comes back and sets the candle on the table*]: He's gone . . .

VOINITSKY [*Has added the numbers on the abacus and writes it down*]: Grand total . . . fifteen . . . twenty-five . . .

> *Sonya sits down and writes.*

MARINA [*Yawns*]: Oh, the sin . . .

Telegin tiptoes in, sits down by the door, and quietly tunes his guitar.

VOINITSKY [*To Sonya after stroking her hair*] Oh, my child, I'm so miserable! If you only knew how miserable I am!

SONYA: What can you do, we have to keep on living!

A pause.

We, Uncle Vanya, will live. We'll live through a very long row of days and slow evenings; we'll patiently put up with hardships that fate sends our way; we'll toil for others without rest now and when we're old; and when our time comes, we'll die calmly, and there, within the veil, we'll say how we suffered and cried, and how bitter we felt, and God will take pity on us, and Uncle, dear Uncle, we will see a bright, beautiful, and fine life, and we'll feel happy and we'll look back on our present sorrows with tenderness, with a smile—and we will rest. Uncle, I believe, believe passionately, fervently . . . [*Sonya kneels before her uncle and lays her head on his hands; she speaks in a weary voice*] We will rest!

Telegin plays softly on the guitar.

We will rest! We'll hear angels, we'll see the sky studded with diamonds, we'll see all earthly evil and all our suffering drown in mercy that will fill the world, and our life will become quiet, tender, and sweet as a caress. I believe, I do . . . [*She wipes his tears with a handkerchief*] Poor, poor Uncle Vanya, you're crying . . . [*Through tears*] You haven't known joy in your life, but just wait, Uncle Vanya, wait . . . We will rest . . . [*Embraces him*] We will!

The Watchman taps.

Telegin strums the guitar softly; Maria Vasilyevna writes in the margins of her pamphlet; Marina knits her stocking.

We will rest!

The curtain slowly comes down.

THREE SISTERS

A Drama in Four Acts

Characters

PROZOROV, ANDREY SERGEYEVICH

NATALIA IVANOVNA, his fiancée, later his wife

OLGA
MASHA } his sisters
IRINA

KULYGIN, FEDOR ILYCH, a teacher at a secondary school, Masha's husband

VERSHININ, ALEXANDER IGNATIEVICH, lieutenant colonel and battery commander

TUZENBACH, NIKOLAI LVOVICH, baron, lieutenant

SOLYONY, VASILY VASILIEVICH, captain

CHEBUTYKIN, IVAN ROMANOVICH, army doctor

FEDOTIK, ALEXEY PETROVICH, second lieutenant

RODEH, VLADIMIR KARLOVICH, second lieutenant

FERAPONT, caretaker at the county council offices, an old man

ANFISA, nanny, old woman aged 80

The action takes place in a provincial town.

ACT ONE

The Prozorovs' house. A drawing room with columns; on the other side—a large reception room. It is noon; outside the weather is sunny and cheerful. In the dining room, the table is being set for lunch. Olga, wearing the regulation dark blue dress of a teacher at a secondary school for girls is continuously correcting students' exercise books, standing and pacing about the room; Masha, in a black dress, sits with her hat on her lap reading a book; Irina, in a white dress, stands lost in thought.

OLGA: Father died exactly a year ago, this very day, May fifth, your name day,[1] Irina. It was very cold then, and snowing. I thought that I'd never get over it, and you fainted: were lying there lifeless. But now, a year later, it is easy for us to think back on it, and you're already in a white dress, looking radiant . . .

The clock strikes twelve.

The clock was striking then, too.

I remember when they were carrying Father, the band was playing, and shots were fired at the cemetery. He was a general, a brigade commander, and yet, there were very few people there. Probably because it was raining. A heavy rain with snow.

IRINA: Why bring that up!

Baron Tuzenbach, Chebutykin, and Solyony appear behind the columns, near the table in the dining room.

OLGA: It's warm today; you can keep the windows wide open, but the leaves on the birch trees haven't opened yet. Father was given a brigade here and left Moscow with us eleven years ago, and I remember it so well; it was early May then too, and everything is in bloom in Moscow; it's warm and everything is bathed in sunlight. Eleven years ago, but I remember it all as though we left just yesterday. Oh, my God! I woke up this morning, saw all this light, saw the spring, and joy stirred in my heart, and I wanted so much to go back home.

CHEBUTYKIN [*To Solyony and Tuzenbach*]: The hell you will!

TUZENBACH: Of course, that's all nonsense.

Masha, absorbed in reading, softly whistles a song.

OLGA: Stop whistling, Masha. How can you do that!

A pause.

Because I'm at school every day and then I give private lessons into the evening, my head hurts all the time, and the thoughts that come to me . . . as if I were already old. Come to think of it, in the four years that I've been working at the school, I feel my youth and energy draining out of me every day, drop by drop. And only one hope keeps getting stronger . . .

IRINA: To go to Moscow. To sell the house, drop everything here, and go to Moscow . . .

OLGA: Yes! To Moscow, as soon as possible.

Chebutykin and Tuzenbach laugh.

IRINA: Our brother will probably become a professor, and he won't live here anyway. The only thing keeping us from going is poor Masha.

OLGA: Masha will come to Moscow for the summer every year.

Masha whistles a tune softly.

IRINA: With God's help everything will work out. [*Looking out of the window*] The weather's beautiful today. I don't know why I feel so blissful! This morning, I remembered it was my name-day and I suddenly felt such joy, and I remembered my childhood when Mama was still alive. And such delightful thoughts stirred inside me!

OLGA: You're so radiant today and you look unbelievably beautiful. Masha's beautiful, too. Andrey would look good, except that he's put on too much weight and it doesn't suit him. And I've aged and lost a lot of weight—probably because I get upset with the girls at school. Today I'm free; I'm home, and my head doesn't hurt, and I feel younger than I did yesterday. I'm only twenty-eight . . . Everything's all right, it's God's will, but I think if I'd been married and stayed home all day, it would be better.

A pause.

I would love my husband.

TUZENBACH [*To Solyony*]: What you're saying is such nonsense; I'm fed up listening to you. [*Entering the drawing room*] Oh, I forgot to tell you that our new battery commander, Vershinin, is going to call on you today. [*Sits down at the piano*]

OLGA: Well, then! I'm glad to hear it.

IRINA: Is he old?

TUZENBACH: No, not particularly. Forty, forty-five at the most. [*Plays softly*] Seems like a good fellow. Definitely not stupid. Only he talks a lot.

IRINA: Is he good-looking?

TUZENBACH: He's all right; only he has a wife, a mother-in-law, and two girls. It's his second marriage. He calls on everyone and tells them that he has a wife and two girls. He'll tell you, too. His wife's loony: she wears her hair in a long braid like a schoolgirl, speaks always in this high-flown manner, philosophizes, and attempts suicide frequently, probably to spite her husband. I would've left a woman like that long ago, but he puts up with her and only complains.

SOLYONY [*Walking with Chebutykin from the dining room into the living room*]: With one hand I can lift only fifty-five pounds, but with both, I can lift over two hundred pounds. From this I deduce that two men are not twice as strong as one, but three times as strong, and even more . . .

CHEBUTYKIN [*Reading a newspaper as he walks in*]: To prevent hair loss . . . eight grams of naphthalene to a half bottle of pure alcohol . . . dissolve and apply daily . . . [*Writes in his notebook*] We'll make a note of it! [*To Solyony*] So, as I was saying, you put a little cork into a little bottle and you have a small glass tube running through it . . . Then you take a pinch of ordinary, everyday alum . . .

IRINA: Ivan Romanych, dear Ivan Romanych!

CHEBUTYKIN: What is it, my darling little girl?

IRINA: Tell me, why do I feel so happy today? As if I had wind in my sails, this immense blue sky, and big white birds soaring above me. Why is that? Why?

CHEBUTYKIN [*Kisses both her hands, tenderly*]: My white bird . . .

IRINA: When I woke up this morning, got up, washed my face, I suddenly got this feeling that everything in the world was clear to me, and I knew how to live. Dear Ivan Romanych, I know everything. People must work by the sweat of their brow, no matter who they are, and that's the meaning and goal of their lives; their happiness and joy. How good it feels to be a worker who gets up at dawn and crushes stones in the street, or a shepherd, or a schoolteacher who teaches children, or a machinist on the railroad . . . Heavens, forget being human, I'd rather be an ox or even an ordinary horse, as long as I could work, rather than a young woman who wakes up at noon, drinks her coffee in bed, and then spends two hours getting dressed . . . oh, how awful! In hot weather, you sometimes crave something to drink, that's how I crave to work. And if I won't get up early and work, then, Ivan Romanych, you must refuse me your friendship . . .

CHEBUTYKIN [*Tenderly*]: I'll refuse, I will . . .

OLGA: Father taught us to get up at seven o'clock. Now Irina wakes at seven and stays in bed at least till nine thinking of something. And such a serious face! [*Laughs*]

IRINA: You always see me as a little girl, and you think it's strange that I have a serious face. I'm twenty years old!

TUZENBACH: This longing for work, my God, I understand it so well! I've never worked in my life, not once. I was born in cold and idle St. Petersburg, to a family that never knew work and never had any concerns. I remember when I'd come home from military school, the lackey would pull my boots off and I'd be fussing, but my mother always looked at me with awe, and was surprised when not everyone else did. They shielded me from work. Only they didn't succeed! The time has come and some big massive thing is coming towards us all, and a big and mighty storm's brewing; it's coming, it's getting close and it'll soon free our society from laziness, indifference, contempt for work, and this putrid boredom. I will work, and in some twenty-five or thirty years, everybody will work. Everybody!

CHEBUTYKIN: Well, I won't work.

TUZENBACH: You don't count.

SOLYONY: Thank God, you won't even be here in twenty-five years. In two-three years you will die of a stroke or I'll fly into a rage, my dear angel, and put a bullet through your head. [*Takes a bottle of scent from his pocket and sprinkles it on his chest and hands*]

CHEBUTYKIN [*Laughs*]: It's true, I've never done anything. I haven't lifted a finger since I graduated from the university. I haven't even read a single book, only newspapers . . . [*Takes another newspaper out of his pocket*] See . . . I know from reading the newspapers that there was someone, say, by the name of Dobrolyubov,[2] but what it was he wrote, I don't know . . . God knows what . . .

Knocking on the floor is heard; it is coming from below.

See . . . They're calling me downstairs; someone's here to see me. I'll be right back . . . wait . . . [*Hurries out while combing his beard*]

IRINA: He's up to something.

TUZENBACH: Yes. He left with a solemn expression and most likely will come back with a present for you.

IRINA: This is so unpleasant!

OLGA: Yes, it's awful. He's always doing silly things like that.

MASHA: "A green oak stands by a curving seashore,/ And on that oak a golden chain"[3] . . . And on that oak a golden chain . . . [*Gets up and hums quietly*]

OLGA: You're not cheerful today, Masha.

Masha is humming and puts on her hat.

Where are you going?

MASHA: Home.

IRINA: That's strange . . .

TUZENBACH: Leaving in the middle of your sister's name-day party!

MASHA: It doesn't matter . . . I'll come tonight. Good-bye, my dear . . . [*Kisses Irina*] I wish you once more good health and much happiness. In the old days, when Father was alive, we would have thirty or forty officers at our parties; they were loud, but today it's one-and-a-half officers and quiet like a hermit's cell . . . I have to go . . . I'm in gloomlandia[4] today, sad, don't listen to me. [*Laughing through tears*] We'll talk later, good-bye for now, my dear; I'll go somewhere.

IRINA [*Displeased*]: You are so . . .

OLGA [*With tears*]: I know how you feel, Masha.

SOLYONY: When a man talks philosophy, it's called philosophistry or just plain sophistry, but when a woman or two women go at it, then it's wake me up when it's over.

MASHA: What do you mean by that, you awful, terrible man?

SOLYONY: Nothing. "No time to say a prayer,/ He was knocked down by a bear."[5] *A pause.*

MASHA [*Sternly to Olga*]: Stop bawling!

Enter Anfisa and Ferapont with a cake.

ANFISA: This way, dear sir. Come in, your feet are clean. [*To Irina*] This is from the county council, from Protopopov, Mikhail Ivanych . . . A pie.

IRINA: Thank you. Please express thanks to him. [*Accepts the cake*]

FERAPONT: Wha?

IRINA [*Louder*]: Express thanks!

OLGA: Nanny dear, give him some pie. Ferapont, go, they'll give you some pie.

FERAPONT: Wha?

ANFISA: Come on, dear sir, Ferapont Spiridonych. Come . . . [*Leaves with Ferapont*]

IASHA: I don't like this Protopopov, Mikhail Potapych or Ivanych. You shouldn't have invited him.

IRINA: I didn't invite him.

MASHA: So much the better.

Enter Chebutykin followed by a soldier carrying a silver samovar; a buzz of astonishment and displeasure.

OLGA [*Covering her face with her hands*]: A samovar! How awful![6] [*Walks toward the table in the dining room*]

IRINA: Ivan Romanych, dear, what are you doing!

TUZENBACH [*Laughing*]: I told you!

MASHA: You should be ashamed of yourself!

CHEBUTYKIN: My dear, my darling girls, you're all I've got; you're the most precious thing in the whole world to me. I'm almost sixty. I'm an old man, a lonely, worthless old man . . . The only good thing left in me is my love for you, and if it wasn't for you I would've been dead long ago . . . [*To Irina*] My dear child, I've known you from the day you were born . . . carried you in my arms . . . I loved your dear, late mother . . .

IRINA: But why give such expensive presents!

CHEBUTYKIN [*Through tears, crossly*]: Expensive presents . . . How can you say that! [*To the orderly*] Take the samovar over there . . . [*Mockingly*] Expensive presents . . .

The orderly takes the samovar into the reception room.

ANFISA [*Walking through the drawing room*]: My dears, a colonel I don't recognize! He already took off his coat, my children, and he's coming this way. Arinushka, be sweet and politest . . . [*Leaving*] And it's lunchtime already . . . Goodness me . . .

TUZENBACH: It must be Vershinin.

Enter Vershinin.

Lieutenant Colonel Vershinin!

VERSHININ [*To Masha and Irina*]: I'd like to present myself: Vershinin. I'm so glad that I'm here at last. Oh, look at you! Oh, my word!

IRINA: Please, have a seat. We're very happy to meet you.

VERSHININ [*With joy*]: I'm so glad, so glad! But there were three of you sisters. I remember: three girls. I can't remember the faces now, but I remember very well that your father, Colonel Prozorov, had three little girls, and I saw you with my own eyes. How time flies! Oh, my, how time flies!

TUZENBACH: Alexander Ignatievich is from Moscow.

IRINA: From Moscow? You are from Moscow?

VERSHININ: Yes, from Moscow. Your late father was battery commander there, and I was an officer in the same brigade. [*To Masha*] Your face I remember a little, I think.

MASHA: I don't remember yours!

IRINA: Olia! Olia! [*Shouts into the dining room*] Olia, come here, come!

Olga comes from the drawing room into the reception room.

It turns out, Lieutenant Colonel Vershinin is from Moscow.

VERSHININ: Then you must be Olga Sergeyevna, the eldest . . . You're Maria . . . And you—Irina—the youngest . . .

OLGA: You are from Moscow?

VERSHININ: Yes. I studied in Moscow, entered the service and served there a long time, and finally received my own battery assignment and, as you can see, transferred here. I don't really remember you, I only remember that there were three of you. Your father, I remember vividly; I close my eyes and I see him just like it was yesterday. I used to visit you in Moscow . . .

OLGA: I thought I remembered everyone, and all of a sudden . . .

VERSHININ: My name is Alexander Ignatievich . . .

IRINA: Alexander Ignatievich, you are from Moscow . . . What a surprise!

OLGA: Because we're moving there.

IRINA: We hope to be there already by autumn. It's our hometown, we were born there . . . On Old Basmanny Street . . .

Both laugh happily.

MASHA: All of a sudden to see someone from our hometown. [*Lively*] Now I remember! Olia, do you remember they used to say "lovestruck major." You were a lieutenant and in love with someone then, and everyone teased you with "major" for some reason.

VERSHININ [*Laughs*]: Yes, yes . . ."Lovestruck major," exactly right . . .

MASHA: Only then you had a moustache . . . Oh, how you have aged! [*Through tears*] How you have aged!

VERSHININ: Yes, when they called me lovestruck major, I was young and in love. Not anymore.

OLGA: But you don't have a single gray hair. You've aged, but you're not old yet.

VERSHININ: Still, I'm forty-two. How long ago did you leave Moscow?

IRINA: Eleven years. Masha, what an oddball you are, why are you crying? [*Through tears*] I'll start crying too . . .

MASHA: Never mind. What street did you live on?

VERSHININ: On Old Basmanny Street.

OLGA: And so did we . . .

VERSHININ: I lived on Nemetskaia[7] Street at one time. I used to walk to the Red Barracks from there. There you cross a glum bridge on the way and under the bridge the water's rushing. When you're all alone, it fills your heart with sadness.

   A pause.

   And here, you have a wide and plentiful river! A wonderful river!

OLGA: Yes, only it's cold. It's cold here and a lot of mosquitoes . . .

VERSHININ: Oh, no! Here you have a good, healthy Slavic climate. The woods, the river . . . and birch trees, too. Dear, modest, birch trees; I love them more than all other trees. It's a good place to live. It's strange that the railway station is twelve miles away, though . . . And nobody knows why.

SOLYONY: But I know why it's like that.

   Everyone looks at him.

   Because if the station was nearby, then it wouldn't be far away, but if it's far away, then it's not nearby.

   An awkward pause.

TUZENBACH: Vasily Vasilych[8] is a real joker.

OLGA: Now I, too, remember you. I remember.

VERSHININ: I knew your dear mother.

CHEBUTYKIN: She was a good woman, may she rest in peace.

IRINA: Mother's buried in Moscow.

OLGA: At the Novodevichy[9] . . .

MASHA: To think that I'm already starting to forget her face. The same way people won't remember us, either. They'll forget.

VERSHININ: Yes. They'll forget. It's our fate and there's nothing we can do about it. What we think as serious, significant, very important—a day will come—will all be forgotten or seem unimportant.

A pause.

And what's interesting is that we can't know now what will be considered sublime, important, and what—pitiful and ridiculous. Didn't the discoveries of Copernicus or, say, Columbus seem pointless and absurd at first, while gibberish written by some crank was taken as supreme truth? And it may very well turn out that our life now—to which we resign ourselves—in time, will seem strange, awkward, foolish, insufficiently pure, and maybe even sinful . . .

TUZENBACH: Who can say? Perhaps they'll think highly of it and will remember it with respect. We don't have tortures, executions, invasions, but at the same time, so much suffering!

SOLYONY [*In a high-pitched voice*]: Chicka, chicka, chicka . . . No need to feed the baron, just give him a chance to philosophize.

TUZENBACH: Vasily Vasilyevich, please leave me alone . . . [*Sits down in another chair*] It's boring after all.

SOLYONY [*In a high-pitched voice*]: Chicka, chicka, chicka . . .

TUZENBACH [*To Vershinin*]: The suffering observed nowadays—and there's so much!—speaks, nonetheless, to a high moral level already attained by society . . .

VERSHININ: Yes, yes, of course.

CHEBUTYKIN: You've just said, Baron, that they'll think highly of our life, but the people are still pretty low . . . [*Stands up*] Look how low I am. It's to make me feel better that you, obviously, have to speak highly of my life.

Sounds of violin playing coming from offstage.

MASHA: That's Andrey, our brother, playing.

IRINA: He's our scholar. He'll probably be a professor. Papa was a military man, but his son has chosen a learned career for himself.

MASHA: In keeping with Papa's wishes.

OLGA: We've teased him to death today. He seems to be in love a little.

IRINA: With one of the local young ladies. She'll be here today most likely.

MASHA: Oh, the way she dresses! It's not that it's ugly or out of fashion; it's just pitiful. An odd-looking bright-yellowish skirt with a vulgar fringe and a red top. And those scrubbed-scrubbed cheeks! Andrey's not in love—I don't believe it; he's got taste after all; he's just teasing us, pulling our leg. Yesterday I heard that she's marrying Protopopov,[10] the chairman of the local council. So much the better . . . [*Speaking in the direction of the side door*] Andrey, come here! Come, my dear, just for one minute!

Andrey comes in.

OLGA: This is my brother, Andrey Sergeyich.

VERSHININ: Vershinin.

ANDREY: Prozorov. [*Wipes his sweaty face*] You're our new battery commander, aren't you?

OLGA: Can you imagine, Colonel Vershinin's from Moscow?

ANDREY: Really? Oh, well, now my dear sisters won't leave you in peace.

VERSHININ: They're already fed up with me.

IRINA: Look at the little picture frame Andrey gave me today! [*Shows him the frame*] He made it himself.

VERSHININ [*Looking at the little frame and not knowing what to say*]: Yes . . . indeed . . .

IRINA: And the frame that's above the piano, he made that too.

Andrey makes an impatient gesture with his hand and steps away.

OLGA: He's a scholar and he plays the violin, and he can carve different things—in other words, he's a jack of all trades. Andrey, don't leave! He always does that—always slips out. Come over here!

Masha and Irina take him arm in arm and bring him back, laughing.

MASHA: Come, come!

ANDREY: Leave me alone, please.

MASHA: How silly you are! We used to call the colonel the "lovestruck major," and he never got upset.

VERSHININ: Not at all!

MASHA: And I want to call you: the lovestruck fiddler!

IRINA: Or lovestruck professor! . . .

OLGA: He's in love! Andriusha's[11] in love!

IRINA [*Clapping her hands*]: Bravo, bravo! Encore! Andriushka's in love!

CHEBUTYKIN [*Coming up behind Andrey, takes him by the waist*]: "*For love alone dear nature has given birth to us.*"[12] [*Bursts out laughing, never letting go of his newspaper*]

ANDREY: All right, enough, that's enough ... [*Wipes his face*] I couldn't sleep all night and now I'm a little out of sorts, as they say. I read till four, then went to bed, but to no avail. I was thinking about this and that, but then the early sunrise and the sun's just pushing itself into the bedroom. While I'm here for the summer, I want to translate a book from the English.

VERSHININ: Do you read English?

ANDREY: Yes. Our father, God rest his soul, oppressed us with education. It's silly and ridiculous, but I have to say that after he died I started putting on weight, and in one year I've gained all this weight as if my body freed itself from oppression. Thanks to our father, my sisters and I know French, German, and English, and Irina speaks Italian, too. But at what cost!

MASHA: In this town knowing three languages is an unnecessary luxury. Not even a luxury, but some sort of an unneeded appendage, like a sixth finger. We know a lot of superfluous things.

VERSHININ: Come now! [*Laughs*] You know a lot of superfluous things! I don't think there is or could ever exist a town so boring and dreary that it would not need someone intelligent and educated. Let's suppose that among one hundred thousand inhabitants of this town, of course, backward and crude, there are only three people like you. Well, it goes without saying, you can't prevail against the dark throngs surrounding you; during your lifetime, little by little, you'll have to give in and lose yourself in this crowd of a hundred thousand; life will choke you, but you won't disappear, you won't be without influence; after you, already six people like you will emerge, then twelve and so on until people like you finally become the majority. In two or three hundred years, life on earth will be incredibly beautiful and exquisite. One needs a life like that, and if it's not here yet, then one must anticipate it, wait and dream about it, and prepare for it, and to do this one must see and know more than our grandfathers and fathers ever saw or knew. [*Laughs*] And you're complaining that you know a lot of superfluous things.

MASHA [*Takes off her hat*]: I'm staying for lunch.

IRINA [*With a sigh*]: I really ought to write this all down ...

Andrey is not there; he has slipped out of the room.

TUZENBACH: Many years from now you're saying that life on earth will be beautiful and exquisite. That's true. But to take part in it now, even if from afar, we have to prepare for it, we have to work . . .

VERSHININ [*Stands up*]: Well. All these flowers, however! [*Looking around*] And a wonderful place. I envy you! All my life I've been knocking around from place to place, with two chairs, a sofa, and smoky stoves always. All my life I've been lacking precisely these flowers . . . [*Rubs his hands*] Oh, well! Never mind!

TUZENBACH: Yes, we have to work. I bet you're thinking: that German's wallowing in sentiment. But, word of honor, I'm Russian, I really am, and I don't even speak German. My father's Russian Orthodox . . .

A pause.

VERSHININ [*Walking up and down the stage*]: I often think: what if we were to begin our life again, but this time consciously? If only the life we've already lived was just a rough draft, so to speak, and the other one—a final draft! Then each one of us, I think, would try their best not to repeat themselves and at least create different living conditions for himself, making sure that it's a place like this one, with flowers and a mass of light . . . I have a wife, two girls; besides, my wife is a lady who is not well, and so on and so forth—and so, if I were to begin my life anew, I wouldn't get married . . . I wouldn't, no!

Enter Kulygin wearing tails.

KULYGIN [*Walks up to Irina*]: Dear sister,[13] allow me to wish you many happy returns on your name-day and sincerely and from the heart wish you good health and everything else that one can wish a young woman of your age. And also to offer you as a gift this little book. [*Hands her the book*] It's the history of our high school for fifty years, written by me. A trifle of a book, written for lack of anything better to do, but do read it all the same. Hello, ladies and gentlemen! [*To Vershinin*] Kulygin, a teacher at the local secondary school. Civil servant, seventh rank. [*To Irina*] In this book you'll find a list of all those who graduated from our secondary school in the last fifty years. *Feci quod potui, faciant meliora potentes.*[14] [*Kisses Masha*]

IRINA: But you already gave me the same book for Easter.

KULYGIN [*Laughs*]: Oh, you don't say! In that case give it back, or better yet, give it to the colonel here. Take it, colonel. Read it some day when you are bored.

VERSHININ: Thank you. [*Getting ready to leave*] I'm extremely glad to have made your acquaintance ...

OLGA: You are leaving? No, don't!

IRINA: Stay for lunch. Please.

OLGA: Please, do!

VERSHININ [*With a bow*]: I think you're celebrating a name-day. I didn't know, forgive me, and didn't wish you many happy returns ... [*Goes into the reception room with Olga*]

KULYGIN: Ladies and gentlemen, today's Sunday, a day of rest; so let us rest and enjoy ourselves, each in the manner befitting his age and station. The rugs should be rolled up for the summer and put away till winter ... with Persian powder or naphthalene ... The Romans were healthy people because they knew how to work and how to rest; they had *mens sana in corpore sano.*[15] Their life followed predictable forms. Our headmaster says that the most important thing in life is form ... Whatever loses form is finished—and our daily life is the same way. [*Putting his arm round Masha's waist, laughing*] Masha loves me. My wife loves me. And the curtains, too, with the carpets ... I feel cheerful today, I'm in very good spirits. Masha, today at four we're at the headmaster's. There's an outing for the teachers and their families.

MASHA: I'm not going.

KULYGIN [*Agitated*]: My dear Masha, why not?

MASHA: I'll tell you later ... [*Angrily*] All right, I'll go, just leave me alone, please ... [*Walks away*]

KULYGIN: And then we'll spend the evening at the headmaster's. Despite his ailing health, this man tries above all to be sociable. Such an outstanding and enlightened personality. A splendid man. Yesterday, after the meeting, he says to me, "I'm tired, Fedor Ilych. I'm tired." [*Looks at the clock, then at his watch*] Your clock is seven minutes fast. "Yes," he says, "tired."

Sounds of violin playing are coming from offstage.

OLGA: Ladies and gentlemen, lunch is served! Hot pie!

KULYGIN: Ah, dear Olga, my dear Olga! Yesterday I worked from early morning till eleven o'clock at night, I was tired, and today I feel happy. [*Goes
to the table in the reception room*] My dear . . .

CHEBUTYKIN [*Puts the newspaper in his pocket and combs his beard*]: A pie?
Splendid!

MASHA [*Sternly to Chebutykin*]: Only I warn you: no drinking today. Do you
hear me? Drinking's bad for you.

CHEBUTYKIN: Ugh! I'm over it. I haven't had a drinking binge in two years.
[*Impatiently*] Hey, my good woman, what does it matter!

MASHA: Still, don't you dare drink. Don't you dare. [*In anger, but making sure
that her husband cannot hear*] Damn it, another boring evening at the
headmaster's!

TUZENBACH: I wouldn't go if I were you . . . Just like that.

CHEBUTYKIN: Don't go, my sweetie-pie.

MASHA: Sure, don't go . . . This damn life, it's unbearable . . . [*Goes into the
reception room*]

CHEBUTYKIN [*Follows her*]: Now, now . . .

SOLYONY [*Going through to the reception room*]: Chicka, chicka, chicka . . .

TUZENBACH: Enough, Vasily Vasilych. That's enough!

SOLYONY: Chicka, chicka, chicka . . .

KULYGIN [*Cheerfully*]: To your health, Colonel! I'm a pedagogue and here,
at the house, I'm one of the family, Masha's husband . . . She's good-
hearted, very good-hearted . . .

VERSHININ: I'll drink some of that dark vodka . . . [*Drinks*] To your health!
[*To Olga*] It's good to be here!

Irina and Tuzenbach remain in the drawing room.

IRINA: Masha's in a bad mood today. She got married at eighteen when she
thought he was the most intelligent person. But not anymore. He is
most good-hearted, but not the most intelligent.

OLGA [*Impatiently*]: Andrey, we're waiting, are you coming?

ANDREY [*Offstage*]: Coming. [*Comes in and walks to the table*]

TUZENBACH: What are you thinking about?

IRINA: Nothing. I don't like your friend Solyony and I'm scared of him. He's
always saying stupid things . . .

TUZENBACH: He's a strange man. I feel sorry for him, and he annoys me, but
it's mostly I feel sorry. I think he's a little shy . . . When it's just the two

of us, he can be very intelligent and affectionate, but in company, he's crude and a *bretteur*.[16] Don't leave, let them take their seats at the table. Allow me to stay near you a little longer. What are you thinking about?

A pause.

You're twenty and I'm not yet thirty. We have so many years ahead of us—a long, long succession of days filled with my love for you . . .

IRINA: Nikolai Lvovich, don't talk to me about love.

TUZENBACH [*Not listening*]: I have a burning hunger for life, for struggle, work, and this hunger has merged with my love for you, Irina; and as if on purpose, you're beautiful and I think that life's so beautiful! What are you thinking about?

IRINA: You say: life's beautiful. But what if it only appears beautiful! For us, the three sisters, life hasn't been beautiful yet; it's been choking us like weeds . . . Tears are rolling down . . . I really shouldn't . . . [*Quickly wipes her eyes, smiling*] We have to work, to work. The reason we're so unhappy and take such a gloomy view of life is because we don't know how to work. We're born to people who despised labor . . .

Natalia Ivanovna comes in; she is wearing a pink dress with a green sash.

NATASHA: They're sitting down to lunch already . . . I'm late . . . [*Glances in the mirror and fixes herself up*] My hair seems all right . . . [*Upon seeing Irina*] Many happy returns, dear Irina Sergeyevna! [*Gives her a vigorous and prolonged kiss*] You have many guests; I am a little embarrassed, really . . . Hello, Baron!

OLGA [*Coming into the drawing room*]: Oh, and here is Natalia Ivanovna. Hello, my dear!

They kiss.

NATASHA: Many happy returns. Such a large gathering, I feel terribly awkward . . .

OLGA: Stop it. We're all friends here. [*In a horrified undertone*] A green sash! My dear, that's not right!

NATASHA: Is it bad luck?

OLGA: No, it just doesn't go together . . . it looks a little strange . . .

NATASHA [*In a tearful voice*]: Really? But it's not green; it's closer to matte. [*Follows Olga into the reception room*]

*In the reception room everybody is in the process of sitting down. The draw-
ing room is empty.*

KULYGIN: Let's hope you find yourself a good fiancé, Irina. It's time for you
to marry.

CHEBUTYKIN: Natalia Ivanovna, I hope you land a fiancé, too.

KULYGIN: Natalia Ivanovna already has a fiancé.

MASHA: I'll have a little glass of this wine! Ah, this sweet life of mine, come
what may!

KULYGIN: You get C minus for conduct.

VERSHININ: The brandy is good. What's it made with?

SOLYONY: Roaches.

IRINA [*In a tearful voice*]: Ugh! Disgusting!

OLGA: For supper tonight we're having roast turkey and sweet apple pie.
Thank goodness I'm home all day and in the evening, too. Ladies and
gentlemen, come see us tonight, all of you.

VERSHININ: Allow me to join you tonight as well!

IRINA: Please do.

NATASHA: They don't stand on ceremony.

CHEBUTYKIN: *For love alone dear nature has given birth to us.* [*Laughs*]

ANDREY [*Angry*]: Ladies and gentlemen, stop it! Haven't you had enough?

Fedotik and Rodeh come in with a large basket of flowers.

FEDOTIK: They're eating already.

RODEH [*Loudly and pronouncing the letter* R *the French way*]: Already? Yes,
they're celebrating . . .

FEDOTIK: Hold on a minute! [*Takes a picture*] One! Hold it again . . . [*Takes
another picture*] Two! All done now!

*They take the basket and go into the reception room where they receive a
noisy greeting.*

RODEH [*Loudly*]: Many happy returns and best, best wishes. The weather's
charming today, absolutely splendid. I was out all morning today walking with the boys. I teach sports at the school.

FEDOTIK: You can move now, Irina Sergeyevna, you can! [*Takes another picture*] You are remarkably good-looking today. [*Takes a humming-top
from his pocket*] Here, by the way, is a top . . . It makes an amazing
sound . . .

IRINA: Oh, it's lovely!

MASHA: *"A green oak stands by a curving seashore, / And on that oak a golden chain"* . . . *And on that oak* . . . *a golden chain. And on that oak* . . . *a golden chain* . . . [*Plaintively*] But why do I keep saying that? I haven't been able to get this phrase out of my head since morning.

KULYGIN: Thirteen at table!

RODEH [*Loudly*]: Ladies and gentlemen, how can you believe in superstition?

Laughter.

KULYGIN: If you have thirteen at the table, it means that two people are in love. Could it be you, Doctor, by any chance?

Laughter.

CHEBUTYKIN: Oh, I'm an old sinner, but why Natalia Ivanovna is blushing, I don't understand at all.

Loud laughter; Natasha runs from the reception room to the drawing room; Andrey runs after her.

ANDREY: It's all right, don't pay attention to them! Wait . . . please, I entreat you . . .

NATASHA: I'm ashamed . . . I don't know what's happening to me, and they're making a laughingstock of me. Getting up from the table like this is not polite, but I can't, I can't . . . [*Covers her face with her hands*]

ANDREY: My dear, please, I beg you, don't worry! I assure you they are joking, they mean well. My dear, my darling, they're warm and good-hearted people, and they love me and you both. Come over here, by the window, where they can't see us . . . [*Looks around*]

NATASHA: I'm just not used to being in company!

ANDREY: Oh youth, wonderful, beautiful youth! My dearest, my darling, don't worry! . . . Believe me, believe me . . . I feel so good; my heart is bursting with love and joy . . . Oh, they can't see us! They can't see! Why did I fall in love with you when I did—oh, I don't understand anything. My dear, my good, innocent girl, be my wife! I love you, love you . . . like I've never loved anyone before . . .

A kiss.

Two officers enter and, seeing the kissing couple, stop in surprise.

Curtain.

ACT TWO

The set is the same as in Act One.

It is eight o'clock in the evening. From the street, the faint sounds of accordion playing are heard. The stage is dark. Enter Natasha, wearing a dressing gown and holding a candle. She crosses the stage and stops at the door to Andrey's room.

NATASHA: Andriusha, what are you doing? Reading? It's nothing, I was just . . . [*Goes and opens another door, glances through the doorway, then closes it*] No flame left burning . . .

ANDREY [*Comes in carrying a book*]: What is it, Natasha?

NATASHA: Making sure there's no light left burning . . . It's carnival week and the servants are beside themselves, better watch out, anything might happen. Last night, at midnight, I walk through the dining room and see a candle burning there. But who lighted it, I couldn't get out of them. [*Puts down the candle*] What time is it?

ANDREY [*Glancing at his watch*]: Quarter past eight.

NATASHA: Olga and Irina aren't back yet. They're working hard, poor things. Olga's at the pedagogical council and Irina's at the telegraph office . . . [*Sighing*] I said to your sister this morning: "Take care of yourself, Irina, my dear girl." She doesn't listen. You said quarter past eight? I'm afraid little Bobik is not well at all. Why does he feel so cold? Yesterday he had a fever and today he feels cold all over . . . I'm so afraid!

ANDREY: It's all right, Natasha, the boy's fine.

NATASHA: But still, it's better to keep him on a diet. I'm afraid. And I heard that the revelers are coming over 'round nine; Andriusha, it'd be better if they didn't come.

ANDREY: I don't really know. They're invited, after all.

NATASHA: The little boy woke up this morning and looks at me, and suddenly he smiled: you see, he recognized me. "Hello, Bobik!" I say. "Hello, dear." And he laughs. Children understand, understand so well. All right then, dear, I'll tell them not to let in the revelers.

ANDREY [*Timidly*]: It's really up to my sisters. They are in charge, you know.

NATASHA: And they are too, I'll tell them. They're so good-hearted . . . [*Walks away*] I told them to serve yogurt for supper. The doctor says you should eat only yogurt, otherwise you'll never lose weight. [*Stops*]

Bobik feels cold. I'm afraid that maybe he is cold in his room. We ought to put him, at least until it gets warmer, in another room. For instance, Irina's room is perfect for the baby: it's dry and sunny all day long. We should tell her; she can stay in the same room with Olga for the time being . . . She's not home during the day anyway; she only sleeps here . . .

A pause.

Andriushanchik,[17] sweetie, why don't you say something?

ANDREY: Just thinking . . . And there's nothing to say . . .

NATASHA: Oh . . . there's something else I was going to tell you . . . Oh yes, Ferapont's here, from the council, he's asking for you.

ANDREY [*Yawns*]: Send him in.

Natasha exits; Andrey bends over the forgotten candle and reads his book. Enter Ferapont wearing an old shabby overcoat with a turned-up collar and a scarf wrapped over his ears.

ANDREY: Hello, my dear man. What's new?

FERAPONT: The chairman sent this book and some papers. Here . . . [*Hands over a book and a packet*]

ANDREY: Thank you. Very good. But why did you come so late? It's after eight already.

FERAPONT: Wha?

ANDREY [*Speaking louder*]: I'm saying you came late; it's after eight.

FERAPONT: Yes, sir! When I came here it was still light out, but they wouldn't let me in. The master's busy, they tell me. Well then. I wait; I was in no hurry. [*Thinking Andrey is asking him something*] Wha?

ANDREY: Nothing. [*Looking at the book*] Tomorrow is Friday, the offices are closed, but it doesn't matter, I'll go in . . . do something. I'm bored at home . . .

A pause.

My dear old man, how things change, and how life deceives us! Today, I was bored, had nothing to do, I picked up this book—my old university lectures, and it made me laugh . . . My goodness, I'm secretary of the district council, the same council chaired by Protopopov; I'm secretary, and the most I can ever hope for—is to be a member of the district council! Me—a member of the local district council; me—who dreams every night of being a professor at Moscow University, a famous scholar, the pride of all Russia!

FERAPONT: I dunno, sir . . . Hard of hearing . . .

ANDREY: If you could hear me properly, I wouldn't probably be talking to you at all. I have to talk to someone, but my wife doesn't understand me; for some reason, I'm afraid of my sisters, afraid that they would laugh at me, put me to shame . . . I don't drink, I don't go to taverns, but, my dear friend, how I'd love to be sitting at a table at Testov's or the Grand Muscovy in Moscow.

FERAPONT: In Moscow, at the office a workman was just saying, some merchants were eating bliny,[18] and the one who ate forty kicked the bucket. Forty or fifty. I can't 'member.

ANDREY: You're sitting at a big restaurant in Moscow, you don't know anyone and no one knows you, and yet you don't feel like an outsider. But here, you know everybody and everybody knows you, but you're an outsider, an outsider . . . An outsider and all alone.

FERAPONT: Wha?

A pause.

The same fella was saying—maybe he's lying—that supposedly there's a rope stretched all across Moscow.[19]

ANDREY: What for?

FERAPONT: I dunno, sir. The contractor was saying.

ANDREY: Nonsense. [*Reads the book*] Have you ever been to Moscow?

FERAPONT [*After a pause*]: No, wasn't God's will.

A pause.

Can I go?

ANDREY: Yes, you can go. Be well.

Ferapont goes out.

Take care. [*Reading*] Come back for the papers tomorrow morning . . . Go now . . .

A pause.

He left.

The bell rings.

Oh, well . . . [*Stretches and walks slowly to his room*]

Offstage, the nanny is singing while rocking the baby to sleep. Masha and Vershinin come in. While they are talking to each other, the maid lights the lamp and candles.

MASHA: I can't say.

A pause.

I don't know. Of course, habit means a lot. After Father died, for instance, it took us a long time to get used to not having orderlies in the house. But apart from habit, I think I'm being only fair. Other places may be different, but in our town, the most decent, noble, and well mannered are—the military.

VERSHININ: I feel like something to drink. I'd have some tea.

MASHA [*Glancing at the clock*]: They'll be bringing it soon. They married me off when I was eighteen; I was afraid of my husband because he was a teacher and I had only just graduated. He seemed to me terribly scholarly, so intelligent, and important. But not anymore, unfortunately.

VERSHININ: So I see . . .

MASHA: I'm not talking about my husband, I'm used to him, but among civilians there are so many rude, unpleasant, and just ill-mannered people. Rudeness upsets and offends me, and I suffer when someone's not delicate enough, or gentle, or courteous enough. Whenever I spend time in the company of schoolteachers, my husband's colleagues, I plain suffer.

VERSHININ: Well . . . But I don't think it matters, civilian or military, at least not in this town. It doesn't matter! Just talk here to anyone educated, civilian or military, he is utterly exhaused with his wife, exhaused with his house, his estate, and his horses . . . It's natural for a Russian to have, to the highest degree, this elevated way of thinking, but, tell me, why in life does he fall so short? Why?

MASHA: Why?

VERSHININ: Why is he utterly exhaused with his children and his wife—why? And why are his wife and children utterly exhaused with him?

MASHA: You're out of sorts today.

VERSHININ: Maybe. I didn't have lunch; I haven't eaten since morning. One of my daughters is a little sick, and when my girls are sick I get worried and raked over with guilt because they have a mother like that. Oh, if you only saw her today! What a nobody! We started quarrelling at seven in the morning, and at nine I slammed the door and left.

A pause.

I never talk about it and, oddly enough, complain only to you. [*Kisses her hand*] Don't be angry with me. I have no one besides you in the whole world, no one . . .

A pause.

MASHA: What a din in the chimney. Shortly before Father died, we heard the same kind of din in the chimney. Just like that.

VERSHININ: Are you superstitious?

MASHA: Yes.

VERSHININ: That's strange. [*Kisses her hand*] You're a marvelous and wonderful woman. Marvelous and wonderful! It's dark here, but I see your eyes sparkling.

MASHA [*Sits down on another chair*]: There's more light here . . .

VERSHININ: I love, love, I love . . . I love your eyes, your movements, I dream about them . . . You're a marvelous and wonderful woman!

MASHA [*Laughing softly*]: When you talk to me like this, it makes me laugh for some reason although I feel scared. I beg you, don't say it again . . . [*Under her breath*] Then again, say it, I don't care . . . [*Covers her face with her hands*] I don't care. Somebody is coming, talk about something else . . .

Irina and Tuzenbach come in through the reception room.

TUZENBACH: I have a triple last name. My name's Baron Tuzenbach-Krone-Altschauer, but I'm Russian, Russian Orthodox like you. There's very little German left in me, except for patience, perhaps, that stubbornness that you are getting fed up with. I walk you home every night.

IRINA: I'm so tired!

TUZENBACH: And every day I'll come to the telegraph office and walk you home, and I'll be doing it ten, twenty years, until you drive me away . . . [*Noticing Masha and Vershinin, delightedly*] Oh, it's you? Hello.

IRINA: Well, I'm home at last. [*To Masha*] Just now a lady comes in to send a telegram to her brother in Saratov, to tell him that her son died today, but she can't remember the address. And so she sent it without the address, to Saratov. She's crying. And I was rude to her for no reason at all. "I've no time," I tell her. It's so stupid. The revelers are coming tonight, right?

MASHA: Yes.

IRINA [*Sitting down in an armchair*]: Just to get a decent rest. I'm tired.

TUZENBACH [*With a smile*]: When you come back from work, you seem so little, so unhappy . . .

A pause.

IRINA: I'm tired. I don't like the telegraph office, I don't like it.

MASHA: You've lost weight . . . [*Whistles*] You look younger and your face looks more like a boy's . . .

TUZENBACH: It's the hair.

IRINA: I have to look for another position because this one's not for me. It has none of the things I wanted and dreamed so much about. It's work without poetry or thought . . .

Knocking on the floor.

The doctor's knocking. [*To Tuzenbach*] Dear, knock back . . . I can't . . . I'm tired . . .

Tuzenbach knocks on the floor.

IRINA: He'll be right over. We need to take some measures. Yesterday, the doctor and our Andrey went to the club and lost again. I heard Andrey lost two hundred rubles.

MASHA [*Indifferently*]: There's nothing you can do about it now!

IRINA: He lost money gambling two weeks ago, and he lost in December. I wish he'd lose it all, then maybe we would leave this town. Goodness gracious, I dream about Moscow every night as if I'm crazy. [*Laughs*] We're moving there in June, but until June, we still have . . . February, March, April, May—almost half a year!

MASHA: We have to be careful so Natasha doesn't find out about his gambling loss.

IRINA: I don't think it matters to her.

Chebutykin, who has just woken up from an after-lunch nap, comes into the reception room combing his beard and then sits down at the table and takes a newspaper out of his pocket.

MASHA: Here he is . . . Has he paid the rent?

IRINA [*Laughing*]: No. Nothing in eight months. He must've forgotten.

MASHA [*Laughing*]: Sitting tall there!

Everyone laughs. A pause.

IRINA: Why are you so quiet, Alexander Ignatych?

VERSHININ: I don't know. I'd like some tea. A kingdom for a glass of tea! I haven't had anything since this morning . . .

CHEBUTYKIN: Irina Sergeyevna!

IRINA: What is it?

CHEBUTYKIN: Please come here. *Venez ici.*[20]

Irina goes over and sits at the table.

I can't do it without you.

Irina lays out the cards for a game of patience.

VERSHININ: Well? If I can't get my tea, then let's philosophize at least.

TUZENBACH: Fine. About what?

VERSHININ: About what? Let's, for instance, imagine . . . life after we're gone, in, say, two, three hundred years.

TUZENBACH: Well? After we're gone, people will fly around in air balloons, men's jackets will change, they'll discover a sixth sense, maybe, and develop it, but life itself will remain the same; a hard life, full of mystery, and happy. Even in a thousand years, man will still sigh his usual "oh, life's hard!" but at the same time, just like now, he will be afraid of death and won't want to die.

VERSHININ [*After some thought*]: How shall I put it? I think that little by little everything on earth will change, and it has been changing already, right before our eyes. In two or three hundred, or a thousand years, if you like—how long is not the point—a new and happy life will come. We won't be part of it, of course, but we live and work for it now, we suffer, we create it—and that's the purpose of our being here, and our happiness, if you will.

Masha laughs quietly.

TUZENBACH: What's the matter?

MASHA: I don't know. I've been laughing since morning.

VERSHININ: I finished same as you, didn't go to the academy; I read a lot but I don't know how to choose books, and I may be reading not what I should be reading, but in the meantime, the longer I live the more I want to know. My hair is turning gray and I'm almost an old man already, but I know so little, oh, how little! But still, it seems to me that I know what's most important and real, and I know it well. And how I would love to prove to you that there's no happiness, there shouldn't be and there won't be any for us . . . We need to work and work, and happiness—is for our distant offspring.

A pause.

If not for me, then at least for the descendants of my descendants.

Fedotik and Rodeh appear in the reception room. They sit down and sing quietly, strumming a guitar.

TUZENBACH: You're saying I shouldn't even be dreaming of happiness! But if I'm happy!

VERSHININ: No.

TUZENBACH [*Throwing up his arms and laughing*]: We obviously don't understand each other. Now how can I convince you?

Masha laughs quietly.

[*Gesturing to her*] Go ahead, laugh! [*To Vershinin*] Not only in two or three hundred years from now, even a million years from now, life will still be same as ever; it doesn't change, it is continuous, it follows its own laws, which you can't know or, at least, which you'll never learn about. Birds of passage, cranes, for instance, fly and keep flying regardless of ideas, high or low, that pop into their heads; they will keep flying without knowing where or what for. They fly and keep flying no matter what kind of philosophers turn up in their midst; and let them philosophize all they want as long as they keep flying . . .

MASHA: Still, the meaning of it?

TUZENBACH: The meaning . . . Look, it's snowing. What's the meaning?

A pause.

MASHA: I think a person must be a believer or search for something to believe in; otherwise their life is empty, empty . . . To live not knowing why cranes fly, why children are born, or why there're stars in the sky . . . Either you know why you live, or it's all nonsense, not worth two straws.

A pause.

VERSHININ: Still, I'm sorry that my youth is gone . . .

MASHA: Gogol said somewhere: "life on this earth is a bore, ladies and gentlemen!"[21]

TUZENBACH: And I'm saying: it's hard to argue with you, ladies and gentlemen. Forget it . . .

CHEBUTYKIN [*Reading the newspaper*]: "Balzac got married in Berdichev."[22]

> *Irina sings softly.*

I'll make a note in my book. [*Makes a note*] Balzac got married in Berdichev. [*Reads the newspaper*]

IRINA [*Laying out a solitaire game, pensive*]: Balzac got married in Berdichev.

TUZENBACH: Well, the die is cast. Maria Sergeyevna, you know, I'm resigning my commission.

MASHA: I heard. I don't see what's so good about it. I don't like civilians.

TUZENBACH: It doesn't matter . . . [*Gets up*] I'm not handsome, what kind of a military man am I? Well, it doesn't matter anyway . . . I'll work. To work hard at least one day in my life, to come home in the evening and in exhaustion collapse on the bed and fall asleep instantly. [*Going into the reception room*] Workers must be sound sleepers!

FEDOTIK [*To Irina*]: I've bought you color pencils at Pyzhikov's on Moscow Street. And this little penknife . . .

IRINA: You're always treating me like a child, but I'm grown up . . . [*Takes the pencils and penknife, with delight*] Oh, how adorable!

FEDOTIK: For myself here I bought a knife . . . Here, look . . . one blade, another blade, a third, and this one is for picking your ears, and tiny scissors, and this is to clean under your nails . . .

RODEH [*Loudly*]: Doctor, how old are you?

CHEBUTYKIN: Me? I'm thirty-two.

> *Laughter.*

FEDOTIK: I'll show you another solitaire . . . [*Lays out the cards*]

> *The samovar is brought in and Anfisa tends to it; a little later Natasha comes in and also busies herself at the table; Solyony comes in, says hello, and sits down at the table.*

VERSHININ: Oh, this wind!

MASHA: Yes. I'm fed up with winter. I already forgot what summer's like.

IRINA: I can see the solitaire's going to come out. We'll go to Moscow.

FEDOTIK: No it's not. See, the eight is on top of the two of spades. [*Laughs*] It means you won't go to Moscow.

CHEBUTYKIN [*Reads his newspaper*]: "Tsitsihar.[23] Smallpox is raging there."

ANFISA [*Going up to Masha*]: Masha, have some tea, my dearest. [*To Vershinin*] Please have some, your Excellency . . . forgive me, sir, I forgot your name, your patronymic[24] . . .

MASHA: Bring it here, Nanny. I'm not going there.

IRINA: Nanny!

ANFISA: Coh-mmming!

NATASHA [*To Solyony*]: Infants understand just fine. "Hello, Bobik," I say. "Hello, dear!" And he looked at me a certain way. You think it's the mother speaking in me, but no, no, I assure you! He's an extraordinary child.

SOLYONY: If this child was mine, I'd fry him up in a pan and eat him. [*Takes his tea into the drawing room and sits in a corner*]

NATASHA [*Covering her face with her hands*]: A rude, ill-mannered man!

MASHA: Happy are those who don't notice whether it's summer or winter. I think that if I lived in Moscow, I would be indifferent to the weather . . .

VERSHININ: The other day I read the diary of a French minister written in prison. The minister had been sentenced over the Panama scandal.[25] He talks about the birds he sees from his prison window with such joy and elation, the birds he had never noticed when he was minister. Now, of course, he is out of prison, he already doesn't notice the birds, like before. The same way you won't notice Moscow when you live there. We have no happiness, and we can't have any, we can only wish for it.

TUZENBACH [*Takes a box from the table*]: Where is the candy?

IRINA: Solyony ate them.

TUZENBACH: All of them?

ANFISA [*Handing round tea*]: A letter for you, dear sir.

VERSHININ: For me? [*Takes the letter*] From my daughter. [*Reads it*] Yes, of course . . . Forgive me, Maria Sergeyevna, I'll slip out quietly. I won't have tea. [*Stands up upset*] It's the same old story . . .

MASHA: What is it? Is it a secret?

VERSHININ [*Quietly*]: My wife's taken poison again. I have to go. I'll leave quietly. It's all so terribly unpleasant. [*Kisses Masha's hand*] My dear, lovely, good woman . . . I'll go out quietly . . . [*Leaves*]

ANFISA: Where's he going? I just served him tea . . . The likes of him.

MASHA [*Losing her temper*]: Leave me alone! Stop bothering me all the time, can't leave me in peace . . . [*Goes towards the table carrying her tea*] I'm fed up with you, old woman!

ANFISA: Why are you upset? My dear!

Andrey's voice offstage: Anfisa!

ANFISA [*Mimicking him*]: Anfisa! Himself just sitting there . . . [*Goes out*]

MASHA [*By the table in the reception room, in anger*]: Let me sit down at least!
[*Jumbles up the cards on the table*] Sprawled out with your cards here.
Drink your tea!

IRINA: You're mean, Mashka.

MASHA: If I'm mean, then don't talk to me. Leave me alone!

CHEBUTYKIN [*Laughing*]: Leave her alone, leave her alone . . .

MASHA: You're sixty years old but, but you're like a schoolboy, always saying
damn nonsense.

NATASHA [*Sighs*]: Dear Masha, why use these expressions in a conversation?
With your beautiful looks, I'm telling you straight, in decent high company, you'd be simply charming if it wasn't for these words. *Je vous prie,
pardonnez-moi, Marie, mais vous avez des manières un peu grossières.*[26]

TUZENBACH [*Trying not to laugh*]: Please, may I have some . . . some . . .
There's cognac there, I think . . .

NATASHA: *Il parait que mon Bobik déjà ne dort pas,*[27] he woke up. My boy is
not well today. I'll go see him, excuse me . . . [*Goes out*]

IRINA: And where did Alexander Ignatych go?

MASHA: Home. Something out of the ordinary again with his wife.

TUZENBACH [*Approaches Solyony with a decanter of cognac*]: You're always sitting by yourself, thinking about something—don't know what. Come
on, let's make peace. Let's drink some cognac.

They drink.

Tonight I will have to play the piano all night, play all that nonsense . . .
Why not!

SOLYONY: Make peace, why? I didn't quarrel with you.

TUZENBACH: You always make me feel as if something bad happened between
us. I have to admit that your personality is somewhat strange.

SOLYONY [*Reciting*] "I may be somewhat strange, but tell me who is not?"[28]
"Do not be angry, Aleko!"[29]

TUZENBACH: What does Aleko have to do with it . . .

A pause.

SOLYONY: When I'm one-on-one with someone, I'm all right and the same as everybody else, but in company, I'm dispirited, shy, and . . . I talk nonsense. But still, I'm better and more noble than many, many others. And I can prove it.

TUZENBACH: I often get angry at you when you're constantly picking on me in company, but I still like you for some reason. Why not, I'm getting drunk tonight. Let's have a drink!

SOLYONY: Let's have a drink!

They drink.

I've never had anything against you, Baron. But I have Lermontov's[30] personality. [*Quietly*] I even look a little like Lermontov . . . so they say . . . [*Takes a bottle of scent from his pocket and pours it on his hands*]

TUZENBACH: I'm resigning my commission. *Basta!*[31] I thought about it for five years and, finally, I made up my mind. I'll work.

SOLYONY [*Declaiming*]: Do not be angry, Aleko . . . Forget, forget your dreams . . .

While they are talking, Andrey comes in quietly with a book and sits down by the candle.

TUZENBACH: I will work . . .

CHEBUTYKIN [*Walking into the drawing room with Irina*]: And they also served us genuine food from the Caucasus—soup with onion, and for the second course—chekhartma,[32] a meat dish.

SOLYONY: Cheremsha is not meat at all, but a plant similar to our onion.

CHEBUTYKIN: No, sir, my angel. Chekhartma isn't onion but roast mutton.

SOLYONY: And I'm telling you, cheremsha is onion.

CHEBUTYKIN: And I'm telling you, chekhartma is mutton.

SOLYONY: And I'm telling you, cheremsha is onion.

CHEBUTYKIN. There's no point in arguing with you. You've never been to the Caucasus and never had their chekhartma.

SOLYONY: I haven't had it because I can't stand it. Cheremsha smells just like garlic.

ANDREY [*Imploringly*]: That's enough, gentlemen!

TUZENBACH: What time are the revelers coming?

IRINA: They said around nine; should be here any minute.

TUZENBACH [*Embraces Andrey*]: "Oh, my porch, my porch, my brand-new porch . . ."[33]

ANDREY [*Dancing and singing*]: "My brand new porch, my porch of maple . . ."

CHEBUTYKIN [*Dancing*]: "And the lattice work!"

Laughter.

TUZENBACH [*Kisses Andrey*]: Andriusha, damn it, let's drink, let's drink to our friendship.[34] Andriusha, I'll come with you to Moscow, to the University.

SOLYONY: Which one? There're two universities in Moscow.

ANDREY: There's one university in Moscow.

SOLYONY: And I'm telling you—two.

ANDREY: Let it be three. Even better.

SOLYONY: There're two universities in Moscow!

Sounds of grumbling and shushing.

There're two universities in Moscow: the old and the new. And if you don't wish to listen, if my words irritate you, then I don't have to speak. I can even go in the other room . . . [*Goes out through one of the doors*]

TUZENBACH: Bravo! Bravo! [*Laughs*] Ladies and gentlemen, let's begin, I'm sitting down to play. That Solyony is a funny fellow . . . [*Sits down at the piano and plays a waltz*]

MASHA [*Waltzing alone*]: The baron is drunk, he's drunk, he's drunk!

Enter Natasha.

NATASHA [*To Chebutykin*]: Ivan Romanych! [*Says something to Chebutykin, then goes out quietly*]

Chebutykin touches Tuzenbach on the shoulder and whispers something to him.

IRINA: What's wrong?

CHEBUTYKIN: It's time for us to go. Good-bye.

TUZENBACH: Good night. Time to go.

IRINA: But wait . . . And the revelers?

ANDREY [*Embarrassed*]: There won't be any revelers. You see, my dear, Natasha says that Bobik's not all well and that's why . . . In short, I don't know and it doesn't matter in the least!

IRINA [*Shrugging her shoulders*]: Bobik is unwell!

MASHA: Come what may! If they're kicking us out, we'd better go. [*To Irina*] It's not Bobik who's unwell, she is . . . Here! [*Taps her forehead*] A commoner!

Andrey leaves through the door on the right to his room. Chebutykin follows him and everyone says good-bye in the reception room.

FEDOTIK: What a shame! I was counting on spending a pleasant evening here, but if the baby's sick, then of course . . . I'll bring him some toys tomorrow . . .

RODEH [*In a loud voice*]: I purposely took a long nap after lunch today thinking that I'd be dancing all night. It's only nine o'clock!

MASHA: Let's go outside and talk it over. We'll decide what's what.

> *Voices are heard saying "Good-bye," "Be well." Tuzenbach's happy laughter is heard. Everyone leaves. Anfisa and the maid clear the table and put out the lights. The nanny's singing is heard. Enter quietly Andrey, wearing an overcoat and a hat, and Chebutykin.*

CHEBUTYKIN: I didn't have time to get married because life flashed by me, and also because I was madly in love with your mother, who was already married . . .

ANDREY: There's no need to marry. No need because it's boring.

CHEBUTYKIN: It may all very well be so, except for loneliness. However you philosophize, my dear boy, loneliness is a dreadful thing . . . Though in essence . . . of course, it doesn't matter in the least!

ANDREY: Let's go quickly.

CHEBUTYKIN: What's the rush? We'll make it.

ANDREY: I'm afraid the wife might stop me.

CHEBUTYKIN: Oh!

ANDREY: I'm not going to play tonight, I'll just sit and watch. I'm not feeling well . . . What should I do, Ivan Romanych, for shortness of breath?

CHEBUTYKIN: Why ask me? I don't remember, my dear boy. I don't know.

ANDREY: We'll walk through the kitchen.

> *The doorbell rings and then it rings again; voices and laughter are heard. They leave.*

IRINA [*Comes in*]: Who's that?

ANFISA [*Whispering*]: The revelers!

> *The bell rings again.*

IRINA: Nanny, tell them there's no one home. Tell them to excuse us.

> *Anfisa goes out. Irina paces around the room lost in thought. She is upset. Enter Solyony.*

SOLYONY [*Perplexed*]: No one's here . . . Where is everybody?

IRINA: They went home.

SOLYONY: That's strange. Are you alone here?

IRINA: Yes, alone.

> *A pause.*

> Good-bye.

SOLYONY: Just now, I wasn't sufficiently restrained and was tactless. But you're not like everyone else, you're above them and more pure and you can see the truth . . . Only you alone can understand me. I love deeply, I love infinitely . . .

IRINA: Good-bye. Go.

SOLYONY: I can't live without you. [*Follows her*] Oh, my bliss! [*Through tears*] Oh, happiness! Your gorgeous, wonderful, exquisite eyes, the likes of which I've never seen on any woman . . .

IRINA [*Coldly*]: Stop it please, Vasily Vasilych!

SOLYONY: This is the first time I speak of my love for you, and it's as if I've left the earth for another planet. [*Rubs his forehead*] Well, it doesn't matter. Love cannot be compelled, of course . . . But I'll have no lucky rivals either . . . I shall not . . . I swear to you by everything that I hold sacred, I'll kill my rival . . . Oh, wonderful!

> *Natasha passes by with a candle.*

NATASHA [*Opens and looks into one door, then another, and walks past the door to her husband's room*]: Andrey's there. Let him read. I'm sorry, Vasily Vasilych, I didn't know you were here, I'm not properly dressed . . .

SOLYONY: I don't care. Good-bye! [*Goes out*]

NATASHA: Oh, you are tired, my dear, my poor girl! [*Kisses Irina*] You should go to bed earlier.

IRINA: Is Bobik asleep?

NATASHA: Asleep. But a restless sleep. By the way, dear, I've been meaning to tell you, it's always either you're not here or I'm busy . . . I think Bobik's room is too cold and damp for him. And your room is just right for the baby. My dear, my love, move in with Olia for the time being!

IRINA [*Not understanding*]: Where?

> *A troika with bells is heard driving up to the house.*

NATASHA: You'll be in the same room with Olia, and Bobik will have your room. He's such a sweetie; today I say to him, "Bobik, you're mine! Mine!" And he just looks at me with his sweet little eyes.

The doorbell.

It must be Olga. How late she is!

The maid comes in and whispers in Natasha's ear.

NATASHA: Protopopov? Oh, he is such an oddball. Protopopov's here, asking me to go with him for a ride in a troika. [*Laughs*] Men are so strange ...

The doorbell.

Someone's here. Why don't I go for a ride for just a quarter of an hour ... [*To the maid*] Tell him I'm coming.

The doorbell.

The door bell again ... it must be Olga ... [*Goes out*]

The maid runs out. Irina sits deep in thought, Kulygin and Olga come in, followed by Vershinin.

KULYGIN: That's odd! And they said they were going to have a party.

VERSHININ: That's strange; I left only a half hour ago, and they were waiting for the revelers ...

IRINA: Everybody's left.

KULYGIN: Did Masha leave too? Where did she go? And why is Protopopov waiting in a troika downstairs? Who's he waiting for?

IRINA: Don't ask questions ... I'm tired.

KULYGIN: Such a pouter ...

OLGA: The council meeting has just ended. I'm utterly exhausted. Our headmistress is ill and now I'm taking her place. My head, my head hurts, my head ... [*Sits down*] Andrey lost two hundred rubles at cards yesterday ... The whole town's talking about it ...

KULYGIN: Yes, I got tired at the council, too. [*Sits down*]

VERSHININ: My wife thought she'd give me a little scare and almost poisoned herself. I'm glad everything worked out, and I can relax now ... So we need to leave then? Well, allow me to wish you all the best. Fedor Ilych, let's go somewhere! I can't stay at home, I simply can't ... Come with me!

KULYGIN: I'm tired. I'm not going. [*Stands up*] I'm tired. Did my wife go home?

IRINA: Probably.

KULYGIN [*Kisses Irina's hand*]: Good-bye. Tomorrow and the day after we can rest all day. All the best! [*Moves off*] I would really like some tea. I was looking forward to spending an evening in pleasant company, and—*o, fallacem hominum spem!*[35] The accusative with exclamation . . .

VERSHININ: I'll go by myself, then. [*Goes out with Kulygin, whistling*]

OLGA: My head hurts, my head . . . Andrey lost gambling . . . the whole town is talking about it . . . I'll go lie down. [*Walks off*] I'm free tomorrow . . . Oh, my God, how nice it feels! I'm free tomorrow, and the day after tomorrow . . . My head hurts, my head . . . [*Goes out*]

IRINA [*Alone*]: Everybody left. No one's here.

Outside sounds of an accordion; nanny is singing.

NATASHA [*In a fur coat and hat crosses the reception room followed by her maid*]: I'll be home in half an hour. I'll just go for a short ride. [*Goes out*]

IRINA [*Alone on the stage, with longing*]: To Moscow, to Moscow! To Moscow!

Curtain.

ACT THREE

Olga and Irina's bedroom. Two beds, one on the right and one on the left fenced in by folding screens. It's past two in the morning. Offstage bells are ringing the alarm because of a fire that started a long time ago. It is clear that no one has gone to bed yet. Masha is lying on the sofa; as usual, she is wearing a black dress. Enter Olga and Anfisa.

ANFISA: They're sitting down there now under the stairs . . . I tell them "please come upstairs, you can't just sit here"—they're crying. "We don't know," they say, "where our papa is. God forbid," they say, "he might have burnt to death," they say. Oh, the things they say! And in the yard, too, those people . . . with hardly anything on.

OLGA [*Takes a dress out of a wardrobe*]: Take this gray one . . . And this, too. And the shirt too . . . And this skirt, Nanny dear, as well. Oh, for heaven's sake, this is awful! Kirsanovsky Lane must've all burnt down . . . Take this . . . And this . . . [*Throws a dress over Anfisa's arms*] The poor Vershinins had a scare . . . Their house barely escaped going up in flames. They should spend the night here . . . we can't let them go home . . . And poor Fedotik's lost everything in the fire, nothing's left . . .

ANFISA: You'd better call Ferapont, Oliushka, I can't carry it all . . .

OLGA [*Rings*]: You can't get anyone ... [*Calls through the door*] Come up here, whoever's there!

Through the open door a window is visible glowing red from the fire; you can hear a team of firemen go by the house.

How awful! And I'm so fed up with it!

Enter Ferapont.

OLGA: Here, take all this downstairs. The Kolotilin girls are standing there, under the stairs, give it to them ... And give this, too ...

FERAPONT: Yes, ma'am. In 1812 Moscow burned too. Good God! The French were amazed.

OLGA: Go, go now.

FERAPONT: Yes, ma'am. [*Goes out*]

OLGA: Nanny, dear, give them everything. We don't need anything, Nanny dear, give it all to them ... I'm so tired; I can hardly stand on my feet ... We can't let the Vershinins go home ... The girls can sleep in the drawing room, and Alexander Ignatych downstairs with the baron ... Fedotik, too, with the baron, or he can stay here in the reception room ... The doctor, wouldn't you know it, is drunk, horribly drunk, and we can't put anyone in with him. And we'll put Vershinin's wife in the drawing room, too.

ANFISA [*Tired*]: Don't send me away, Oliushka, dear! Please don't.

OLGA: You are talking nonsense, Nanny. No one's sending you away.

ANFISA [*Puts her head on Olga's chest*]: My dear, my golden girl, I toil, I work ... When I get too weak, they'll all say: Get out! But where? I'm eighty years old ... eighty-one ...

OLGA: Nanny, have a seat ... You're tired, poor thing ... [*Helps her sit down*] Take a rest, my dear. How pale you are!

Natasha comes in.

NATASHA: They're saying that we should set up as soon as possible a society to help the victims of the fire. Well? It's a splendid idea. We always have to help the poor; it's the obligation of the rich. Bobik and little Sophie are sleeping through it all like nothing happened. There're so many people everywhere, wherever you turn, a full house. And with the *influenza* in town now, I worry the children might catch it.

OLGA [*Not listening to her*]: From this room, you can't see the fire, it's peaceful here . . .

NATASHA: Well . . . My hair probably looks disheveled. [*In front of the mirror*] They say I've put on weight . . . it's not true! Not at all! And Masha's asleep—poor girl, she's exhausted . . . [*To Anfisa, coldly*] Don't you dare sit in my presence! Get up! Get out of here!

Anfisa goes out. A pause.

Why you keep this old woman, I never understand!

OLGA [*Struck dumb*]: I'm sorry, I don't understand either . . .

NATASHA: There's no need for her here. She's a peasant and should live in a village . . . The frivolity! I like order in the house! No superfluous people in the house. [*Patting Olga on the cheek*] Poor girl, you are tired! Our headmistress is tired! When my little Sophie grows up and starts school, I'll be afraid of you.

OLGA: I won't be headmistress.

NATASHA: They'll pick you, Olga, dear. It's done.

OLGA: I'll refuse. I can't . . . It's more than I can bear. [*Drinks water*] You were just so rude to Nanny . . . Forgive me, I can't tolerate it . . . Everything went dark before my eyes . . .

NATASHA [*Uneasy*]: Forgive me, Olia, forgive me . . . I didn't mean to upset you.

Masha gets up, takes a pillow and leaves in anger.

OLGA: Dear, you've got to understand: maybe it's the way we were brought up, but I can't tolerate this. Seeing how you just treated her oppresses me, makes me ill . . . I lose heart! . . .

NATASHA: Forgive me, forgive me . . . [*Kisses her*]

OLGA: Any, even the slightest discourteousness, a rude remark, upsets me . . .

NATASHA: I often say things I shouldn't, that's true, but my dear, you have to agree that she could live in a village.

OLGA: She has been with us already thirty years.

NATASHA: But now she can't work! Either I don't understand you or you simply don't want to understand me. She's incapable of work; all she does is sleep or sit around.

OLGA: So let her sit.

NATASHA [*Surprised*]: What, let her sit around? She's a servant, isn't she? [*Through tears*] I don't understand you, Olia. I have a nanny, a wet nurse, a maid and a cook . . . then what do we need that old woman for? What for?

Offstage, the fire alarm bells are heard.

OLGA: Tonight I've aged ten years.

NATASHA: We've got to come to terms, Olga. You're at school, I'm at home; you have your teaching, I have the house. And if I say something about a servant, then I know what I'm talking about. I know what I am *talking a-bout* . . . And I don't want to see this old thief, this old hag here tomorrow . . . [*Stamps her feet*] That witch! . . . Don't you dare irritate me! Don't you dare! [*Regaining self-control*] You see, if you don't move downstairs we'll always be quarrelling. It's just awful.

Kulygin comes in.

KULYGIN: Where's Masha? It's time to go home. They say the fire's dying out. [*Stretches*] Only one block burnt down, but it was windy, and in the beginning it looked as if the whole town was on fire. [*Sits down*] I'm exhausted. My dear Olechka[36] . . . I often think: if it hadn't been for Masha, I would have married you, Olechka. You're so good . . . I'm utterly exhausted. [*Listens*]

OLGA: What is it?

KULYGIN: The doctor, wouldn't you know it, he's gone on a bender; he's hideously drunk. Wouldn't you know it! [*Getting up*] I think he's coming here . . . Can you hear him? Yes, here he comes . . . [*Laughs*] He is so . . . I'm going to hide . . . [*Goes towards the wardrobe and stands in the corner*] That rascal.

OLGA: He didn't touch a drop for two years and suddenly he ups and gets drunk . . . [*Moves to the back of the room with Natasha*]

Chebutykin comes in; steadily as if sober, he walks across the room, stops, looks, then goes to the washstand and starts washing his hands.

CHEBUTYKIN [*Morosely*]: To hell with them . . . Damn them all. They think I'm a doctor, can treat different diseases, but I don't know anything at all, I've forgotten it all, what I once knew, I don't remember anything, nothing at all.

Olga and Natasha go out without his noticing.

To hell with them. Last Wednesday, I treated a woman at Zasyp—she died, and it's my fault that she died. Well . . . , I knew a thing or two twenty-five years ago, but now I don't remember any of it. None of it. Maybe I'm not even human; maybe I only pretend that I have arms, and legs, and a head; maybe I don't exist at all, and I only think that I walk, and eat, and sleep. [*Crying*] Oh, if only it was possible not to exist! [*Stops crying, morosely*] Who the hell knows . . . The day before yesterday, at the club, they're saying: Shakespeare, Voltaire . . . I didn't read them, nothing at all, but I made a face like I did. And the others did the same, too. So vulgar! So low! And the woman I killed on Wednesday, it all came back to me . . . everything came back, and everything twisted up inside, and it felt so vile and sickening . . . I went and started drinking . . .

Irina, Vershinin, and Tuzenbach come in. Tuzenbach wears a civilian suit, new and stylish.

IRINA: We'll sit here for a bit. No one will come in here.

VERSHININ: If it wasn't for the soldiers, the whole town would've burned down. What terrific boys! [*Rubs his hands with pleasure*] What a treasure they are! What terrific boys!

KULYGIN [*Coming to them*]: What time is it?

TUZENBACH: It's past three. It's getting light out.

IRINA: They're all sitting in the reception room, nobody's leaving. And your Solyony's sitting there . . . [*To Chebutykin*] Why don't you go to bed, Doctor.

CHEBUTYKIN: It's all right, ma'am . . . Thank you, ma'am. [*Combs his beard*]

KULYGIN [*Laughs*]: Soused, aren't you, Ivan Romanych? [*Taps him on the shoulder*] What a terrific boy! *In vino veritas,*[37] as the ancients used to say.

TUZENBACH: Everyone's asking me to arrange a concert for the benefit of the victims.

IRINA: Oh, who would . . .

TUZENBACH: We could do it if we really wanted to. Maria Sergeyevna, in my opinion, plays the piano beautifully . . .

KULYGIN: Plays beautifully!

IRINA: She's already forgotten. She hasn't played in three years . . . or four.

TUZENBACH: Here in town, decidedly no one appreciates music, not a soul, but I, I understand and, honestly, trust me, Maria Sergeyevna's playing is magnificent, almost gifted.

KULYGIN: Quite right, Baron. I love her, I love Masha very much. She's lovely.

TUZENBACH: To be able to play so marvelously and at the same time to know that no one, no one understands you!

KULYGIN [*Sighs*]: Well . . . But would it be proper for her to participate in a concert?

A pause.

After all, ladies and gentlemen, I don't know anything. Maybe it will be good. I have to say, our school principal is a good man, even a very good man, a most intelligent man, but his views . . . Of course, it's none of his business, but still, if you wish, maybe I'll talk to him.

Chebutykin picks up a porcelain clock and examines it.

VERSHININ: I got all dirty at the fire, just look at me.

A pause.

Yesterday I heard in passing that they want to transfer our brigade somewhere far away. Some say, to the Polish Kingdom, others say, to Chita.[38]

TUZENBACH: I heard it, too. Well . . . The town will become completely deserted.

IRINA: And we're going too!

CHEBUTYKIN [*Drops the clock and it breaks*]: To smithereens!

A pause. Everyone is sad and embarrassed.

KULYGIN [*Picking up the pieces*]: Ivan Romanych, oh, Ivan Romanych, to break such a valuable thing! You get an F minus for conduct!

IRINA: This was our late mother's clock.

CHEBUTYKIN: Maybe it was . . . So it's your mother's. But maybe I didn't break it, it only seems that I did? Maybe it only seems to us that we exist, and in reality we don't? I don't know anything, nobody knows anything. [*At the door*] What are you looking at? Natasha's having her fling with Protopopov, and you don't see it . . . You're sitting here not noticing a thing while Natasha's having a fling with Protopopov . . . [*Sings*] "*Would you kindly take this date . . .*" [*Goes out*]

VERSHININ: Well . . . [*Laughs*] It's all really very strange!

A pause.

When the fire broke out, I immediately ran home; I run up to the house and I see that it's safe and sound and not in any danger, but my two girls are standing at the doorway in their nightgowns; their mother isn't there; people scurry about, horses, dogs running around, and the girls have this look of terror, a look of horror, pleading, God knows what else; my heart sank when I saw their faces. I'm thinking, my God how much more they'll have to go through during their long lifetime! I grab them, and as I run, I can think of one thing only: how much suffering they'll have to endure in this world!

The fire bells sound; a pause.

I come here and their mother is here, yelling and upset.

Masha comes in with a pillow and sits down on the sofa.

And when my girls were standing by the front door in their nightgowns, and the street was red from flames, and the overwhelming noise, and I thought: something similar already happened many years ago, when an enemy would suddenly invade, loot, set fire . . . But at the same time, what a big change there is between now and what used to be! And soon, not too far in the future, in just two or three hundred years, they'll look at how we live now with the same sense of horror and ridicule; and everything we do today will seem awkward, hard, very uncomfortable, and strange. Oh, but what a life it will be then, what a life! [*Laughs*] Forgive me, I've been philosophizing again. Allow me to continue. I very much want to philosophize, that's the kind of mood I'm in.

A pause.

As if they're all asleep. Anyway, as I was saying: what a life it'll be! Can you only imagine . . . Like you, there are only three in this town, but in generations to come there'll be more, and then more and even more people like you, and a time will come when everything will change your way, and people will live your way too, and then you'll become obsolete, and other people, better than you, will come into this world . . . [*Laughs*] I'm in a funny mood today. Damn, how I long to live . . . [*Sings*] "*True love knows neither age nor station. Its transports are pure invigoration . . .*"[39] [*Laughs*]

MASHA: Drum-dee-dum . . .

VERSHININ: Dee-dum . . .

MASHA: Druh-ruh-ruh?

VERSHININ: Druh-dee-duh. [*Laughs*]

Fedotik comes in.

FEDOTIK [*Dances*]: I've lost everything! Everything! Everything!

> *Laughter.*

IRINA: That's not a joke. Did everything burn down?

FEDOTIK [*Laughs*]: Burned clean. Nothing's left. The guitar burned too, the photography, and all my letters . . . And I wanted to give you a little notebook—it, too, burned up.

> *Enter Solyony.*

IRINA: Oh, no, Vasily Vasilych, please go. You can't come in here.

SOLYONY: Why is it then that the baron can and I can't?

VERSHININ: We should be going. Really, how's the fire?

SOLYONY: They say it's dying down. I find it positively strange: why is it that the baron can and I can't. [*Takes out a bottle of eau de cologne and sprinkles it on himself*]

VERSHININ: Drum-dee-dum . . . ?

MASHA: Drum-dum.

VERSHININ [*Laughing, to Solyony*]: Let's go to the reception room.

SOLYONY: Very well, we'll make a note of it. This thought I could elaborate on here, but the geese will get annoyed, I fear . . . [*Looking at Tuzenbach*] Chicka, chicka, chicka . . . [*Goes out with Vershinin and Fedotik*]

IRINA: Oh, look how Solyony smoked up the place . . . [*Bewildered*] The baron's asleep. Baron! Baron!

TUZENBACH [*Waking up*]: However, I'm tired . . . A brick factory . . . No, I'm not delirious, I'm in fact leaving for a brick factory soon, and I'll start working . . . We already talked about it. [*To Irina, tenderly*] You're so pale, beautiful, and charming . . . It seems that your pallor, like light, brightens the dark air . . . You are sad and unhappy with life . . . Oh, would you come with me, we'll go together to work! . . .

MASHA: Oh Nikolai Lvovich, please go.

TUZENBACH [*Laughing*]: You're here? I can't see. [*Kisses Irina's hand*] Good-bye, then, I'm leaving . . . I'm looking at you now and I am reminded of the day long ago, your name-day celebration, when you, so lively and cheerful, talked about the joys of working . . . And what a happy life I imagined then! Where is it? [*Kisses her hand*] You've tears in your eyes. Go to bed, it's getting light out . . . the morning's breaking . . . If only I was allowed to sacrifice my life for you!

MASHA: Nikolai Lvovich, please go . . . That's enough, really . . .

TUZENBACH: I'm going . . . [*Leaves*]

MASHA [*Lying down*]: Fedor, are you sleeping?

KULYGIN: Eh?

MASHA: Just go home.

KULYGIN: My darling Masha, my dear Masha . . .

IRINA: She's exhausted. Fedya, why don't you let her rest.

KULYGIN: I'm going . . . My good wife, my lovely wife . . . I love you, my one
and only . . .

MASHA [*Angrily*]: *Amo, amas, amat, amamus, amatis, amant.*[40]

KULYGIN [*Laughs*]: No, she's so amazing! I've been married to you seven years,
but it seems that we got married just yesterday. Honestly. No, really,
you're an amazing woman. I'm content, content, content!

MASHA: I'm fed up with it, fed up, fed up with it . . . [*Sits up and talks while
sitting*] I can't get it out of my head . . . It's just outrageous. It's like a nail
driven into my head, and I can't keep it to myself anymore. I'm talking
about Andrey . . . He's mortgaged this house at the bank and his wife
took all the money, but the house isn't only his, it belongs to the four of
us! He must know this if he has any decency left in him.

KULYGIN: What's the point, Masha! Why bother? Andriusha owes money right
and left, so forget about it.

MASHA: In any case, it's outrageous. [*Lies down*]

KULYGIN: You and I aren't poor. I work; I work at the school, then I give private lessons . . . I'm an honest man. Without airs . . . *Omnia mea mecum
porto*, as they say.[41]

MASHA: I don't need anything, but this injustice infuriates me.

A pause.

Go, Fedor.

KULYGIN [*Kisses her*]: You're tired, rest for a half-hour, and I'll sit there and
wait. Go to sleep . . . [*Walks*] I'm content, I'm content, I'm content.
[*Goes out*]

IRINA: Indeed, how petty our Andrey has become, how worn out and how
old he's grown next to this woman! He was at one point preparing to
become a professor, and yesterday he boasted that he'd finally made it
to the District Council. He's a member, and Protopopov's the chairman . . . The whole town's talking and laughing about it, and he alone
knows and sees nothing . . . And here, everyone's rushed to the fire, and

he just sits in his room oblivious to it all. All he does is play his violin. [*Agitated*] Oh, this is awful, awful, just awful! [*Crying*] I can't, I can't take it any more! . . . I can't, I just can't! . . .

Olga comes in and tidies up by her bedside table.

[*Sobs loudly*]: Get rid of me, get rid of me, I can't take it any more! . . .

OLGA [*Frightened*]: What is it? What is it? My darling!

IRINA [*Sobbing*]: Where? Where did it all go? Where is it? Oh, my God, I've forgotten, forgotten everything . . . It's all mixed up in my head . . . I can't remember the Italian for *window* or even *ceiling* . . . I'm forgetting it all, I'm forgetting something every day, and life's slipping away, and it's not coming back, never, and we'll never go to Moscow . . . I can see now that we won't . . .

OLGA: My dear, my darling . . .

IRINA [*Trying to control herself*]: Oh, I'm so miserable . . . I can't work, I will not work. Enough, that's enough! I worked at the telegraph office, now I'm at the town council, and I loathe and despise everything they ask me to do . . . I'm twenty-three, I've been working a long time, and my brain's completely dried up, I'm losing weight, my looks, my youth, and I get no satisfaction from any of it; but the time passes and it feels that I keep moving farther and farther away from the beautiful life and into some kind of an abyss. I'm desperate, and how come I'm still alive and haven't killed myself yet . . . I don't understand . . .

OLGA: Don't cry, my girl, don't . . . It pains me.

IRINA: I'm not crying, I'm not. That's enough. Here, I'm not crying anymore. That's enough . . . Enough!

OLGA: My darling, I say it to you as a sister and a friend; if you want my advice, marry the baron!

Irina quietly crying.

After all, you respect and value him . . . It's true, he's homely, but he's so decent and pure . . . After all, people marry not out of love, you know, but out of duty. At least, that's what I think, and I'd marry without love. I would marry whoever proposed to me, as long as he's a decent person. I'd even marry an old man . . .

IRINA: I kept waiting, thinking that we'd move to Moscow, and that there I'd meet the real one, I dreamed about him, loved him . . . But it turned out to be all nonsense, all nonsense . . .

OLGA [*Embraces her sister*]: My darling, my beautiful sister, I understand everything; when Baron Nikolai Lvovich left the military service and came to see us in a civilian jacket, I thought he looked so homely that I even started crying . . . He asks: "Why are you crying?" How can I tell him! But, God willing, if he was to marry you, I'd be happy. This is something different.

Natasha with a candle crosses the stage, entering through the door on the right and exiting through the door on the left, all in complete silence.

MASHA [*Sits up*]: She walks around as if she herself started the fire.

OLGA: Masha, you're silly. You're the silliest one in our family. Please, forgive me.

MASHA: My dearest sisters, I feel like confessing. My heart's uneasy. I'll confess to you, and then I'll never breathe a word about it to anyone, ever . . . I'll tell it to you now. [*Quietly*] It's my secret, but you should know it . . . I can't keep it to myself anymore . . .

A pause.

I love, I love . . . I love this man . . . You just saw him . . . Oh, come what may. In other words, I love Vershinin . . .

OLGA [*Goes to her side of the room behind the screen*]: Stop it. I can't hear you anyway.

MASHA: What can I do! [*Clutches her head*] At first I thought he was odd, then I felt sorry for him . . . then I fell in love . . . fell in love with his voice, his words, his misfortunes, his two girls . . .

OLGA [*Behind the screen*]: I still can't hear you. Whatever nonsense you talk, I can't hear you.

MASHA: Oh, Olia, you are the silly one. I love him—then such is my fate. Such is my lot . . . And he loves me . . . It's all frightening, isn't it? So it's not good? [*Pulls Irina by the arm towards herself*] Oh, my dear . . . How will we live out our lives, and what will become of us . . . When you read a novel, you think that it's so old and obvious, but when you fall in love yourself, then you see that nobody knows anything and everybody decides for themselves . . . My dear, dear sisters . . . I've confessed to you, and now I'll keep silent. I'll be like Gogol's madman[42] . . . silence . . . silence . . .

Andrey with Ferapont behind him.

ANDREY [*Irritated*]: What d'you need? I don't understand.

FERAPONT [*Standing in the doorway, impatiently*]: Andrey Sergeyevich, I've told you ten times already.

ANDREY: First of all, I'm not Andrey Sergeyevich to you but Your Honor!

FERAPONT: The firemen, Your Highness,⁴³ are asking to please let them get to the river through the garden. They keep going round and round—a big pain.

ANDREY: Fine. Tell them it's all right.

Ferapont leaves.

I'm fed up with them. Where's Olga?

Olga comes out from behind the screen.

I've come to see you, give me the key to the case, I've lost mine. You have a little key like that.

Olga hands him the key silently. Irina goes behind her screen. A pause.

What a huge fire! It's started dying down now. Ferapont, damn it, made me so angry, and I said something stupid to him . . . Your Honor . . .

A pause.

Olga, why are you so quiet?

A pause.

It's time to stop this nonsense, this sulking for no rhyme or reason. Masha, you're here and Irina's here, very well then—let's talk it over frankly, once and for all. What do you have against me? What?

OLGA: Leave it, Andriusha. We'll talk it over tomorrow. [*Nervously*] What an excruciating night!

ANDREY [*Very embarrassed*]: Don't worry. I'm asking you very objectively what it is you have against me? Say it.

Vershinin's voice: "Drum-dee-dum . . . !"

MASHA [*Gets up, saying loudly*]: Druh-dee-duh. [*To Olga*] Good-bye, Olga. God bless you. [*Goes behind the screen and kisses Irina*] Sleep well . . . Good-bye, Andrey. Go, they're exhausted . . . you'll talk it over with them tomorrow . . . [*Goes out*]

OLGA: Yes, Andriusha, let's put it off till tomorrow . . . [*Goes behind her screen*] It's time for bed.

ANDREY: I will say it and then I'll go. I will . . . First of all, you have something against Natasha, my wife, and I've noticed it since the day I got married.

Natasha is a fine, honest, frank, and noble person—that's my opinion. I love my wife and respect her, you understand, I respect her and I demand that others do the same. I repeat, she's an honest, noble person, and your objections to her, forgive me, are just childish.

A pause.

Second, it's as if you're angry with me because I'm not a professor or a scholar. But I work for the district; I'm a member of the District Council, and I consider my service every bit as sacred and noble as being a scholar. I'm a member of the District Council, and I'm proud of it, if you wish to know . . .

A pause.

And third . . . I have this to say . . . I've mortgaged the house without asking you . . . It's my fault, yes, and I'm asking you to forgive me . . . Debts compelled me to do it . . . thirty-five thousand . . . I don't play cards anymore, I gave that up long ago, but the main thing in my defense is that you, young ladies, you receive a pension, whereas I had no . . . earnings so to speak . . .

KULYGIN [*Through the door*]: Masha's not here? [*Anxiously*] Where could she be? That's odd . . . [*Goes out*]

ANDREY: They aren't listening. Natasha's an outstanding, honest person. [*Paces up and down the stage silently, then stops*] When I got married, I thought that we would all be happy . . . all happy . . . But oh, my God . . . [*Cries*] My dear sisters, my darling sisters, don't believe me, don't . . . [*Goes out*]

KULYGIN [*Into the doorway, anxiously*]: Where's Masha? Masha's not here? That's most unusual. [*Leaves*]

Fire alarm rings, empty stage.

IRINA [*Behind the screen*]: Olia! Who is that knocking on the floor?

OLGA: It's Doctor Ivan Romanych. He's drunk.

IRINA: What a restless night!

A pause.

Olia! [*Looks out from behind the screen*]: Have you heard? They are taking the brigade from here and transferring it somewhere far away.

OLGA: It's just rumors.

IRINA: Then we'll be left alone . . . Olia!

OLGA: What?

IRINA: My dear, darling, I respect the baron, I value him; he's a fine man, I will marry him, all right; only let's go to Moscow! I beg you, let's go! There is nothing in the whole wide world better than Moscow! Let's go, Olia! Let's go!

Curtain.

ACT FOUR

The old garden at the Prozorovs' house. A long path of spruce trees, at the end of which the river is visible. On the other side of the river—a forest. On the right—the terrace of the house; here, on the table, bottles and champagne glasses; it appears that they have just finished drinking champagne. It's noontime. From time to time, passersby from the street walk across the garden to the river. Five or so soldiers walk briskly past.

Chebutykin is in a benevolent mood that he maintains throughout the act. He is sitting in an armchair in the garden waiting to be called; he is wearing his military cap and holding a stick. Irina, Kulygin, with a medal around his neck and without his moustache, and Tuzenbach, are standing on the terrace and saying good-bye to Fedotik and Rodeh, who are coming down the steps; both officers are in field uniform.

TUZENBACH [*Kisses Fedotik*]: You're such a good man, we got along so well. [*Kisses Rodeh.*] One more . . . Good-bye, my dear!

IRINA: Good-bye.

FEDOTIK: It's not good-bye, it's farewell: we'll never see each other again!

KULYGIN: Who knows! [*Wipes his eyes and smiles*] Now I'm crying too.

IRINA: We'll meet again sometime.

FEDOTIK: In ten or fifteen years? By then we'll hardly recognize each other and give each other the cold shoulder . . . [*Takes a picture*] Stay still . . . Just one last one.

RODEH [*Embraces Tuzenbach*]: We won't see each other again. [*Kisses Irina's hand*] Thank you for everything, for everything!

FEDOTIK [*Annoyed*]: Can't you stay still!

TUZENBACH: God willing, we'll see each other again. Make sure you write to us. Be sure to write.

RODEH [*Looking around the garden*]: Farewell trees! [*Shouts*] Hup-hup!

A *pause*.

Farewell, echo!

KULYGIN: Watch out, you might get married over there in Poland . . . Your Polish wife will put her arms 'round you and say to you *kohanie*.[44] [*Laughs*]

FEDOTIK [*After glancing at his watch*]: We've less than an hour left. From our battery only Solyony is taking the barge; we're with the combat maneuver unit. Three of the batteries are leaving today as a battalion, and another three tomorrow, and then the town will be all peace and quiet.

TUZENBACH: And dreadful boredom.

RODEH: And where's Maria Sergeyevna?

KULYGIN: Masha's in the garden.

FEDOTIK: I'll go say good-bye to her.

RODEH: Farewell, I'd better go or I'll start crying . . . [*Quickly embraces Tuzenbach and Kulygin, kisses Irina's hand*] We had a fine time here . . .

FEDOTIK [*To Kulygin*]: Here's a small souvenir . . . a notebook with a little pencil . . . We'll walk to the river right through here . . .

Fedotik and Rodeh go off, both glance back.

RODEH [*Yells*]: Hup-hup!

KULYGIN [*Shouts*]: Farewell!

At the rear of the stage Fedotik and Rodeh meet Masha and say good-bye to her. She goes off with them.

IRINA: They left . . . [*Sits down on the bottom step of the terrace*]

CHEBUTYKIN: But they forgot to say good-bye to me.

IRINA: Why didn't you?

CHEBUTYKIN: Well, I forgot, too, I suppose. But I'll be seeing them soon anyway; I'm leaving tomorrow. Well . . . Just one more day left. A year from now they'll retire me and I'll come back here to spend the rest of my life near you . . . I have only one little year left until my retirement . . . [*Puts one newspaper in his pocket and takes out another one*] I'll come back to you here and will change my life radically . . . I'll become so quiet, so pi . . . pious, and so very decent . . .

IRINA: And you really ought to change your life, my dear. You ought to somehow.

CHEBUTYKIN: Yes. I feel it. [*Sings quietly*] *Ta-ra-ra boom-de-ay, / Sit on a tomb today* . . .

KULYGIN: Ivan Romanych is unreformable! Simply unreformable!

CHEBUTYKIN: If you'd train me, then I would reform.

IRINA: Fedor has shaved off his moustache. I can't bear looking at him.

KULYGIN: Why not?

CHEBUTYKIN: I would tell you what your face reminds me of, but I can't.

KULYGIN: Well then! By convention, it's modus vivendi.[45] Our director is clean-shaven, and as soon as I became inspector, I shaved, too. Nobody likes it, but for me, it matters not. I'm content. With or without a moustache I'm just as content. [*He sits down*]

In the back of the garden, Andrey is pushing a stroller with a sleeping baby.

IRINA: Ivan Romanych, dear, darling, I am terribly worried. Last night you were on the boulevard; tell me, what happened there?

CHEBUTYKIN: What happened? Nothing. Nothing of any importance. [*Reads his paper*] It doesn't matter!

KULYGIN: They are saying that Solyony and the baron met yesterday on the boulevard by the theater . . .

TUZENBACH: Stop it! Why, really, please . . . [*Waves his hand and goes into the house*]

KULYGIN: By the theatre . . . Solyony started picking on the baron, and the baron couldn't take it and said something offensive . . .

CHEBUTYKIN: I don't know. It's all nonsense.

KULYGIN: At one of the seminaries, a teacher once wrote *nonsense* on a student's composition, and the student read it as *non sense*—he thought it was in Latin . . . [*Laughs*] So funny really. I heard that Solyony's in love with Irina and hates the baron . . . Well, it's understandable. Irina's a very nice young lady. She's even a little like Masha, just as pensive. Only Irina you're a little sweeter. Although Masha's disposition is also very good. I love her, my Masha.

From the back of the garden, coming from offstage: "Halloo-oo! Hup-hup!"

IRINA [*Shudders*]: For some reason, everything frightens me today.

A pause.

I've everything ready to go and I'm sending my things off after lunch. Tomorrow the baron and I are getting married, and tomorrow we're also leaving for the brick factory, and the day after tomorrow I start teaching, a new life is beginning. With God's help! When I was taking the teacher's exam, I was even crying from joy, from goodness . . .

A pause.

The cart's coming any minute to pick up the things . . .

KULYGIN: It certainly is, but it's not very serious. It's all just ideas, and not much substance. From the bottom of my heart, though, I wish you the best.

CHEBUTYKIN [*Deeply moved*]: My lovely girl, my darling . . . My precious girl . . . You're so far ahead of me, there's no catching up. I'm left behind like a bird of passage that's too old and can't fly. Fly away, my dears, fly away and God bless!

A pause.

You shouldn't have shaved off your moustache, Fedor Ilych.

KULYGIN: That's enough! [*Sighs*] Well, as soon as the soldiers leave today, everything will go back the way it was. No matter what they say, Masha is a good and honest woman, I love her very much, and I thank my fate . . . People's lots are all so different . . . There is this Kozyrev fellow in the excise-tax office. We went to school together, but he was let go in fifth grade because he just couldn't get the *ut consecutivum.*⁴⁶ Now he's sick, lives in poverty, and when I see him, I always say, "Hello, *ut consecutivum.*" And he says, "Yes, exactly, *consecutivum*," as he coughs . . . But I've been fortunate all my life; I'm happy, I even have the Stanislaus, second class, and I now teach others this *ut consecutivum*. Of course, I'm intelligent, more intelligent than many, but that's not what makes me happy . . .

*In the house, "A Maiden's Prayer"*⁴⁷ *is played on the piano.*

IRINA: Tomorrow evening, I won't have to listen to "A Maiden's Prayer," I won't be running into Protopopov . . .

A pause.

And Protopopov is sitting there in the drawing room; he came today, too . . .

KULYGIN: Has the headmistress come yet?

IRINA: No, not yet. They sent for her. If you only knew how hard it's been for me to live here alone, without Olia . . . She lives at the high school; she's headmistress, busy all day long, and I'm all alone, bored, I have nothing to do, and I abhor the room I live in . . . So this is what I decided: since I'm not meant to live in Moscow, so be it. Such is my fate. I can't do anything about it . . . It's all God's will, yes, it is. Nikolai Lvovich proposed to me . . . And so? I thought about it and made my decision. He's a good man, amazing what a good man he is . . . And suddenly I felt as if my soul had sprung wings, and I cheered up and lightened up, and I felt again like working, working . . . Only something happened yesterday, and this secret's been hanging over me . . .

CHEBUTYKIN: *Non sense.* It's all nonsense.

NATASHA [*Through the window*]: The headmistress!

KULYGIN: The headmistress has arrived. Come.

> *Goes in with Irina.*

CHEBUTYKIN [*Reads the paper and sings softly*]: *Ta-ra-ra boom-de-ay, / Sit on a tomb today . . .*

> *Masha walks up to him. Andrey at the back of the stage pushes the pram.*

MASHA: Sitting there, lolling about . . .

CHEBUTYKIN: And why not?

MASHA [*Sits down*]: Oh, nothing . . .

> *A pause.*

Did you love my mother?

CHEBUTYKIN: Very much.

MASHA: And did she love you?

CHEBUTYKIN [*After a pause*]: That I don't remember anymore.

MASHA: Is mine here? That's how our cook Marfa used to talk about her policeman—"mine." Is mine here?

CHEBUTYKIN: Not yet.

MASHA: When you steal happiness in dribs and drabs, and then you lose it, like me, a shred at a time, then little by little you grow crude and embittered . . . [*Points to her chest*] I'm boiling inside . . . [*Looking at Andrey as he pushes the baby carriage past*] There's our Andrey, our dear brother . . . All our hopes are lost. Thousands of people helped hoist a huge bell, it took so much effort and money, and it suddenly dropped down and shattered. All of a sudden, just like that. Same with Andrey . . .

ANDREY: When will they finally quiet down in the house? Making a hubbub.

CHEBUTYKIN: Soon. [*Looks at his watch*] I have an old-fashioned striking watch . . . [*Winds the watch; it strikes*] The first, second and fifth batteries are leaving at one o'clock sharp . . .

> *A pause.*

And I'm tomorrow.

ANDREY: For good?

CHEBUTYKIN: I don't know, I may come back after a year. Although, who the hell knows . . . it doesn't matter . . .

> *Sounds of a harp and violin are coming from somewhere in the distance.*

ANDREY: The town will be deserted. Snuffed out.

> *A pause.*

Something did happen yesterday by the theatre; everyone's talking about it, but I don't know.

CHEBUTYKIN: It's nothing. It's nonsense. Solyony started picking on the baron, the baron lost his temper, insulted him, and Solyony, in the end, was obliged to challenge him to a duel. [*Looks at his watch*] I think it's time already . . . At half-past twelve in the state grove, that one that you see across the river . . . Bang, bang! [*Laughs*] Solyony imagines himself Lermontov and even writes poetry. Joking aside, it's his third duel already.

MASHA: Whose?

CHEBUTYKIN: Solyony's.

MASHA: And the baron?

CHEBUTYKIN: What about the baron?

> *A pause.*

MASHA: I'm all confused . . . Still, I'm saying that we shouldn't let them do it. He could injure the baron or even kill him.

CHEBUTYKIN: The baron's a good man, but one baron more, one baron less—what does it matter? Let them! It doesn't matter!

> *Shouts are heard coming from the other side of the garden: "Halloo-oo! Hup-hup!"*

You'll have to wait. That's Skvortsov calling, the second. He's sitting in the boat.

> *A pause.*

ANDREY: In my opinion, taking part in a duel or attending it, even as a doctor, is morally wrong.

CHEBUTYKIN: It only seems that way . . . We're not here, nothing's here, and we only think that we exist . . . And what does it matter!

MASHA: And all day they talk, talk, talk . . . [*Walking*] Living in this climate where it could start snowing any minute, and these conversations, to boot . . . [*Stops*] I'm not going inside the house; I can't go in there . . . when Vershinin gets here, tell me . . . [*Walks along the path*] And birds of passage are flying already . . . [*Looks up*] Swans or geese . . . My dear birds, the lucky ones . . . [*Walks away*]

ANDREY: Our house will become empty. The officers will leave, you're leaving, my sister's getting married, and I'll be all alone in the house.

CHEBUTYKIN: And the wife?

Enter Ferapont with some papers.

ANDREY: A wife is a wife. She's honest, decent, well, good-hearted, but at the same time she has something in her that debases her to a petty, blind, sort of a scaly creature. In any case, she's not a person. I'm talking to you like a friend, the only person I can open up to. I love Natasha, I do, but sometimes she seems so incredibly vulgar, and then I'm completely at a loss and don't understand why, how come I love her so—or at least used to . . .

CHEBUTYKIN [*Stands up*]: My friend, I'm leaving tomorrow, and we may never see each other again, so here's my advice to you. You know, put on your cap, pick up a walking stick and leave . . . walk and keep walking without a backward glance. And the farther you get away the better.

In the background, Solyony and two officers cross the stage; upon seeing Chebutykin, he turns towards him; the officers continue walking.

SOLYONY: Doctor, it's time! It's already twelve-thirty. [*Greets Andrey*]

CHEBUTYKIN: Coming. I'm fed up with all of you. [*To Andrey*] Andriusha, if anyone asks for me, tell them I'll be right back . . . [*Sighs*] Ohhh . . . !

SOLYONY: "No time to say a prayer,/ He was knocked down by a bear." [*Walks beside him*] What are you groaning about, old man?

CHEBUTYKIN: So!

SOLYONY: How's the health?

CHEBUTYKIN [*Angry*]: Like the wealth.

SOLYONY: The old man worries for no reason. I won't allow myself much and will just wing him like a woodcock. [*Takes out the perfume and sprinkles it on his hands*] I've used up a full bottle today, but my hands still smell. They smell of corpse.

A pause.

So . . . Do you remember the poem? "*And restless, he is seeking tempests, / As if in tempests he'd find rest.*"[48]

CHEBUTYKIN: Yes. "No time to say a prayer, / He was knocked down by a bear."

Leaves with Solyony.

Shouts are heard: "Hup-hup! Halloo-oo!" Enter Andrey and Ferapont.

FERAPONT: Papers to sign . . .

ANDREY [*Irritably*]: Get away from me! Get away! I entreat you! [*Walks away with the baby carriage*]

FERAPONT: But that's what papers are for, for signing them. [*Walks towards the back of the stage*]

Enter Irina and Tuzenbach wearing a straw hat. Kulygin crosses the stage shouting, "Haloo-oo! Masha! Haloo-oo!"

TUZENBACH: He's probably the only person in town who's glad that the soldiers are going.

IRINA: That's understandable.

A pause.

Our town will feel deserted now.

TUZENBACH [*Looking at his watch*]: Darling, I'll be right back.

IRINA: Where are you going?

TUZENBACH: I have to go into town, to . . . see my friends off.

IRINA: That's not true . . . Nikolai, why are you so absent-minded today?

A pause.

What happened yesterday by the theatre?

TUZENBACH [*With an impatient gesture*]: I'll come back in an hour and I'll be with you again. [*Kisses her hands*] My precious . . . [*Peers at her intently*] I've loved you for five years, and I still can't get used to it, and you seem to me ever more beautiful. What lovely, beautiful hair! What eyes! Tomorrow I'll take you away from here, and we'll work, we'll be rich, and my dreams will come to life. You will be happy. There's just one thing, just one: you don't love me!

IRINA: It's not in my power. I'll be your wife, faithful and obedient, but there is no love, what can I do! [*Crying*] I've never loved, not once in my life. Oh, how I've dreamed about love, have been dreaming about it for a long time, but my heart is like an expensive grand piano, it's locked up and the key is lost.

A pause.

You seem restless.

TUZENBACH: I didn't sleep last night. There's nothing terrible in my life to frighten me, but this lost key torments my soul, doesn't let me sleep . . . Say something to me.

A pause.

Say something to me . . .

IRINA: What? Say what? What?

TUZENBACH: Anything . . .

IRINA: Enough! That's enough!

A pause.

TUZENBACH: Sometimes in life, out of the blue, these little things, these nothings, acquire such significance. You still laugh at them, still think them trifles, but you keep going realizing that you don't have the strength to stop yourself. Oh, let's not talk about that! I feel cheerful. It's as if I'm seeing these pines, maples, and birch trees for the first time in my life, and everything looks at me with anticipation. What beautiful trees, and come to think of it, how beautiful life must be around them!

Shouts of: "Yoo-hoo! Halloo-oo!"

I have to go, it's time . . . There, a dead tree, and yet it's swaying with the others in the wind. That's how I imagine, even if I die, I will be part of life one way or another. Farewell, my darling . . . [*Kisses Irina's hands*] The papers that you gave me are on my desk under the calendar.

IRINA: I'm coming with you.

TUZENBACH [*Alarmed*]: No, no! [*Walks quickly and stops on the path*] Irina!

IRINA: What?

TUZENBACH [*Not knowing what to say*]: I didn't have coffee this morning. Tell them to make me some . . . [*Leaves quickly*]

Irina stands pensive, then walks to the back of the stage and sits on a swing. Enter Andrey with the baby carriage; Ferapont appears.

FERAPONT: Andrey Sergeyich, these aren't my papers, see, they're official. I didn't make them up.

ANDREY: Oh, where is it, where did my past go—when I was young, cheerful, intelligent, when I dreamed and thought beautiful thoughts, when my present and future were full of hope? Why is it that the moment we begin to live, we become boring, drab, tedious, lazy, indifferent, useless, and unhappy . . . Our town has existed for two hundred years, a hundred thousand inhabitants, and yet not one of them who doesn't look like the rest; not a single hero, not in the past, not in the present; not a scholar or an artist, not even someone a tiny bit noticeable to awaken envy or a desire to emulate . . . They only eat, drink, sleep, then die . . . others are born and also eat, drink, and sleep, and so as not to sink into torpor from this boredom, they spice their lives with vile gossip, vodka, cards, litigiousness; and the wives deceive their husbands, and husbands lie, pretending they don't see anything, don't hear anything, and this devastating vulgar influence oppresses the children, and the divine spark goes out in them, and they turn into the same pitiful corpses, like their fathers and mothers, resembling one another . . . [*To Ferapont, angrily*] What do you want?

FERAPONT: Wha? Sign papers.

ANDREY: I am fed up with you.

FERAPONT [*Handing over the documents*]: Just now, a doorman from the treasury was saying . . . He says in St. Petersburg last winter it was two hundred degrees of frost.

ANDREY: The present's revolting, but how good it feels to think about the future! It feels free and open; and in the distance—a glimmering light, and I see freedom, and I see myself and my children free ourselves from idleness and drinking kvass,[49] from goose with cabbage and after-lunch naps, and from this vile sponging . . .

FERAPONT: Two thousand people froze suppos'ly. The people, he says, were horrified. Maybe in Petersburg or maybe in Moscow—can't 'member.

ANDREY [*In a sudden rush of tenderness*]: My dear sisters, my remarkable sisters! [*Through tears*] Masha . . . my sister . . .

NATASHA [*In the window*]: Who's talking so loud here? Is that you, Andriusha? You'll wake up little Sophie. *Il ne faut pas faire du bruit, la Sophie est dormée deja. Vous êtes un ours.*[50] [*Angry*] If you want to talk, then let someone else take the baby carriage. Ferapont, take the baby carriage from the master!

FERAPONT: Yes, ma'am. [*Takes the carriage*]

ANDREY [*Flustered*]: I'm speaking softly.

NATASHA [*From behind the window, caressing her little boy*]: Bobik! Naughty Bobik! Bad Bobik!

ANDREY [*Glancing over the papers*]: All right, I'll go over these and sign what's needed, and you'll take them back to the office . . . [*Goes inside the house reading the papers; Ferapont wheels the baby carriage towards the back of the garden*]

NATASHA [*From behind the window*]: Bobik, what's your mama's name? My dear, my dear! And who's this? This is Aunt Olia, say to your aunt: "Hello, Olia!"

Wandering musicians, a man and a young woman, play a violin and a harp; Vershinin, Olga and Anfisa come out of the house and for a minute listen in silence; Irina walks up to them.

OLGA: Our orchard's like a public thoroughfare, people walk and drive through it all the time. Nanny, give the musicians something! . . .

ANFISA [*Hands the musicians money*]: You'd better go, God bless, my dears.

The musicians bow and leave.

The poor people, the bitter fate. No one plays on a full stomach! [*To Irina*] Hello, Arisha! [*Kisses her*] Eeeee! What a good life! What a good life! A free apartment at the school, my precious girl, together with Oliushka—God's found me a place in my old age. Never in my life have I had it better, sinner that I am . . . The apartment's large, belongs to the school, and I've a whole li'l room and a little bed. Everything belongs to the school. I wake up at night—and oh, Lord and goodness gracious, there's no one more fortunate than me!

VERSHININ [*After glancing at his watch*]: We're leaving, Olga Sergeyevna. It's time for me to go.

A pause.

I wish you all the very best . . . Where's Maria Sergeyevna?

IRINA: Somewhere in the garden . . . I'll go look for her.

VERSHININ: Please. I'm in a hurry.

ANFISA: I'll go look, too. [*Yells*] Mashenka, yoo-hoo! [*She and Irina go deep into the garden*] Haloo-oo!

VERSHININ: Everything comes to an end. And so we part ways. [*Looking at his watch*] The town served us a sort of lunch, we drank champagne, the town head gave a speech; I was eating and listening but in my soul, I was here with you . . . [*Glancing around the garden*] I've become so attached to you.

OLGA: Will we ever see each other again?

VERSHININ: Most likely not.

A pause.

My wife and both girls will be staying here for another two months or so; please, if anything happens, if they need anything . . .

OLGA: Yes, yes, of course. Rest assured.

A pause.

Tomorrow there won't be a single soldier left in town; it'll all be a distant memory, and, of course, for us, a new life will begin . . .

A pause.

Nothing works out the way we want it: I didn't want to be headmistress, and yet I've became one. I'll never be in Moscow then . . .

VERSHININ: Well . . . Thank you for everything . . . Forgive me if I did anything wrong . . . I've talked much too much—please forgive me, and don't think ill of me.

OLGA [*Wiping her eyes*]: Why isn't Masha here . . .

VERSHININ: What else can I say to you by way of parting? What's there to philosophize about? . . . [*Laughs*] Life is hard. To many of us it appears dead-ended and hopeless, but still, we have to admit that it's becoming more clear and easier all the time, and most likely, it won't take long before it becomes altogether bright. [*Looks at his watch*] It's time for me to go, it's time! In the past, mankind was busy making wars; filling its existence with campaigns, incursions, victories, but now all that has outlived itself, leaving behind an immense void with nothing to fill it yet; mankind is desperately looking for it, and will find it, of course. Oh, if only it could be sooner!

A pause.

You know, if only we could add education to love of work, and love of work to education. [*Looks at his watch*] Well, it's time for me to go . . .

OLGA: Here she comes.

Enter Masha.

VERSHININ: I've come to say good-bye . . .

Olga moves a little to the side so as not to interfere with their saying good-bye.

MASHA [*Looking into his face*]: Farewell . . .

A prolonged kiss.

OLGA: That's enough, enough . . .

Masha is sobbing hard.

VERSHININ: Write[51] to me . . . Think of me! Let me go, it's time . . . Olga Ser-geyevna, take her, it's time . . . for me . . . I'm late . . . [*Deeply moved, he kisses Olga's hands, embraces Masha again and leaves quickly*]

OLGA: That's enough, Masha! Stop it, dear . . .

Enter Kulygin.

KULYGIN [*Embarrassed*]: It's all right, let her cry, let her . . . My good Masha, my kind Masha . . . You're my wife, and I'm happy no matter what . . . I am not complaining, not reproaching you in the least . . . Here, Olia is my witness . . . We'll go back to live like before, and I won't say a word to you, not even one hint . . .

MASHA [*Holding back her sobs*]: "*A green oak stands by a curving seashore, / And on that oak a golden chain*" . . . and on that oak a golden chain. I am los-ing my mind . . ."*A green oak stands . . . by a curving seashore.*"

OLGA: Calm down, Masha . . . Calm down . . . Give her some water.

MASHA: I'm not crying anymore . . .

KULYGIN: She's already stopped crying. She's so good-hearted . . .

The muffled sound of a distant shot is heard.

MASHA: "A green oak stands by a curving seashore, / And on that oak a golden chain." Green cat . . . Green oak . . . I'm mixing up . . . [*Drinks water*] An unfortunate life . . . I don't need anything now . . . I'll calm down in a moment . . . It doesn't matter . . . What does "by a curving seashore" mean? Why can't I get these words out of my head? My thoughts are all mixed up.

Enter Irina.

OLGA: Calm down, Masha. See, what a good girl . . . Let's go in the room.

MASHA [*Angry*]: I won't go in there. [*Starts sobbing again, but stops immediately*] I don't go in the house anymore and I'm not going to . . .

IRINA: Let's sit together quietly for a bit. You know, I'm leaving tomorrow . . .

A pause.

KULYGIN: Yesterday, I took away this beard and moustache from a junior at the school . . . [*Puts on the beard and moustache*] I look like the German teacher . . . [*Laughs*] Don't I? These boys are funny.

MASHA: You do look like your German teacher.

OLGA [*Laughs*]: He does.

Masha is crying.

IRINA: Masha, that's enough!

KULYGIN: Just like him . . .

Enter Natasha.

NATASHA [*To the maid*]: What? Protopopov, Mikhail Ivanych, will keep an eye on Sophie and Andrey Sergeyevich will take the baby carriage with Bobik. Children are so much work . . . [*To Irina*] Irina, you're leaving tomorrow—what a pity. Stay another week at least. [*Upon seeing Kulygin, she shrieks; he laughs and removes the beard and moustache*] Stop that, you scared me! [*To Irina*] I've gotten so used to you, and you think it'll be easy for me to say good-bye to you? I'll have them move Andrey with his violin into your room—let him saw away there!—and we'll put Sophie in his room. An amazing, marvelous child! What a dear little girl! She looked at me today with these eyes and—"mama!"

KULYGIN: A fine baby, that's true.

NATASHA: So starting tomorrow, I'm here alone. [*Sighs*] First of all, I'll make them cut down this spruce tree path, then this maple . . . At nighttime it looks so ugly . . . [*To Irina*] My dear, that sash does not suit you at all . . . It's in bad taste . . . You need something a little brighter there. And here I'll have them plant all over lots of flowers, lots of flowers, and it'll smell . . . [*Sternly*] What is this fork doing on the bench? [*Going indoors, to the maid*] I'm asking, what is the fork doing on the bench here? [*Shouts*] Be quiet!

KULYGIN: She's on a rampage!

A march is heard being played by a band offstage; everyone listens.

OLGA: They're leaving.

> *Enter Chebutykin.*

MASHA: Our dear ones are going away. Well then . . . Safe journey to them! [*To her husband*] We have to go home. Where's my hat and cape?

KULYGIN: I took them in the house . . . I'll go get them.

OLGA: Well, now we can all go to our respective homes. It's time.

CHEBUTYKIN: Olga Sergeyevna!

OLGA: What?

> *A pause.*

What?

CHEBUTYKIN: Nothing . . . I don't know how to tell you . . . [*Whispers in her ear*]

OLGA [*Stunned*]: No!

CHEBUTYKIN: Yes . . . That's how it goes . . . I'm exhausted, utterly exhausted, I don't want to talk anymore . . . [*Annoyed*] However, it doesn't matter!

MASHA: What happened?

OLGA [*Embraces Irina*]: Today's a terrible day . . . I don't know how to tell you, my dear . . .

IRINA: What? Tell me quickly: what? For God's sake! [*Crying*]

CHEBUTYKIN: The baron was killed in a duel just now . . .

IRINA [*Weeps quietly*]: I knew it, I knew it . . .

CHEBUTYKIN [*At the back of the stage sits down on a bench*]: I'm exhausted . . . [*Takes a newspaper out of his pocket*] Let them cry a little . . . [*Sings softly*] Ta-ra-ra boom-de-ay, / Sit on a tomb today . . . What does it matter!

> *The three sisters stand snuggling up to each other.*

MASHA: Oh, listen to the music! They're going away from us, and one is gone, gone forever, we'll be left all alone to begin our life anew. We must go on living . . . We must . . .

IRINA [*Puts her head on Olga's breast*]: A time will come when everyone will know what it's all about, why all this suffering; there won't be any mystery, but in the meantime, we must go on living . . . we must work, just work! Tomorrow I'll go by myself; I'll teach school and devote my life to those who may need it. It's fall now; winter will be here soon, the snow will bury everything, and I will work, I will work . . .

OLGA [*Embraces both sisters*]: The music is so cheerful, lively, and I feel like living! Oh, my God! Time will pass and we'll be gone forever, we'll be forgotten, our faces will be forgotten, our voices, and how many of us there were, but our suffering will turn to joy for those who'll live after us; peace and happiness will come to earth, and they'll remember kindly and bless those who live now. Oh, my dear sisters, our life isn't over yet. We will live! The music is so cheerful, so joyous, and it seems just a little bit longer and we'll know why we live, why we suffer . . . If only we could know! If only we could know!

The music becomes more and more faint; Kulygin, cheerful, smiling, carries a hat and cape; Andrey pushes the baby carriage with Bobik sitting in it.

CHEBUTYKIN [*Singing softly*]: *Ta-ra-ra boom-de-ay, / Sit on a tomb today . . .*
[*Reads a newspaper*] It doesn't matter! Doesn't matter!

OLGA: If only we could know, if only we could know!

Curtain.

THE CHERRY ORCHARD
A Comedy in Four Acts

Characters

RANEVSKAYA, LIUBOV ANDREYEVNA, a landowner

ANYA, her daughter, 17

VARYA, her adopted daughter, 24

GAEV, LEONID ANDREYEVICH, Mme Ranevskaya's brother

LOPAKHIN, ERMOLAI ALEXEYEVICH, a merchant

TROFIMOV, PYOTR SERGEYEVICH, a student

SIMYONOV-PISCHIK, BORIS BORISOVICH, a landowner

CHARLOTTA IVANOVNA, a governess

EPIKHODOV, SEMYON PANTELEYEVICH, a clerk

DUNYASHA, a maid

FIERS, a footman, an old man, 87

YASHA, a young footman

PASSERBY

STATIONMASTER

POST OFFICE OFFICIAL

GUESTS, SERVANTS

The action takes place on L. A. Ranevskaya's estate.

ACT ONE

A room still called the nursery. One of the doors leads to Anya's room. It is almost dawn; the sun is about to rise. It's already May and the cherry trees are in bloom but outside in the orchard it is chilly—morning frost. The windows in the room are closed.

Dunyasha comes in with a candle, and Lopakhin holding a book.

LOPAKHIN: The train's arrived, thank God. What time is it?

DUNYASHA: It's almost two. [*Puts out the candle*] It's light out.

LOPAKHIN: How late was the train, then? At least two hours. [*Yawns and stretches himself*] Look at me, what an ass I made of myself! I came here expressly to meet them at the station, and suddenly overslept . . . Dozed off sitting up. Most annoying . . . I wish you'd woken me up.

DUNYASHA: I thought you'd gone. [*Listening intently*] Here, I think they're coming.

LOPAKHIN [*Listens attentively*]: No . . . They've got to collect their luggage, this and that . . .

A pause.

Liubov Andreyevna has lived abroad for five years; I don't know what she's like now . . . She's a good person. Easy to take, without airs. I remember when I was a mere boy of fifteen, my late father—he worked in a little shop here in the village—punched me in the face so my nose was bleeding . . . He was drunk, and for some reason or other we'd come into the courtyard together. Liubov Andreyevna was young and so slim then, and I remember it so clearly; she took me to the washstand here in this very room, the nursery. She said, "Don't cry, little peasant, it'll all heal in time for the wedding . . ."

A pause.

Little peasant . . . True, my father was a muzhik, a peasant, but here I am decked out in a white waistcoat and yellow shoes. A pig in a china shop . . . The only thing is I'm rich now and I've lots of money, but take a good look at me, I'm as peasant as they come . . . [*Flips pages of the book*] I was reading this but I couldn't understand anything. I fell asleep reading it.

A pause.

DUNYASHA: The dogs didn't sleep all night; they sense that their masters are returning.

LOPAKHIN: What's with you, Dunyasha . . .

DUNYASHA: My hands are trembling. I'm going to faint.

LOPAKHIN: You're too sensitive, Dunyasha. Dressing like a lady, and your hair is like a lady's. You mustn't do that. Know your place always.

Enter Epikhodov—with a bouquet. He wears a short jacket and shiny polished boots, which squeak loudly. He drops the bouquet upon entering.

EPIKHODOV [*Picking up the bouquet*]: These are from the gardener and he says to put them in the dining room. [*Gives the bouquet to Dunyasha*]

LOPAKHIN: And bring me some kvass.[1]

DUNYASHA: Yes, sir. [*Goes out*]

EPIKHODOV: The morning frost now—three degrees below freezing, but the cherry trees are all in bloom. I can't approve of our climate. [*Sighs*] I can't. Our climate can't conduce itself at all. And, Ermolai Alexeyevich, allow me to append that I bought myself new boots two days ago, and they, I assure you, they squeak just impossible. What can I grease them with?

LOPAKHIN: Leave me alone. Im fed up with you.

EPIKHODOV: A new disaster befalls me every day. But I don't gripe; I'm used to it, and I smile even. [*Dunyasha comes in and brings Lopakhin some kvass*] I'm going. [*Knocks over a chair*] There . . . [*As if triumphantly*] There, you see, excuse the expression, by the way, such a circumstance . . . It's remarkable! [*Goes out*]

DUNYASHA: The truth, Ermolai Alexeyevich, is that Epikhodov has proposed to me.

LOPAKHIN: Ah!

DUNYASHA: I don't even know what . . . He's a quiet man, but sometimes he starts talking and you can't understand anything. It's nice and full of feeling; only you can't understand any of it. I think I may even like him. He's madly in love with me. He's so unfortunate, though; every day something happens to him. We tease him about it: twenty-two disasters.

LOPAKHIN [*Listens*]: There, I think they're coming . . .

DUNYASHA: Coming! What's the matter with me? . . . I have the chills.

LOPAKHIN: They're here. Let's go greet them. Will she recognize me? We haven't seen each other for five years.

DUNYASHA [*Excited*]: I'm going to faint . . . Oh, faint!

The sounds of two carriages driving up to the house. Lopakhin and Dunya-sha quickly go out. The stage is empty. Then, from the adjacent rooms come sounds of people arriving. Fiers, having gone to meet Liubov Andreyevna, walks quickly across the stage leaning on a stick. He is wearing old-fashioned livery and a tall hat. He is mumbling to himself, but you can't make out a single word. The noise behind the stage gets louder and louder. A voice is heard: "Let's go through here." Enter Liubov Andreyevna, Anya, and Char-lotta Ivanovna with a little dog on a chain; they are all dressed in travel-ing clothes; Varya is wearing a long coat and a kerchief on her head. Gaev, Simyonov-Pischik, Lopakhin, Dunyasha with a bundle and an umbrella, and a servant with luggage—all walk across the room.

ANYA: Let's walk through here. Do you remember, Mama, what room this is?

LIUBOV ANDREYEVNA [*Joyfully, through her tears*]: The nursery!

VARYA: It's so cold! My hands are frozen stiff. [*To Liubov Andreyevna*] Your rooms, the white one and the violet one, are just as they were, Mamochka.

LIUBOV ANDREYEVNA: My nursery, my darling, beautiful room . . . I used to sleep here when I was little . . . [*Crying*] And now I'm like a little girl again. [*Kisses her brother, Varya, then her brother again*] And Varya is just the same as ever, like a nun. And I recognize Dunyasha . . . [*Kisses her*]

GAEV: The train was two hours late. How do you like that!

CHARLOTTA [*To Pischik*]: My dog eats nuts too.

PISCHIK [*Amazed*]: Imagine that!

All go out except Anya and Dunyasha.

DUNYASHA: We've been waiting so long for you! [*Takes off Anya's coat and hat*]

ANYA: I haven't slept for four nights on the road . . . I have the chills now.

DUNYASHA: You left during Lent; it was freezing and snowing, but now? My dear! [*Laughs and kisses her*] We've been waiting for you, my dear, my light and joy . . . I have to tell you now, I can't wait another minute . . .

ANYA [*Sleepy*]: Something again . . .

DUNYASHA: The clerk Epikhodov proposed to me right after Easter.

ANYA: You're always talking about that . . . [*Fixing her hair*] I lost all my hair-pins . . . [*She is exhausted and even staggers a little as she walks*]

DUNYASHA: I don't even know what to make of it. He loves me; he loves me so!

ANYA [*Looks into her room; in a gentle voice*]: My room, my windows, it's as if I had never left. I'm home! Tomorrow morning I'll get up and run out into to the orchard . . . Oh, if I could only fall sleep! I didn't sleep the whole way; I was all worried.

DUNYASHA: Pyotr Sergeyevich arrived here two days ago.

ANYA [*With joy*]: Petya!

DUNYASHA. He's sleeping in the bathhouse, he's staying there. He doesn't want to be in the way, he says. [*Looks at her pocket watch*] I ought to wake him, but Varvara Mikhailovna told me not to. "Don't wake him," she says.

Enter Varya with a bunch of keys on her belt.

VARYA: Dunyasha, coffee, quick. Mama wants some.

DUNYASHA: Just a minute. [*Goes out*]

VARYA: Well, thank God you're here. You're home again. [*Snuggling up to her*] My darling's back! My beautiful girl's back!

ANYA: What I've been through.

VARYA: I can imagine!

ANYA: I left during Passion week; it was cold then. Charlotta talked the whole way doing her magic tricks. Why did you foist her on me?

VARYA: You can't go by yourself, darling. At seventeen!

ANYA: We get to Paris and it's cold and snowing there. My French is awful. Mama lives on the fifth floor. I come up and she's there with some Frenchmen, ladies, an old *abbé* with a book, and the room is smoky, it's not homey. It suddenly made me feel so sorry for Mama, so sorry, I hugged her head and couldn't let go. Later Mama kept snuggling up to me and crying . . .

VARYA [*Weeping*]: Don't, please don't . . .

ANYA: She'd already sold the summerhouse near Mentone; she had nothing left, nothing. And I didn't have a penny, either; we barely made it back. And Mama just doesn't understand! We sit down for dinner at the station, and she orders the most expensive things and tips the waiters a ruble each. Charlotta does the same. And Yasha, too, demands a serving—it's just awful. You know, Mama's lackey, Yasha; we brought him back with us.

VARYA: I saw the rascal.

ANYA: How are things? Have you paid the interest?

VARYA: Not a bit of it.

ANYA. Oh my God, oh my God . . .

VARYA: They will settle the estate in August . . .

ANYA: Oh, my God. . . .

LOPAKHIN [*Looks into the room and bellows*] Baaaah! . . . [*Exit*]

VARYA [*Through tears*]: I feel like smacking him . . . [*Shakes her fist*]

ANYA [*Embraces Varya, softly*]: Varya, has he proposed to you? [*Varya shakes her head in the negative.*] But he loves you . . . Why don't you have a talk? What are you waiting for?

VARYA: I think that nothing will come of it. He's busy and has no time for me . . . pays no attention to me. Never mind, it's so hard for me to look at him . . . Everybody talks about our wedding, everybody congratulates me, but there's nothing there; it's all like a dream . . . [*In a changed voice*] Your brooch is kind of like a little bee.

ANYA [*Sadly*]: Mama bought it. [*Walks into her room and speaks in a cheerful voice like a child*] In Paris, I flew on a hot air balloon!

VARYA: My darling's back! My beautiful girl's back!

Dunyasha has already returned with the coffeepot and is making coffee.

[*Standing by the door*] I go about all day, darling, taking care of the house, and I dream that we marry you off to a rich man, then I'd be at peace and I would then go see the elders at the monastery then to Kiev . . . to Moscow, and so on. To walk from one holy place to another. Just walk and walk . . . So heaven-like! . . .

ANYA: The birds are singing in the orchard. What time is it now?

VARYA: It must be after two. Time for bed, darling. [*Goes into Anya's room*] So heaven-like!

Enter Yasha with a heavy shawl and a small traveling bag.

YASHA [*Crossing the stage, politely*]: May I pass through this way?

DUNYASHA: I can hardly recognize you, Yasha. You've changed so much abroad.

YASHA: Hmm . . . And who are you?

DUNYASHA: When you went away I was this tall. [*Showing with her hand*] I'm Dunyasha, Fedor Kozoyedov's daughter. You don't remember!

YASHA: Hmm . . . Fresh as a cucumber![2] [*Looks round and embraces her; She screams and drops the saucer. Yasha quickly goes out*]

VARYA [*In the doorway with a displeased voice*]: What was that?

DUNYASHA [*Through tears*]: I broke a saucer . . .

VARYA: It's a good sign.[3]

ANYA [*Coming out of her room*]: We should warn Mama that Petya's here . . .

VARYA: I told them not to wake him up.

ANYA [*Pensively*]: Father died six years ago, and a month later my brother Grisha drowned in the river—an adorable seven-year-old boy! Mother couldn't take it and walked away, walked without a backward glance . . . [*Shudders*] How well I understand her, if only she knew!

A pause.

And Petya Trofimov was Grisha's tutor, and he might remind her of it . . .

Enter Fiers in a short jacket and white waistcoat.

FIERS [*Goes to the coffeepot, anxiously*]: The mistress will be served her coffee here . . . [*Puts on white gloves*] Is it ready? [*To Dunyasha, sternly*] You! And the cream?

DUNYASHA: Oh, my goodness . . . [*Leaves quickly*]

FIERS [*Fussing about the coffeepot*]: Oh, you nincompoop . . . [*Murmurs to himself*] Back from Paris . . . the master, too, used to travel to Paris . . . in a carriage . . . [*Laughs*]

VARYA: What was that, Fiers?

FIERS: What's your wish? [*Joyfully*] The mistress is back! I made it till she came! I don't care if I die now . . . [*Weeps with joy*]

Enter Liubov Andreyevna, Gaev, Lopakhin, and Simyonov-Pischik, who is wearing a long jacket of thin cloth and wide trousers.[4] *Gaev comes in, moving his arms and body as if playing billiards.*

LIUBOV ANDREYEVNA: What was it? Let me think . . . The yellow into the corner! A bank shot to the center!

GAEV: A cut shot to the corner! Once upon a time, sister, you and I slept in this room, and now I'm fifty-one years old, strange as it may seem.

LOPAKHIN: Yes, time flies.

GAEV: Who?

LOPAKHIN: I said time flies.

GAEV: It smells of patchouli here.

ANYA: I'm going to bed. Good night, Mama. [*Kisses her*]

LIUBOV ANDREYEVNA: My precious baby girl. [*Kisses her hands*] Glad to be home? I still can't get over it.

ANYA. Good-bye, Uncle.

GAEV [*Kisses her face and hands*]: God bless you. How you resemble your mother! [*To his sister*] Liuba, when you were her age, you looked just like her.

> *Anya shakes hands with Lopakhin and Pischik and goes out and shuts the door behind her.*

LIUBOV ANDREYEVNA: She's exhausted.

PISCHIK: It's a long journey, I guess.

VARYA [*To Lopakhin and Pischik*]: Well, gentlemen? It's after two, it's high time.

LIUBOV ANDREYEVNA [*Laughs*]: You're the same as ever, Varya. [*Draws her close and kisses her*] I'll finish my coffee and we'll all go.

> *Fiers lays a cushion under her feet.*

Thank you, dear. I drink coffee all the time. I drink it day and night. Thank you, my dear old man. [*Kisses Fiers*]

VARYA: I'll go make sure they've brought in all the luggage ... [*Goes out*]

LIUBOV ANDREYEVNA: Is it me really sitting here? [*Laughs*] I feel like jumping and waving my arms in the air. [*Covers her face with her hands*] What if I'm only dreaming! God knows I love my homeland, I love it dearly, I couldn't even look out the window without crying. [*Through tears*] But I must have my coffee. Thank you, Fiers. Thank you, dear old man. I'm so glad you're still around.

FIERS: The day before yesterday.

GAEV: He's hard of hearing.

LOPAKHIN: I've got to catch a five o'clock train to Kharkov.[5] That's annoying! I wanted to see you and to talk a little ... You're still as magnificent as ever.

PISCHIK [*Breathes heavily*]: Even prettier ... wearing Parisian styles ... she'll make me lose my head, hook, line, and sinker ...

LOPAKHIN: Your brother, Leonid Andreyevich, says that I'm a boor and just a rich peasant, but I don't care in the least. Let him talk. I only hope that you trust me as before and that your amazing, touching eyes always go on gazing at me as before. God have mercy! My father was your grandfather's and father's serf, but you, you did so much for me at one point, more than anybody else, that I've forgiven it all and love you like family ... and even more than family.

LIUBOV ANDREYEVNA: I can't sit still, I can't. [*Jumps up and paces in great excitement*] I'll never get over this joy ... You can laugh at me; I'm a foolish woman ... My dear little bookcase ... [*Kisses the bookcase*] My little table.

GAEV: You know that Nanny died while you were away.

LIUBOV ANDREYEVNA [*Sits down and drinks coffee*]: Yes, may she rest in peace. I read it in a letter.

GAEV: And Anastasy died too. Peter the Squint-eye left us and is now living in town at the police commissioner's. [*Takes a box of sugar hard candy out of his pocket and sucks on one*]

PISCHIK: My daughter, Dashenka . . . sends her regards . . .

LOPAKHIN: I feel like saying something nice and cheerful to you. [*Looking at his watch*] I have to leave, no time to talk . . . well, I'll do it briefly. You already know that your cherry orchard is being sold to pay off your debts. The auction is set for the twenty-second of August; but don't you worry, my dear, no need to lose sleep over it, there's a way out . . . Here's my plan. May I have your attention! Your estate is only sixteen miles from the town, the railway was built nearby, and if you were to take the cherry orchard, and the land by the river, and split it into lots and then lease them for summer cottages, you'll have at the least twenty-five thousand rubles a year in income.

GAEV: Pardon me, what nonsense!

LIUBOV ANDREYEVNA. I don't quite understand you, Ermolai Alexeyevich.

LOPAKHIN: You will charge the summer people, at the very least, twenty-five rubles a year per three acres, and if you publicize it now, I'm willing to bet you anything that come fall you won't have a single plot left; they'll all be taken. In short, congratulations, you've been saved. The location's perfect, the river's deep. Only, of course, you'll need to fix up and clean out some things . . . for instance, you'll need to tear down the old buildings, this house, which is no longer any good, and cut down the old cherry orchard . . .

LIUBOV ANDREYEVNA: Cut it down? My dear, forgive me, but you don't understand anything. If there's one interesting or even remarkable thing at all in this district, it's our cherry orchard.

LOPAKHIN: The only remarkable thing about the orchard is that it's very big. It produces cherries once every two years, and even then you don't know what to do with them; nobody wants to buy them.

GAEV: This orchard is even mentioned in the *Encyclopedic Dictionary*.

LOPAKHIN [*Looks at his watch*]: Unless we can think of something and come up with a plan, then on the twenty-second of August, both the cherry orchard and the estate will be sold at an auction. Make up your mind! I swear to you, there's no other way out. No, none.

FIERS: In the olden days, forty or fifty years back, they used to dry the cherries, soak them, marinate them, and make jam with them, and sometimes . . .

GAEV: Be quiet, Fiers.

FIERS: And sometimes, they would send carts of dried cherries off to Moscow and Kharkov. And make so much money! The dried cherries were soft, juicy, sweet, and fragrant . . . They had a way to prepare them . . .

LIUBOV ANDREYEVNA: So what happened to it?

FIERS: They forgot. Nobody remembers it.

PISCHIK [*To Liubov Andreyevna*]: What was it like in Paris? Eh? Did you eat frogs?

LIUBOV ANDREYEVNA: I ate crocodile.

PISCHIK: Imagine that . . .

LOPAKHIN: Up until now, in the countryside, we only had landlords and peasants, but now we have summer people. All the towns, even the smallest ones are surrounded by summer cottages now. And it's a sure thing that in twenty years' time summer people will have multiplied to an incredible extent. Today a person is sitting on his balcony drinking tea, but he could start cultivating his land, and then your cherry orchard will become a happy, rich, and gorgeous place . . .

GAEV [*Annoyed*]: What nonsense!

Enter Varya and Yasha.

VARYA: Mamochka, there are two telegrams for you here. [*Picks out a key and unlocks the antique bookcase while rattling her keys*] Here they are.

LIUBOV ANDREYEVNA: They're from Paris. [*Tears them up without reading them*] I'm finished with Paris.

GAEV: And do you know, Liuba, how old this bookcase is? A week ago I took out the bottom drawer and I saw some numbers burned into it. The bookcase was made exactly one hundred years ago. How about that! What? We could celebrate its centennial. It is an inanimate object, but still, it's a fine bookcase.

PISCHIK [*Amazed*]: A hundred years . . . Imagine that!

GAEV: Yes . . . that's quite something. [*Touching the bookcase*] Dear, esteemed bookcase! I salute your existence, which has already for over a hundred years been directed towards the bright ideals of goodness and justice;

your silent call to productive work hasn't weakened over a hundred years [*through tears*], supporting for generations in our family the optimism and faith in a better future, and cultivating in us ideals of goodness and social awareness.

A pause.

LOPAKHIN: Well . . .

LIUBOV ANDREYEVNA: You're the same as ever, Lionya.

GAEV [*A little embarrassed*]: From the ball on the right to the corner! Cut to the middle!

LOPAKHIN [*Glances at his watch*]: Well, it's time for me to go.

YASHA [*Offering Liubov Andreyevna medicine*]: Do you want to take your pills now . . . ?

PISCHIK: Don't take any *medicaments*, my dearest . . . No harm or benefit in them . . . Let me have them . . . my dear. [*Takes the pills, places all of them into the palm of his hand, blows on them, puts them in his mouth, and drinks some kvass*] There!

LIUBOV ANDREYEVNA [*Frightened*]: You've lost your mind!

PISCHIK: I swallowed all the pills.

LOPAKHIN: What a bottomless pit!

All laugh.

FIERS: They were here Easter week and ate half a pail of pickled cucumbers . . . [*Mumbles*]

LIUBOV ANDREYEVNA: What was that?

VARYA: He's been mumbling for three years. We're used to it.

YASHA: Advanced in years.

Charlotta Ivanovna, dressed in white, very thin and tightly laced, with a lorgnette dangling at her waist, walks across the stage.

LOPAKHIN: Excuse me, Charlotta Ivanovna, I haven't said hello to you yet. [*Tries to kiss her hand*]

CHARLOTTA [*Taking her hand away*]: If I let you kiss my hand, then you'll want my elbow, then my shoulder . . .

LOPAKHIN: I have no luck today.

All laugh.

Show a magic trick, Charlotta Ivanovna!

LIUBOV ANDREYEVNA: Charlotta, show us a magic trick!

CHARLOTTA: Don't. I wish to sleep. [*Goes out*]

LOPAKHIN: We'll see each other in three weeks. [*Kisses Liubov Andreyevna's hand*] Good-bye for now. It's time to go. [*To Gaev*] Till we meet again. [*Kisses Pischik*] Till we meet again. [*Gives his hand to Varya, then to Fiers and to Yasha*] I don't feel like going. [*To Liubov Andreyevna*] Should you make up your mind on the cottages, let me know, and I'll get you a loan of fifty thousand or so. Think about it.

VARYA [*Crossly*]: Do go, already!

LOPAKHIN: I'm going, I'm going. . . . [*Goes out*]

GAEV: A boor. Actually, excuse me . . . Her suitor; Varya's getting married to him.

VARYA: Uncle, you talk too much.

LIUBOV ANDREYEVNA: Well, Varya, I'll be delighted. He's a good man.

PISCHIK: He is, to tell the truth . . . a most worthy man . . . And my Dashenka . . . also says . . . says many different things. [*Snores, but wakes up immediately*] But still, dear madam, lend me . . . two hundred and forty rubles . . . to pay off the interest on my mortgage tomorrow . . .

VARYA [*Frightened*]: No, we don't have it!

LIUBOV ANDREYEVNA. It's true, I've nothing at all.

PISCHIK: You'll find it. [*Laughs*] I never lose hope. I thought all was lost once and I was done in, but then they built a railway across my land . . . and paid me. Something else will come up if not today, tomorrow. Dashenka will win two hundred thousand . . . she's got a lottery ticket.

LIUBOV ANDREYEVNA: We had our coffee and can go to bed now.

FIERS [*Brushing off Gaev's suit and speaking in a didactic tone*]: You've put on the wrong breeches again. What am I to do with you!

VARYA [*Quietly*]: Anya's asleep. [*Quietly opens the window*] The sun's up already; it's not cold. Take a look, Mamochka: what lovely trees! And, my goodness, the air! The starlings are singing!

GAEV [*Opens the other window*]: The garden's all white. You remember, don't you, Liuba? This long path goes straight all the way, straight like a stretched out strap; it shines on moonlit nights. Do you remember? You haven't forgotten?

LIUBOV ANDREYEVNA [*Looks at the orchard through the window*]: Oh, my childhood, my innocence! I used to sleep in this nursery, look out into the orchard from here, wake up happy every morning, and it was just the same then as it is now; nothing has changed. [*Laughs with joy*] It's all white! Oh, my orchard! After a dark and inclement fall and a cold winter, you're young again, full of joy, and the angels of heaven haven't abandoned you . . . If only I could lift the heavy burden off my shoulders, if only I could forget the past!

GAEV: Yes, and they'll sell the orchard to pay off the debts, as strange as it may seem . . .

LIUBOV ANDREYEVNA: Look, our dead Mama is walking in the orchard . . . in a white dress! [*Laughs with joy*] It's her.

GAEV: Where?

VARYA: God bless you, Mamochka.

LIUBOV ANDREYEVNA: Nobody's there, I imagined that. On the right, at the turnoff to the gazebo, a small white tree is bowing down; it looks like a woman . . .

Enter Trofimov wearing glasses and a worn-out student uniform.[6]

What a marvelous garden! This mass of white flowers, the blue sky . . .

TROFIMOV: Liubov Andreyevna!

She looks round at him.

I only wanted to bow to you, and I'll go away. [*Kisses her hand heartily*] I was told to wait till morning, but I didn't have the patience . . .

Liubov Andreyevna looks at him, perplexed.

VARYA [*Through tears*]: It's Petya Trofimov . . .

TROFIMOV: Petya Trofimov, your Grisha's former tutor . . . Have I changed that much?

Liubov Andreyevna embraces him and weeps softly.

GAEV [*Embarrassed*]: That's enough, that's enough, Liuba.

VARYA [*Crying*]: Petya, I told you to wait till tomorrow.

LIUBOV ANDREYEVNA: My Grisha . . . my boy . . . Grisha . . . my son . . .

VARYA: There's nothing we can do about it now, Mamochka. It's God's will.

TROFIMOV [*Softly, through tears*]: There, there . . .

LIUBOV ANDREYEVNA [*Crying softly*]: The boy perished, drowned . . . What for? What for, my friend? [*Softer yet*] Anya is asleep in there and I'm speaking so loud . . . raising a ruckus . . . Well, Petya? Why have you lost your looks? Why have you grown old?

TROFIMOV: In the train a peasant woman called me a mangy gentleman.

LIUBOV ANDREYEVNA: You were just a boy then, a nice student, and now you
    have thinning hair and these glasses. Don't tell me you're still a student!
    [*Walks to the door*]

TROFIMOV: I guess I'm an eternal student.

LIUBOV ANDREYEVNA [*Kisses her brother, then Varya*]: Well, go to bed . . . You,
    too, have grown old, Leonid.

PISCHIK [*Follows her*]: So, to bed then . . . Oh, my gout! I'll stay the night
    here . . . If only, Liubov Andreyevna, darling, I could get . . . two hun-
    dred and forty rubles tomorrow morning . . .

GAEV: Same old song.

PISCHIK: Two hundred and forty rubles . . . to pay off the interest on the
    mortgage.

LIUBOV ANDREYEVNA: I don't have any money, my dear.

PISCHIK: I'll pay it back, dear . . . A trifling sum . . .

LIUBOV ANDREYEVNA: Well, there is nothing I can do, Leonid will give it to
    you . . . Leonid will give it to you.

GAEV: Nothing doing.

LIUBOV ANDREYEVNA: What are you going to do? Give it to him. He needs
    it . . . He'll pay it back.

*Liubov Andreyevna, Trofimov, Pischik, and Fiers exit. Gaev, Varya, and
Yasha remain.*

GAEV: My sister hasn't lost her habit of squandering money. [*To Yasha*] Get
    away, young man, you smell of chicken.

YASHA [*Grinning*]: You're still the same as ever, Leonid Andreyevich.

GAEV: Who? [*To Varya*] What did he say?

VARYA [*To Yasha*]: Your mother's here from the village; she's been sitting in the
    servants' room since yesterday, she wants to see you . . .

YASHA: What in the world for!

VARYA: Shameless!

YASHA: Who needs it! Couldn't she wait till tomorrow? [*Goes out*]

VARYA: Mamochka's same as ever. Just give her a chance and she'll give every-
    thing away.

GAEV: Well . . .

A pause.

When many different cures are offered to treat an illness, then it means
that the illness is incurable. I'm thinking, straining my brains as hard

as I can, and I've several cures, many cures, and so really none at all. It would be good to inherit a fortune from somebody; it would be good to marry off our Anya to a rich man; it would be good to go to the city of Yaroslavl and try our luck with my aunt the countess. After all, the aunt is very, very rich.

VARYA [*Weeps*]: God willing.

GAEV: Don't cry. My aunt's very rich, but she doesn't like us. In the first place, my sister married a lawyer, not a nobleman . . .

Anya appears in the doorway.

Not a nobleman, and it's not as if she's been virtuous. She's nice and kind and charming, and I'm very fond of her, but no matter what extenuating circumstances you produce in her defense, you have to admit that she's a wanton woman; you sense it in the slightest of her movements.

VARYA [*Whispers*]: Anya's in the doorway.

GAEV: Who?

A pause.

Amazing how I just got something in my right eye . . . I can't see well out of it. And Thursday, when I was at the district court . . .

Enter Anya.

VARYA: Anya, how come you're not asleep?

ANYA: I can't fall asleep. I just can't.

GAEV: My little sweetheart! [*Kisses Anya's face and hands*] My child . . . [*Through tears*] You're not my niece, you're my angel, you're my all . . . Trust me, believe me . . .

ANYA: I trust you, Uncle. Everybody loves you and respects you . . . but, Uncle dear, you need to keep quiet, just keep quiet. What were you saying just now about my mother, your own sister? Why were you saying that?

GAEV: Yes, yes . . . [*Covers his face with her hand*] Yes, really, it's awful. Oh, my God, oh, my God! And today I made a speech to a bookcase . . . it's so stupid! And only when I'd finished did I realize how stupid it was.

VARYA: Dear Uncle, yes, you really ought to keep quiet. Just keep quiet, that's all.

ANYA: You'd feel better yourself if only you would just keep quiet.

GAEV: I'll keep quiet. [*Kisses their hands*] I'll keep quiet. But let's talk about this. On Thursday I was at the district court, and a few of us met there together, and we started talking about this and that and the other, and I think it's possible to arrange a loan against the promissory note to pay off the interest to the bank.

VARYA: With God's help!

GAEV: I'll go in on Tuesday and talk to them again. [*To Varya*] Don't cry. [*To Anya*] Your mother will talk to Lopakhin; he won't refuse her, of course . . . And you, as soon as you are all rested, you'll go to Yaroslavl to visit the countess, your grandmother. So you see, we'll attack it from all three angles and it's in the bag. We'll pay off the interest, I'm sure of it . . . [*Puts a fruit-drop in his mouth*] My word of honor, I swear to you, the estate will not be sold! [*Excited*] I swear on my happiness! Here's my hand. You may call me a dishonorable wretch if I allow the auction to take place! I swear to you with my whole being!

ANYA [*Calm again and in a good mood*]: You are so nice and so clever! [*Embraces her uncle*] Now I feel so much at peace! I'm at peace. I'm happy!

Enter Fiers.

FIERS [*Reproachfully*]: Leonid Andreyevich, have you no shame? When are you going to bed?

GAEV: In a minute, in a minute. You can go, Fiers. All right, I'll get undressed by myself this time. Well, children, nighty-night . . . ! I'll give you the details tomorrow, but now go to bed. [*Kisses Anya and Varya*] I'm a man of the eighties . . .⁷ You don't hear much praise for that period but, still, I can say that I've endured plenty for my convictions. There is a reason the peasants love me, I assure you. We've got to get to know the peasant! We've got to know how . . .

ANYA: You're at it again, Uncle!

VARYA: Please keep quiet, dear Uncle!

FIERS [*Angrily*]: Leonid Andreyich!

GAEV: Coming, coming . . . Go to bed now. Off the two sides and into the middle! Putting the clear one . . . [*Goes out. Fiers, mincing, follows him*]

ANYA: I'm at peace now. I don't feel like going to Yaroslavl, I don't like my grandmother but still, I'm at peace now. Thanks to Uncle. [*Sits down*]

VARYA: It's time for bed. I'm going. We had an unpleasant incident here while you were gone. In the old servants' quarters, as you know, where only the old servants live—Efim and Polya and Evstigney, and Karp, too. They started letting some crooks in for the night there—I didn't say anything. But then I heard they're spreading rumors that I gave orders to feed them only peas. Out of stinginess, you see . . . And it was all Evstigney . . . Very well, I thought, if that's true, I was going to teach him a lesson. So I call Evstigney . . . [*Yawns*] He comes in . . ."How could you," I say to him, "Evstigney . . . you fool" . . . [*Looking at Anya*] Anya, dear!

A pause.

She's asleep! . . . [*Takes Anya's arm*] Let's go beddy-bye . . . Come . . . [*Leads her along*] My darling's asleep! Come . . .

They go.

In the distance, on the other side of the orchard, a shepherd plays his reed pipe. Trofimov crosses the stage and stops upon seeing Varya and Anya.

VARYA: Shh . . . She's asleep . . . asleep . . . Let's go, my darling.

ANYA [*Softly, half-asleep*]: I'm so tired . . . all the bells . . . Dear Uncle . . . Mama and Uncle . . .

VARYA: Let's go, my dear, let's go . . . [*Goes into Anya's room*]

TROFIMOV [*With affection*]: My sweet sunshine! My spring!

Curtain.

ACT TWO

A field. An old, long-ago abandoned, crooked chapel; next to it a well and some large stones, which may have been at one point gravestones, and an old bench. A road to Gaev's estate is visible. Off to the side, dark poplars are rising high; behind them—the beginning of the cherry orchard. In the distance—a row of telegraph poles, and on the horizon, far, far away—faint outlines of a big town, visible only on very nice and clear days. The sun is about to set. Charlotta, Yasha, and Dunyasha are sitting on the bench; Epikhodov stands nearby strumming a guitar; everyone is lost in thought. Charlotta wears an old cap; she has taken a rifle off her shoulder and is adjusting the buckle on the strap.

CHARLOTTA [*Pensively*]: I don't have a real passport; I don't know how old I am; and I keep thinking that I'm still young. When I was a little girl, my father and mother went 'round fairs giving performances, very good ones, and I would jump the *salto mortale*[8] and do other things. And when Papa and Mama died, a German lady took me in and began to teach me. I liked it. I grew up and became a governess. But where I come from and who I am, I don't know ... Who my parents are, maybe they weren't married . . . I don't know. [*Takes a cucumber out of her pocket and eats it*] I don't know anything.

A pause.

I feel like talking to someone, but there's no one ... I don't have anyone.

EPIKHODOV [*Strumming the guitar and singing*]: "I care not for the hectic world,/And not for my friends or foes . . ."⁹ How nice it is to play the mandolin!

DUNYASHA: It's a guitar, not a mandolin. [*Looks in a little mirror and powders herself*]

EPIKHODOV: For a madman who's in love, it's a mandolin. [*Sings*] "As long as the heart is warmed by the flames of love returned . . ."

Yasha sings along, too.

CHARLOTTA: These people sing awful ... Foo! Like jackals.

DUNYASHA [*To Yasha*]: How fortunate you are to have been abroad.

YASHA: Yes, of course. I cannot but agree with you there. [*Yawns and lights a cigar*]

EPIKHODOV: That's understandable. Abroad everything has already come to its full complexion.

YASHA: Naturally.

EPIKHODOV: I'm intelligent, I read different remarkable books, but I cannot figure out the course at all, what it is I want—to live or to shoot myself, as a matter of fact; still, I always carry a revolver on me. Here it is . . . [*Shows a revolver*]

CHARLOTTA: I'm done. I'll go now. [*Slings the rifle over her shoulder*] You, Epikhodov, are a very smart man and very frightening. Women must be crazy about you. Brrr! [*Walks*] These know-it-alls are so stupid, nobody to talk to ... I'm always alone, and I've nobody at all ... and who or why I am, nobody knows ... [*Walks away slowly*]

EPIKHODOV: Properly speaking, not touching upon other subjects, I must articulate about myself that, by the way, fate has shown me no pity in her dealings with me, like a storm tossing a small ship. If, suppose, I'm mistaken, then why do I wake up this morning, for example, and find an enormous spider on my chest . . . This big. [*Uses both hands to show the size*] And also, I drink some kvass to quench my thirst, and then in the glass there's bound to be something most indecent, like a roach.

A pause.

Have you read Buckle?[10]

A pause.

I would like to trouble you, Avdotiya Fedorovna, for a couple of words.

DUNYASHA: Speak.

EPIKHODOV: Preferably alone . . . [*Sighs*]

DUNYASHA [*Embarrassed*]: All right, then . . . only first bring me my cape . . . It's by the bookcase . . . it's a little damp here . . .

EPIKHODOV: All right, ma'am . . . I'll go get it, ma'am . . . Now I know what to do with my revolver . . . [*Takes the guitar and walks off strumming it*]

YASHA: Twenty-two disasters! A stupid man, between you and me. [*Yawns*]

DUNYASHA: I hope to goodness he doesn't shoot himself.

A pause.

I've become so anxious; I worry all the time. I was a little girl when they brought me to work in the house, and I'm not used to common life anymore, and my hands are pure white like a lady's. I'm so sensitive and delicate, everything frightens me . . . I'm so afraid. And, Yasha, if you deceive me, I don't know what it'll do to my nerves.

YASHA [*Kisses her*]: A cucumber! Of course, every girl must know her place; there's nothing I dislike more than crude behavior in a girl.

DUNYASHA: I fell madly in love with you; you're educated, you can talk about anything.

A pause.

YASHA [*Yawns*]: Yes, ma'am . . . I think that if a girl loves somebody, then she's already without morals.

A pause.

It's nice to smoke a cigar in the open air . . . [*Listens*] Somebody's coming . . . It's the masters . . .

Dunyasha suddenly embraces him.

Go home, but pretend you went for a dip in the river. Take this path, otherwise you'll run into them and they might think that I was out with you. I can't stand that sort of thing.

DUNYASHA [*Coughing softly*]: I've a headache from the cigar . . . [*She leaves*]

Yasha is sitting alone by the chapel. Enter Liubov Andreyevna, Gaev, and Lopakhin.

LOPAKHIN: You have to make up your mind—no time to waste. It's a simple question. Are you willing to lease the land for summer cottages or not? Just say the word: yes or no? Only one word!

LIUBOV ANDREYEVNA: Who's been smoking revolting cigars here . . . [*Sits down*]

GAEV: They built the railway and made it very convenient now. [*Sits down*] We went to town and had lunch . . . the yellow ball to the middle! I wouldn't mind going in and playing one game . . . [*She looks vexed*]

LIUBOV ANDREYEVNA: Later.

LOPAKHIN: Just one word! [*Imploringly*] Give me an answer!

GAEV [*Yawning*]: Who?

LIUBOV ANDREYEVNA [*Looks in her purse*]: I had a lot of money yesterday, and very little today. My poor Varya, to save money, feeds everybody milk soup; in the kitchen, the old people get only peas, and I'm dropping money senselessly. [*Drops the purse, scattering gold coins*] There, the coins are tumbling out . . . [*She looks vexed*]

YASHA: Allow me to pick them up. [*Picks up the coins*]

LIUBOV ANDREYEVNA. Thank you, Yasha. And why did I have lunch there? . . . That worthless restaurant of yours with music, the tablecloths smell of soap . . . Why do you drink so much, Lionya? Why do you eat so much? Why do you talk so much? And at the restaurant today you talked too much again, and all of it out of place. About the seventies and about the Decadents.[11] And to whom? To the waiters about the Decadents!

LOPAKHIN: Yes.

GAEV [*Waves his hand*]: Obviously, I'm incorrigible . . . [*Irritably to Yasha*] Why are you always in my face . . .

YASHA [*Laughs*]: I can't listen to you without laughing.

GAEV [*To his sister*]: It's either me or him . . .

LIUBOV ANDREYEVNA: Go, Yasha; go . . .

YASHA [*Hands the purse to Liubov Andreyevna*]: I'm going. [*Hardly able to keep from laughing*] Right this minute . . . [*Leaves*]

LOPAKHIN: A rich man, Deriganov, wants to buy your estate. I heard he's coming to the auction himself.

LIUBOV ANDREYEVNA: Where did you hear that?

LOPAKHIN: In town.

GAEV: Our dear aunt from Yaroslavl has promised to send us money, but when or how much no one knows . . .

LOPAKHIN: How much will she send? A hundred thousand? Two hundred?

LIUBOV ANDREYEVNA: Well . . . I'll be grateful if she sends ten or fifteen thousand.

LOPAKHIN: Excuse me, but I have never met anyone so careless, impractical and strange as you. Here I'm telling you in plain language that your estate is up for sale, and it's as if you don't understand.

LIUBOV ANDREYEVNA: What are we to do? Teach us, what?

LOPAKHIN: I've been instructing you every day. Every day I say the same thing over and over. Both the cherry orchard and the land must be leased for summer cottages and do it now, as soon as possible—the auction is around the corner! Can't you understand! Once you make up your mind to lease the land for cottages, they'll give you as much money as you want, and then you'll be saved.

LIUBOV ANDREYEVNA: Summer cottages and summer residents—forgive me, it's so vulgar.

GAEV: I could not agree more with you.

LOPAKHIN: I'm going to cry, scream, or faint. I can't take it anymore! You wore me out! [*To Gaev*] Old woman, that's what you are!

GAEV: Who?

LOPAKHIN: Old woman! [*Wants to leave*]

LIUBOV ANDREYEVNA [*Frightened*]: No, don't leave, my dear. I beg you. Maybe we'll think of something!

LOPAKHIN: What's there to think about?

LIUBOV ANDREYEVNA: Please don't go away. It's more cheerful with you here . . .

A pause.

I keep waiting for something to happen, as if the house is about to collapse on our heads.

GAEV [*In deep thought*]: A bank shot to the corner . . . a *croiser*[12] into the middle. . . .

LIUBOV ANDREYEVNA: We've sinned too much . . .

LOPAKHIN: What sins . . .

GAEV [*Puts a fruit-drop in his mouth*]: They say that I've sucked my estate dry with fruit-drops. [*Laughs*]

LIUBOV ANDREYEVNA: Oh, my sins . . . I've always squandered money, like a mad woman, and married a man who produced nothing but debts. My husband died from champagne—he was a very heavy drinker—and to make matters worse, I fell in love with another man, had an affair, and just at that time—it was my first punishment, a blow straight to the head—my boy drowned, here, in the river . . . , and I went abroad, never to return, never to see this river . . . I closed my eyes and ran, beside myself, but *he* ran after me . . . pitiless, crude. I bought a villa near Mentone because *he* fell ill there, and for three years I knew no rest day or night. The sick man wore me out, and my heart dried up. And last year, when the villa was sold to pay off my debts, I went to Paris, and there he fleeced me, then left me, took up with another woman, I tried to poison myself . . . It was so stupid, so shameful . . . And suddenly it pulled me back to Russia, to my homeland, to my little girl . . . [*Wipes away tears*] Lord, dear God, be merciful, forgive me my sins! Don't punish me anymore! [*Takes a telegram out of her pocket*] I received this today from Paris . . . He asks for forgiveness, begs me to return . . . [*Tears the telegram to pieces*] Is it music I hear? [*Listens*]

GAEV: That is our famous Jewish orchestra. You remember—four violins, a flute, and a double-bass.

LIUBOV ANDREYEVNA: So it still exists? It would be nice to get them to come over sometime, to have a little party.

LOPAKHIN [*Listens*]: I can't hear it . . . [*Sings softly*] "For the right price even Germans will make a Russian French." [*Laughs*] I saw a play at the theatre last night, so funny.

LIUBOV ANDREYEVNA: There is probably nothing funny about it. Instead of plays, you should take a look at yourself more often. You live such a dull life, and all this empty talk.

LOPAKHIN: It's true. Let's face it, our life is stupid . . .

A pause.

My father was a peasant, an idiot; he understood nothing and didn't teach me anything, and only beat me with a stick when drunk. The point is that I am just as much of a dolt and an idiot as he was. I never studied anything; my handwriting is awful, like a pig, I'm ashamed to let people see it!

LIUBOV ANDREYEVNA: You ought to get married, my friend.

LOPAKHIN: Well . . . That's true.

LIUBOV ANDREYEVNA: And to our Varya. She's a nice girl.

LOPAKHIN: Yes.

LIUBOV ANDREYEVNA: She comes from a simple background, works all day long, but most importantly, she loves you. And you yourself have liked her a long time.

LOPAKHIN: Well? I wouldn't mind . . . She's a nice girl.

A pause.

GAEV: I got an offer to work at a bank. Six thousand rubles a year . . . Have you heard?

LIUBOV ANDREYEVNA: You at a bank? Please . . .

Enter Fiers bringing an overcoat.

FIERS [*To Gaev*]: Please, put it on, sir, it's damp.

GAEV [*Putting it on*]: I'm fed up with you, old man.

FIERS: Enough of that . . . You left this morning without telling me. [*Looking carefully over Gaev*]

LIUBOV ANDREYEVNA: You've grown so old, Fiers!

FIERS: What would you like?

LOPAKHIN: She says you've grown very old!

FIERS: I've been around a long time. They were getting ready to marry me off before your father was even born . . . [*Laughs*] I was the head valet when the freedom came.[13] Only I didn't agree to freedom and stayed with the masters . . .

A pause.

I remember everybody was happy, but why, they didn't know.

LOPAKHIN: Sure, it used to be much better. At least they gave us thrashings.

FIERS [*Not hearing*]: I'd say so. Peasants had their masters, and masters had their peasants. But now everyone's apart and you don't know who's who.

GAEV: Keep quiet, Fiers. I've got to go to town tomorrow. I've been promised an introduction to a general who could give us a loan against a promissory note.

LOPAKHIN: Nothing will come of it. And you won't pay off your interest, take my word for it.

LIUBOV ANDREYEVNA: He's delirious. There are no generals.

Enter Trofimov, Anya, and Varya.

GAEV: Here they come.

ANYA: Mama's here.

LIUBOV ANDREYEVNA [*Tenderly*]: Come, come, my dears ... [*Embracing Anya and Varya*] If you two only knew how much I love you. Sit down next to me, like that.

All sit down.

LOPAKHIN: Our eternal student is always walking with the ladies.

TROFIMOV: Mind your own business.

LOPAKHIN: He's pushing fifty and he's still a student.

TROFIMOV: Enough of your stupid jokes.

LOPAKHIN: Why are you, oddball, getting upset?

TROFIMOV: Stop bothering me.[14]

LOPAKHIN [*Laughs*]: May I ask you what you make of me?

TROFIMOV: I think, Ermolai Alexeyevich, that you're a rich man, and you'll be a millionaire soon. You are needed like a predator to eat everything in your way, and keep nature's digestive cycle going.

All laugh.

VARYA: Better tell us about the planets, Petya.

LIUBOV ANDREYEVNA: No, let's continue with yesterday's conversation!

TROFIMOV: About what?

GAEV: About the proud man.

TROFIMOV: Yesterday we talked for a long time but we didn't come to a conclusion. The way you look at it, there's something mystical about the proud man. You may be right in your own way, but if you just think about it, without any monkeyshines, then what pride are we talking about? And if it even makes sense, when physiologically speaking, man is not put together that well, and in the vast majority of cases he's coarse and stupid, and deeply unhappy? We need to stop admiring ourselves. We just need to work.

GAEV: You'll die all the same.

TROFIMOV: Who knows? And what does it mean—you'll die? Maybe a man has a hundred senses and with death only five of those known to us die with him, leaving the remaining ninety-five alive.

LIUBOV ANDREYEVNA: You're so clever, Petya! . . .

LOPAKHIN [*Ironically*]: Oh, awfully!

TROFIMOV: Mankind is pushing forward and perfecting its power. Things that seem unattainable to us now will some day be familiar and obvious, we just need to work and help with all our might those who seek the truth. Meanwhile, here in Russia, there's only a handful of those who work. The vast majority of the educated class I know seek nothing, do nothing, and are still incapable of work. They call themselves intelligentsia, but they talk down to their servants and treat peasants like animals. They don't learn; they don't read anything serious; they don't do anything; all they can do is talk about science, and they understand little in art. They're all so serious, with stern faces, and talk only about important things, but while they go on philosophizing, right in front of our eyes, the workers are eating garbage, sleeping without pillows, thirty or forty to a room, and everywhere bedbugs, stench, dampness, moral squalor . . . And obviously, all our nice talk is only to turn our eyes and the eyes of others away from what is happening. So where are the public day nurseries we hear so much about, and the reading rooms? In the novels, that's where they are; they don't really exist. What exists is dirt, vulgarity, and Asiatic barbarism. . . . I'm afraid of serious faces and I really don't like serious conversations. It would be better to keep quiet!

LOPAKHIN: You know, I get up a little past four every morning and work from morning till night, well, I always have money—my own and other people's—and I see what people are really like. Just try to get something done and you'll find out how few honest, decent people there really are. Sometimes, when I can't fall asleep, I think: Oh Lord, you give us huge forests, colossal fields, endless horizons and living here we ought to be giants ourselves . . .

LIUBOV ANDREYEVNA: Now you want giants . . . Giants are good only in fairy tales; otherwise they frighten us.

Epikhodov walks in the back of the stage playing his guitar.

[*Pensively*] Epikhodov's coming . . .

ANYA [*Pensively*]: Epikhodov's coming . . .

GAEV: The sun's set, ladies and gentlemen.

TROFIMOV: Yes.

GAEV [*Not loudly, as if declaiming*]: Oh, nature, glorious nature, you shine with eternal radiance, beautiful and indifferent; you're the one we call mother, and you combine in yourself being and death; you sustain life and you destroy . . .

VARYA [*Imploringly*]: Uncle, dear!

ANYA: Uncle, you're at it again!

TROFIMOV: You'd better stick to the yellow to the middle with a bank.

GAEV: I'll keep quiet, I'll keep quiet.

> *They all sit pensively. It's quiet. Only Fiers's mumbling is heard. Suddenly a distant sound is heard, as if coming from the sky, a string breaking; the sound dies mournfully.*

LIUBOV ANDREYEVNA: What's that?

LOPAKHIN: I don't know. Maybe a bucket breaking loose somewhere far away in a mine. But it's very far away.

GAEV: Or maybe it's a bird . . . like a heron.

TROFIMOV: Or an owl . . .

LIUBOV ANDREYEVNA [*Shudders*]: It's very unpleasant somehow.

> *A pause.*

FIERS: Before the disaster, the same thing happened; an owl hooted and a samovar kept humming day and night.

GAEV: Before what disaster?

FIERS: Before freedom.

> *A pause.*

LIUBOV ANDREYEVNA: You know, my friends, let's go in; it's getting dark. [*To Anya*] You have tears in your eyes . . . What is it, my girl? [*Embraces her*]

ANYA. It's nothing, Mama.

TROFIMOV: Someone's coming.

> *Enter Passerby in an old white worn-out cap and overcoat. He is a little drunk.*

PASSERBY: Could you kindly tell me if I can I get to the station through here?

GAEV: You can. Stay on this road.

PASSERBY: I thank you from the bottom of my heart. [*After coughing*] Lovely weather . . . [*Recites*] "Brother, long-suffering brother! Come down to the Volga, whose groan . . ."[15] [*To Varya*] Mademoiselle, please give a hungry Russian thirty kopecks . . .

Varya is frightened, she screams.

LOPAKHIN [*Angrily*]: Every disgrace must know its place!

LIUBOV ANDREYEVNA [*Startled*]: Take this . . . here you are . . . [*Feels in her purse*] I don't have silver . . . It doesn't matter, here's a gold piece . . .

PASSERBY: Deeply grateful! [*Leaves*]

Laughter.

VARYA [*Frightened*]: I'm leaving, I'm leaving . . . Oh, Mamochka, at home there's nothing to eat, and you give him a gold piece.

LIUBOV ANDREYEVNA: What am I to do with myself, fool that I am? At home I'll give you everything I've got. Ermolai Alexeyevich, won't you lend me some more! . . .

LOPAKHIN: As you wish.

LIUBOV ANDREYEVNA: Let's go, it's time. And Varya, we've arranged a match for you; congratulations.

VARYA [*Through tears*]: It's not a joke, Mama.

LOPAKHIN: O-varya, get thee to a nunnery . . .

GAEV: My hands are trembling; I haven't played billiards in a long time.

LOPAKHIN: O-varya, oh, nymph, remember me in thy orisons!

LIUBOV ANDREYEVNA: Let's go, ladies and gentlemen. It's almost suppertime.

VARYA: He frightened me. My heart's still pounding.

LOPAKHIN: I want to remind you, ladies and gentlemen, that on the twenty-second of August, the cherry orchard will be sold. Think about it! . . . Think! . . .

All leave with the exception of Trofimov and Anya.

ANYA [*Laughing*]: Thanks to the passerby who frightened Varya, we're alone now.

TROFIMOV: Varya's afraid that we might fall in love with each other and follows us everywhere. She is narrow-minded and can't see that we're above love. The goal and purpose of our lives is to escape all petty and illusory things, which prevent us from being happy and free. Onward! We move irresistibly towards a bright star burning there in the distance! Onward! Don't fall behind, friends!

ANYA [*Clapping her hands*]: You speak so well!

> *A pause.*

It's delightful here today!

TROFIMOV: Yes, the weather is wonderful.

ANYA: You have done something to me, Petya, that has made me love the cherry orchard less than I used to. I loved it so tenderly, and I used to think there was no better place on earth than our orchard.

TROFIMOV: All of Russia is our orchard. The Earth is grand and beautiful, and there are many wonderful places.

> *A pause.*

Anya, just think about it: Your grandfather, your great-grandfather, and all your ancestors owned serfs; they owned living souls. Can't you see these human beings looking at you from every cherry in the orchard, from every leaf and every trunk? Can't you hear their voices . . . ? Owning lives has distorted all of you—those who lived before and those who are living now—to such an extent that your mother and you and your uncle don't notice anymore that you're living on credit, at the expense of others, at the expense of those whom you don't even let in past the entryway . . . We're behind at least two hundred years, we have nothing yet, no real understanding of the past, all we do is philosophize, complain of hopelessness, or drink vodka. And yet it is so clear that to live in the present, we need to redeem our past and break away from it, and the only way we can redeem it is by suffering and by extraordinary and relentless labor. Try to understand that, Anya.

ANYA: The house we're living in has long ago ceased to be our house. I will leave it, take my word.

TROFIMOV: If you have the keys to the household, throw them down the well and walk away. Be as free as the wind.

ANYA [*Thrilled*]: You said it so well!

TROFIMOV: Believe me, Anya, believe me! I'm not thirty yet, and I'm young and still a student, but I've already been through so much! Like winter, that's how hungry I am, ailing, anxious, poor like a pauper, tossed about everywhere by life! And yet my soul has always, every minute, day and night been filled with inexplicable feelings. I sense happiness, Anya, I can already see it . . .

ANYA [*Pensively*]: The moon's on the rise.

> *Epikhodov's playing his guitar. It's the same sad song. The moon rises.*
> *Somewhere by the poplars Varya is looking for Anya and calling, "Anya,*
> *where are you?"*

TROFIMOV: Yes, the moon's on the rise.

> *A pause.*

Here it is, happiness, here it comes; closer and closer, and I can even hear its steps. And so what if we don't see it and don't know it? Others will see it!

> *Varya's voice: Anya! Where are you?*

That Varya again! [*Sternly*] It's infuriating!

ANYA: Well? Let's go to the river. It's nice there.

TROFIMOV: Let's go.

> *They leave.*
>
> *Varya's voice: "Anya! Anya!"*
>
> *Curtain.*

ACT THREE

> *A drawing room separated from a ballroom by an arch. The chandelier is*
> *lighted. Sounds of a Jewish orchestra, the one mentioned in Act Two, are*
> *coming from the entryway. Evening. In the ballroom—they are dancing*
> *grand-rond. Simyonov-Pischik's voice: "Promenadeà une paire!" Coming*
> *into the drawing room: the first pair are Pischik and Charlotta Ivanovna;*
> *the second, Trofimov and Liubov Andreyevna; the third, Anya and the Post*
> *Office Official; the fourth, Varya and the Stationmaster, and so on. Varya*
> *is crying quietly and wipes away tears as she dances. Dunyasha is in the*
> *last pair. They cross the drawing room and Pischik shouts, "Grand-rond,*
> *balancez!" and "Les cavaliers à genoux et remerciez vos dames!"*
>
> *Fiers, in swallowtail, is bringing in a tray with seltzer water. Enter Pischik*
> *and Trofimov from the ballroom.*

PISCHIK: I'm full-blooded and have had two strokes already. Dancing's hard for me, but, as they say, when running with dogs, barking or not, you've got to wag your tail. I'm as healthy as a horse. My late father, a real joker,

may he rest in peace, used to say that our ancient family line of Simyonov-Pischik descended from the very horse that Caligula made senator . . . [*Sits down*] But the trouble is, we've no money! A hungry dog
believes only in meat. [*Snores and wakes up again immediately*] Same
with me . . . it's all . . . about money . . .

TROFIMOV: There is, indeed, something horselike in your figure.

PISCHIK: Well . . . a horse is a good animal . . . you can sell it . . .

> *In the next room the sounds of billiard playing are heard. Varya appears
> through the arch.*

TROFIMOV [*Teasing*]: Madame Lopakhin! Madame Lopakhin!

VARYA [*Angry*]: A mangy gentleman!

TROFIMOV: Yes, I am a mangy gentleman and I'm proud of it!

VARYA [*Pensive, with bitterness*]: There, hired the musicians, but who is going
to pay them? [*Goes out*]

TROFIMOV [*To Pischik*]: If in the course of your life, the energy you spend trying to find money to pay off the interest had been used for something
else, then you would've been able to turn the earth on its axis.

PISCHIK: Nietzsche . . . the philosopher . . . the greatest, the most celebrated
man . . . a man of immense intellect, writes that it's all right to forge
bank notes.

TROFIMOV: You've read Nietzsche?

PISCHIK: Well . . . Dashenka was telling me. Now I'm in a situation when I
might have to forge them . . . Three hundred and ten rubles are due
the day after tomorrow . . . I've got one hundred and thirty already . . .
[*Feels his pockets, nervously*] The money is gone! I've lost the money!
[*Through tears*] Where's the money? [*Joyfully*] Here it is, under the lin-
ing . . . I've even broken into a sweat . . .

> *Enter Liubov Andreyevna and Charlotta Ivanovna.*

LIUBOV ANDREYEVNA [*Humming a lezginka*[16]]: Why isn't Leonid back yet?
What's he doing in town? [*To Dunyasha*] Dunyasha, offer the musicians
some tea . . .

TROFIMOV: The auction's off, I suppose.

LIUBOV ANDREYEVNA: The musicians are out of place and the dancing party
is out of place . . . Well, never mind. . . . [*Sits down and sings softly*]

CHARLOTTA [*Shows a deck of cards to Pischik*]: Here's a deck of cards. Think
of a card, any card.

PISCHIK: All right.

CHARLOTTA: Now shuffle the deck. All right, now. Give it back to me, my dear
Mr. Pischik. *Ein, zwei, drei!*[17] Now look for it in your side pocket . . .

PISCHIK [*Takes a card out of his pocket*]: Eight of spades, exactly right!
[*Amazed*] Imagine that!

CHARLOTTA [*To Trofimov while holding the deck of cards on the palm of her
hand*]: Now tell me quickly what the top card is.

TROFIMOV: Why not? Well, the Queen of spades.

CHARLOTTA: Right! [*To Pischik*] Well now? What's the top card?

PISCHIK: The ace of hearts.

CHARLOTTA: Right! [*Claps her hands and the cards vanish*] Nice weather today.

   A mysterious woman's voice answers her, as if coming from under the floor,
   "Oh, yes, the weather is lovely, madam."

   You are so good, my ideal . . .

   The voice: "I likes you too, madam, very much."[18]

STATIONMASTER [*Applauds*]: Madame the Ventriloquist, bravo!

PISCHIK [*Amazed*]: Imagine that! The most charming Charlotta Ivanovna . . .
I'm simply in love . . .

CHARLOTTA: In love? [*Shrugging her shoulders*] Are you capable of love? Guter
Mensch aber schlechter Musikant.[19]

TROFIMOV [*Slaps Pischik on the shoulder*]: What a horse you are . . .

CHARLOTTA: May I have your attention please! One more magic trick. [*Takes
a shawl off a chair*] Here's a very nice shawl, I vish sell it . . . [*Shakes it*]
Anybody wish buy?

PISCHIK [*Amazed*]: Imagine that!

CHARLOTTA: Ein, zwei, drei. [*She lifts up the shawl quickly. Anya is standing
behind it; she curtsies and runs to her mother, hugs her and runs back to
the ballroom amid general delight of the audience.*]

LIUBOV ANDREYEVNA [*Applauds*]: Bravo, bravo!

CHARLOTTA: Once again! *Ein, zwei, drei!* [*Lifts the shawl. Varya stands behind
it and takes a bow.*]

PISCHIK [*Amazed*]: Imagine that!

CHARLOTTA: The end! [*Throws the shawl at Pischik, curtseys and runs into the
ballroom*]

PISCHIK [*Hurries after her*]: What a temptress . . . How do you like that? Huh?
[*Goes out*]

LIUBOV ANDREYEVNA: Leonid isn't back yet. What's he doing in town so long, I don't understand! Everything must be over by now. Whether the estate's been sold or the auction's called off, why keep us in the dark so long!

VARYA [*Tries to comfort her*]: Uncle, dear, bought it. I'm sure he did.

TROFIMOV [*Sarcastically*]: Yes.

VARYA: Grandmother sent him power of attorney to buy it in her name and transfer the debt to her. She's doing it for Anya. And I'm sure, with God's help, Uncle will buy it.

LIUBOV ANDREYEVNA: The Yaroslavl grandmother sent fifteen thousand rubles to buy the property in her name—she doesn't trust us—and the money wouldn't have covered even the interest. [*Covers her face with her hands*] My fate is being decided today, my fate . . .

TROFIMOV [*Teasing Varya*]: Madame Lopakhina!

VARYA [*Angry*]: Eternal student! Expelled twice from the university already.[20]

LIUBOV ANDREYEVNA: Why are you so upset, Varya? He's teasing you about Lopakhin; well, so what? You can marry Lopakhin if you want to, he's a good, striking man . . . You don't have to if you don't want to, sweetie; nobody's forcing you . . .

VARYA: To be honest, Mamochka, I'm very serious about it. He's a good man, and I like him.

LIUBOV ANDREYEVNA: Then marry him. I don't understand what you're waiting for!

VARYA: I can't exactly propose to him myself, Mamochka. For two years now, everybody's been talking to me about him; everybody, but he either says nothing, or jokes about it. I understand, he's getting rich; he's busy with work, and he can't be bothered with me. If I had money, even a little, even if only a hundred rubles, I'd leave everything and go as far away as possible. I'd enter a convent.

TROFIMOV: So heaven-like!

VARYA [*To Trofimov*]: Students are supposed to be intelligent! [*Softly with tears in her voice*] You've become so homely, Petya, and so old! [*To Lubov Andreyevna, no longer crying*] I can't stand still for a moment, Mamochka. I have to do something all the time.

Enter Yasha.

YASHA [*Hardly able to keep from laughing*]: Epikhodov broke a billiard cue! . . .
[*Goes out*]

VARYA: Why is Epikhodov here? Who told him he could play billiards? I don't
understand these people . . . [*Goes out*]

LIUBOV ANDREYEVNA: Don't tease her, Petya. She's heartbroken as it is.

TROFIMOV: She's overly zealous and keeps sticking her nose in other people's
business. All summer long, she wouldn't leave Anya and me in peace for
fear that we might fall in love. What's it to her? I never gave her a reason
to think that; I'm not so low. We're above love!

LIUBOV ANDREYEVNA: Then I'm beneath love. [*Greatly agitated*] Why isn't
Leonid back? I just need to know: has the estate been sold or not? The
disaster seems so unlikely that I don't know *what* to think, I'm confused . . . I might scream now . . . or do something stupid. Save me,
Petya. Keep talking, keep talking . . .

TROFIMOV: Whether the estate has been sold today or not, what does it matter? It's been over for a long time, and there's no turning back; the path
is grown over. Calm down, my dear. And don't fool yourself, do, at least
once in your life, look truth in the eyes.

LIUBOV ANDREYEVNA: Which truth? You can tell truth from untruth, but I
feel as if I've lost my sight, I don't see anything. You're fearlessly solving
ever-important questions, but tell me, darling, isn't it because you're
young and you haven't lived and suffered through a single one of your
questions? Isn't the reason you so bravely look ahead that you can't
foresee or expect anything terrible ever happening, because life is still
hidden from your young eyes? You're more honest, braver, and deeper
than we are, but just think about it and try to be more magnanimous,
even if just a tad, and spare me. After all, I was born here, my father, my
mother, and my grandfather all lived here, I love this house, and I can't
imagine my life without the cherry orchard, and if you absolutely need
to sell it, then sell me together with it . . . [*Embraces Trofimov, kisses his
forehead*] After all, my son drowned here . . . [*Cries*] Good, kind man,
have pity on me.

TROFIMOV: I feel for you with all my heart.

LIUBOV ANDREYEVNA: But you need to say it differently, differently . . . [*Takes
out a handkerchief, and a telegram falls on the floor*] I'm so heavy-
hearted today, you can't imagine. It's too noisy for me here, and my

heart shivers at every sound, I shiver all over, and yet I can't go to my room: I'm afraid of being in silence by myself. Don't judge me, Petya . . . I love you like family. I'd gladly give Anya to you in marriage, I swear; only, my dear boy, you need to go back to your studies, finish them. You're not doing anything; life tosses you about from place to place; this is all so strange . . . Isn't it? See? And you must do something about your beard to make it grow or something . . . [*Laughs*] You are so funny!

TROFIMOV [*Picking up the telegram*] I've no desire to look handsome.

LIUBOV ANDREYEVNA: The telegram's from Paris. I get one every day. Yesterday and today. That wild man has fallen ill again, he isn't well . . . He begs me to forgive him, implores me to come back; and perhaps I should go to Paris to be near him. Petya, you're making a stern face, but what can I do, my dear, if he's ill, lonely, and unhappy, and who is there to look after him, who's to keep him from making mistakes and give him his medicine on time? And why conceal it and keep it to myself if clearly I love him. I love, I love him . . . It's a weight around my neck and I'm going down to the bottom with it, but I love this weight and can't live without it. [*Squeezes Trofimov's hand*] Don't think badly of me, Petya, and don't say anything to me, don't . . .

TROFIMOV [*Through tears*] Forgive my frankness, but for God's sake, the man has fleeced you!

LIUBOV ANDREYEVNA: No, no, no, you shouldn't say that! [*Covers her ears with her hands*]

TROFIMOV: But he's a scoundrel, you alone don't know it! He's a petty scoundrel, a nobody . . .

LIUBOV ANDREYEVNA [*Angry, but restrained*]: You're maybe twenty-six or twenty-seven, but you are still a schoolboy!

TROFIMOV: So!

LIUBOV ANDREYEVNA: You have to be a man at your age and understand those who love. And yourself know how to love . . . and fall in love! [*Sternly*] Yes! You are not pure; you are just a prude, a silly oddball, a freak . . .

TROFIMOV [*In horror*] What is she saying?!

LIUBOV ANDREYEVNA: "I'm above love!" You're not above love, you're what our Fiers calls a nincompoop. At your age not to have a mistress! . . .

TROFIMOV [*Horrified*]: This is awful! What is she saying?! [*Walks quickly toward the ballroom, clutching his head*] This is awful . . . I can't take it, I'm leaving ... [*Goes out, but returns at once*] It's all over between us! [*Walks into the entryway*]

LIUBOV ANDREYEVNA [*Shouts after him*]: Petya, wait! You're silly, I was only joking! Petya!

Sounds of somebody going up the stairs and falling suddenly with a crash in the entryway. Anya and Varya scream; then immediately laughter is heard.

What's going on there?

Anya runs in.

ANYA: Petya fell down the stairs! [*Runs out*]

LIUBOV ANDREYEVNA: He's such an oddball, this Petya ...

The Stationmaster stops in the middle of the drawing room and recites "The Sinner Woman" by A. Tolstoy.[21] *People listen to him but as soon as he delivers a few lines, the sounds of a waltz are heard coming from the entryway, and the recitation abruptly ends. Everybody dances. Trofimov, Anya, Varya, and Liubov Andreyevna walk in from the entryway.*

Please, Petya ... pure soul ... please forgive me ... Let's go dance ... [*She dances with Petya*]

Anya and Varya are dancing.

Fiers enters and leans his stick by a side door. Yasha has also come in from the drawing room and is watching the dancers.

YASHA: What, grandpa?

FIERS: Not feeling well. Before, generals and barons, and admirals used to dance at our balls, and now we're sending for the post office official and the stationmaster, and even they aren't too eager to come. I'm feeling weak somehow. The late master, the grandfather, would give us all sealing wax when we got sick. I take sealing wax every day for twenty years now, maybe more. Maybe that's why I'm still around.

YASHA: I'm fed up with you, grandpa. [*Yawns*] Hurry up and croak already.

FIERS: Oh, you ... nincompoop! [*Mutters*]

Trofimov and Liubov Andreyevna dance in the ballroom, then in the drawing room.

LIUBOV ANDREYEVNA: *Merci.* I'll sit it down ... [*Sits down*] I'm tired.

Enter Anya.

ANYA [*Agitated*]: Someone in the kitchen just said that the cherry orchard was already sold today.

LIUBOV ANDREYEVNA: Sold to whom?

ANYA. He didn't say to whom. He left. [*Dances with Trofimov out into the ballroom*]

YASHA: Some old man just wagging his tongue. Not one of ours.

FIERS: And Leonid Andreyich[22] isn't back; hasn't come back yet. He went out in a light overcoat; might catch a cold. Oh, too young, too green to know any better!

LIUBOV ANDREYEVNA: I can't take this. Go, Yasha, and find out who bought it.

YASHA: Oh, but the old man, he left a long time ago. [*Laughs*]

LIUBOV ANDREYEVNA [*Slightly vexed*]: What are you laughing about? Why so happy?

YASHA: Epikhodov's too funny. A stupid man. Twenty-two disasters.

LIUBOV ANDREYEVNA: Fiers, if they sell the estate, where will you go?

FIERS: Wherever you tell me to go.

LIUBOV ANDREYEVNA: You don't look good. Are you sick? Why don't you just go to bed . . .

FIERS: Sure . . . [*With a sneer*] I go to bed, and who'll serve, who'll take charge without me? It's just me for the whole house.

YASHA [*To Liubov Andreyevna*]: Lubov Andreyevna, may I ask you a favor, please? If you go to Paris again, please take me with you; I beg you, please. I positively can't stay here. [*Looking around, in an undertone*] Do I need to tell you? You see for yourself: the country is uneducated, the people have no morals, and it's boring, and the food they serve in the kitchen is awful, and on top of it, here's Fiers walking around mumbling inappropriate things. Would you please take me with you!

Enter Pischik.

PISCHIK: Allow me to ask you . . . for this little tiny waltz, my gorgeous . . . [*Liubov Andreyevna walks with him*] My charmer, all the same, I will borrow one hundred and eighty rubles from you . . . I will . . . [*He dances*] A mere one hundred and eighty rubles . . .

They move into the ballroom.

YASHA [*Sings softly*]: "Will you, oh ever, understand the torment deep inside my heart . . . ?"[23]

In the ballroom, a figure wearing a gray top hat and baggy plaid trousers is jumping and waving its hands about; there are cries of "Bravo, Charlotta Ivanovna!"

DUNYASHA [*Stops to powder her face*]: The young miss wants me to dance— there're a lot of gentlemen and only a few ladies—but my head's spinning from all this dancing, and my heart's pounding, Fiers Niko- layevich, the official from the post office said something to me just now that took my breath away.

The music grows faint.

FIERS: So what did he say to you?

DUNYASHA: He says, "You're like a flower."

YASHA [*Yawns*]: The ignorance . . . [*He leaves*]

DUNYASHA: Like a flower . . . I'm such a delicate girl; I just love sweet words.

FIERS: It'll be your undoing.

Enter Epikhodov.

EPIKHODOV: Avdotiya Fedorovna, you don't want to see me . . . as if I was some kind of insect. [*Sighs*] This life!

DUNYASHA: What is it you want?

EPIKHODOV: Undoubtedly, maybe you are right. [*Sighs*] But, certainly, if you look at it from the point of view, then you, if I may say so, for- give my frankness, have absolutely reduced me to a state of mind. I know my luck, every day a new disaster befalls me, but I got used to it long ago, and I face my fate with a smile. You gave me your word, and although I . . .

DUNYASHA: Please, we'll talk later, but now, leave me alone. I'm dreaming now. [*Plays with her fan*]

EPIKHODOV: I have a disaster every day, and I, if I may say so, only smile, and even laugh at it.

Varya comes in from the ballroom.

VARYA: You are still here, Semyon? You have no respect. [*To Dunyasha*] You go, Dunyasha. [*To Epikhodov*] First, you play billiards and break a cue, and then you walk about the drawing room like an invited guest!

EPIKHODOV: You can't, if I may express myself thus, exact anything from me.

VARYA: I'm not exacting anything from you, I'm only telling you. All you ever do is walk around and never do your job. We hired a clerk, but what for—we don't know.

EPIKHODOV [*Offended*]: Whether I work or walk or eat or play billiards is for my superiors and those in the know to decide.

VARYA: You dare talk to me like that! [*Furious*] You dare? Are you saying I don't know anything? Get out of here! Right now!

EPIKHODOV [*Cowardly*]: I must ask you to be more delicate in expressing yourself.

VARYA [*Losing her composure*]: Get out this minute! Get out! Out!

He goes to the door, she follows.

Twenty-two disasters! Get out of my sight! I don't ever want to see you again!

Epikhodov has gone out; his voice can be heard outside: "I'll lodge a complaint against you."

Ah, coming back? [*Picks up the stick, which Fiers had left standing by the door*] Come on, come on, I'll show you . . . So you're coming in? Well, then take that. [*She brings the stick down as Lopakhin enters*]

LOPAKHIN: Much obliged.

VARYA [*Angry but derisively*]: Sorry!

LOPAKHIN: Never mind, ma'am. Much obliged for a pleasant treat.

VARYA: Don't mention it. [*Walks away, then looks back and asks gently*] Did I hurt you?

LOPAKHIN: No, it's all right. I'll have a huge bump, though.

Voices from the ballroom: Lopakhin is back! Ermolai Alexeyevich!

PISCHIK: I see him, I hear him. [*Kisses Lopakhin*] I smell a little cognac, my dearest friend. But we, too, are having a party.

Enter Liubov Andreyevna.

LIUBOV ANDREYEVNA: Is that you, Ermolai Alexeyevich? What took so long? Where's Leonid?

LOPAKHIN: Leonid Andreyevich came back with me, he's coming . . .

LIUBOV ANDREYEVNA [*Excited*]: Well, and? Was there an auction? Tell me!

LOPAKHIN [*Confused, afraid to show his joy*]: The auction ended by four o'clock . . . We missed the train, and had to wait till nine-thirty. [*Sighs heavily*] Ooph! My head's spinning a little . . .

Enter Gaev. In his right hand he is holding his purchases, with his left he wipes away his tears.

LIUBOV ANDREYEVNA: Lionya, and? Lionya, well? [*Impatiently, in tears*] Quickly, for God's sake . . .

GAEV [*Says nothing to her, only waves his hand; to Fiers, crying*]: Here, take this . . . Here are anchovies, Crimean herring . . . I haven't eaten today . . . Oh, how I've suffered today!

The door to the billiard room is open; the clicking of the balls is heard, and Yasha's voice, "Seven and eighteen!" Gaev's facial expression changes, and he is no longer crying.

I'm awfully tired. Fiers, bring me some clothes to change into. [*Goes out through the ballroom to his room; Fiers follows him*]

PISCHIK: What happened at the auction? Tell us!

LIUBOV ANDREYEVNA: Has the cherry orchard been sold?

LOPAKHIN: It has.

LIUBOV ANDREYEVNA: Who bought it?

LOPAKHIN: I did.

Pause.

Liubov Andreyevna, dispirited, would fall if she were not standing by an armchair and a table. Varya takes the keys off her belt, throws them on the floor in the middle of the drawing room and goes out.

LOPAKHIN: I bought it! Wait, ladies and gentlemen, please, I feel lightheaded, I can't talk . . . [*Laughs*] We came to the auction, and Deriganov was there already. Leonid Andreyevich only had fifteen thousand rubles, and Deriganov, to begin with, tossed another thirty on top of the debt. When I saw it, I locked in with him and bid forty. He bids forty-five, I—fifty-five. He raises it by five but I up it by ten . . . Well, then it was over. I gave ninety above the debt, and I got it. The cherry orchard is mine now, it's mine! [*Bursts out laughing*] My God, the cherry orchard's mine! Tell me that I'm drunk, that I'm out of my mind, or that I'm dreaming . . . [*Stamps his feet*] Don't laugh at me! If only my father and grandfather could rise from their grave to see the whole thing, see their trampled, illiterate Ermolai, their Ermolai, who ran around barefoot in winter, how that same Ermolai has bought the estate, the most beautiful thing in the world. I bought the estate where my grandfather and my father were slaves, where they weren't even allowed in the kitchen. I'm dreaming; I'm imagining it . . . It's a figment of your imagination veiled in obscurity . . . [*Picks up the keys, smiling affectionately*] She threw down the keys to show that she's no longer the mistress of the house . . . [*Jingles the keys*] Well, it doesn't matter.

The sounds of the orchestra's tuning up are heard.

Eh, musicians, play, I wish to hear you! Come, all of you, watch Ermolai Lopakhin take an axe to the cherry orchard and the trees fall to the ground! We'll build summer cottages, and our grandchildren and great-grandchildren will see here a new life . . . Music, play on!

The band plays: Liubov Andreyevna sinks into a chair and weeps bitterly.

[*With reproach*] Why didn't you, why didn't you listen to me? My poor, dear lady, now you can't get it back. [*With tears*] Oh, how I want all this to be over and for our ungainly and unhappy life to change somehow.

PISCHIK [*Takes Lopakhin by the arm and half-whispers*]: She's crying. Let's go into the ballroom and leave her here by herself . . . Come . . . [*Takes him by the arm and escorts him out*]

LOPAKHIN: What's going on? Music, play distinctly! I want everything my way! [*With irony*] Here comes the new landowner, the new owner of the cherry orchard! [*He accidentally bumps into a little table, almost knocking down the candelabra*] I can pay for it all! [*Leaves the room with Pischik*]

There is no one in either the ballroom or the drawing room besides Liubov Andreyevna; she sits huddled over and crying bitterly. The music plays softly. Anya and Trofimov enter quickly. Anya walks up to her mother and kneels before her. Trofimov remains by the entrance to the ballroom.

ANYA: Mama! . . . Mama, are you crying? My dear, kind, good, and beautiful Mama, I love you . . . I bless you! The cherry orchard is sold, it's no more, and that's true, that's true, but don't cry Mama; you've got your life ahead of you, and you still have your good and pure soul . . . Come with me, my dear, come away from here, come! . . . We'll plant a new orchard, even more gorgeous than this one, you will see it, you'll understand, and a deep and gentle joy will envelop your heart, like the sun in the evening, and, Mama, you'll smile! Come, my dear! Come! . . .

Curtain.

ACT FOUR

The same set as in Act One. There are no curtains on the windows and no paintings on the walls; only a few pieces of furniture are piled up in the corner as if for sale. It feels empty. By the main entrance, and in the back of the stage, suitcases, bags, etc. are piled up. The door on the left is open, and Varya's and Anya's voices can be heard. Lopakhin stands waiting. Yasha holds a tray with small glasses of champagne. In the entryway, Epikhodov is tying up a box. A hum of voices is heard coming from behind the stage. It's peasants who have come to say good-bye. Gaev's voice: "Thank you, dear fellows, thank you."

YASHA: The simple folks have come to say good-bye. I'm of the opinion, Ermolai Alexeyevich, that they're kind people, but they don't know much.

The hum dies down. Liubov Andreyevna and Gaev come in from the entryway. She is not crying but her face is pale and trembling; and she is unable to speak.

GAEV: You gave them your purse, Liuba. You can't do that, you can't!

LIUBOV ANDREYEVNA: I couldn't help it! I couldn't help it!

They both leave.

LOPAKHIN [*Through the doorway, calling after them*]: Please, kindly oblige! Have a glass of champagne in parting. I didn't think to bring any from town and they only had one bottle at the station. Here!

A pause.

Well, then, ladies and gentlemen! You won't have any? [*Moves away from the door*] Had I known—I wouldn't have bought it. Well, I won't drink it either.

Yasha carefully puts the tray on a chair.

Yasha, at least you have some.

YASHA: Here's to those departing! Good luck! [*Drinks*] I can assure you, this is not real champagne.

LOPAKHIN: Eight rubles a bottle.

A pause.

It's cold as hell here.

YASHA: They didn't light the stoves today, we're going away anyway. [*Laughs*]

LOPAKHIN: What's with you?

YASHA: I'm happy.

LOPAKHIN: It's October, but it's sunny and quiet like in summertime. It's good weather for building. [*After looking at his watch and speaking through the door*] Ladies and gentlemen, remember that we only have forty-six minutes before the train! This means that in twenty minutes we have to leave for the station. Hurry up.

Trofimov comes in from outside wearing an overcoat.

TROFIMOV: I think it's time to go. Carriages are waiting. Where the hell are my galoshes? I've lost them. [*Through the door*] Anya, I don't have my galoshes! I haven't found them!

LOPAKHIN: And I've got to go to Kharkov. I'm taking the same train as you. I'll spend the winter in Kharkov. I've been hanging 'round with you all, and I'm worn out by doing nothing. I can't live without work, I don't know what to do here with my hands; they're hanging about like they don't even belong to me.

TROFIMOV: We'll leave and you'll go back to your useful work.

LOPAKHIN: Here, drink a glass.[24]

TROFIMOV: I'm not going to.

LOPAKHIN: So you're off to Moscow now?

TROFIMOV: Yes. I'll see them to town and tomorrow I'm off to Moscow.

LOPAKHIN: Well . . . The professors have stopped giving lectures waiting for you to show up!

TROFIMOV: That's none of your business.

LOPAKHIN: How many years have you been studying at the university?

TROFIMOV: Think of something new. That's stale and falls flat. [*Looking for his galoshes*] You know, since we may never see each other again, in parting, let me give you a word of advice: Don't wave your arms about! Break the habit of waving your arms. And this building summer cottages, expecting their residents to become individual landowners in time—it's the same as waving your arms . . . You know, no matter what, I still love you. You have the long, fine fingers of an artist, and a fine and sensitive soul . . .

LOPAKHIN [*Embraces him*]: Good-bye, my dear. Thank you for everything. If you need, here, take some money from me for the journey.

TROFIMOV: What for? I don't need it.

LOPAKHIN: But you don't have any!

TROFIMOV: Yes, I do. Thank you very much. I got paid for a translation. It's right here in my pocket. [*Nervously*] But not my galoshes!

VARYA [*From the other room*]: Take this gross thing out! [*Throws a pair of rubber galoshes on the stage*]

TROFIMOV: Why are you so upset, Varya? Hmm . . . These aren't my galoshes!

LOPAKHIN: In the spring I planted poppies, three thousand acres, and made forty thousand profit, net. And when my poppies were in bloom, what a beautiful sight it was! So, as I was saying, I made forty thousand, and I'm offering you a loan because I can. Why turn up your nose at it? I'm a peasant, a muzhik . . . pure and simple.

TROFIMOV: Your father was a peasant, mine was a pharmacist, and it means absolutely nothing.

Lopakhin takes out his wallet.

Leave it, leave it . . . Even if you were to give me two hundred thousand, I wouldn't take it. I'm a free man. And everything that you all, rich and poor, value so highly and dearly has no sway over me; it's just fluff floating in the air. I can make it without you and I can walk right past you: I'm strong and proud. Mankind's moving toward a higher truth and happiness on earth, and I'm in the vanguard!

LOPAKHIN: Will you get there?

TROFIMOV: I will.

A pause.

I'll either get there or show others the way to get there.

In the distance, sounds of axes striking the trees are heard.

LOPAKHIN: Well, farewell, my dear. Time to go. Here we stand, turning up our noses at each other, but life passes by just the same. When I work for long stretches of time, without getting tired, my thoughts are lighter, and I think I understand why I exist. But how many people in Russia exist without a good reason. Well, it doesn't matter; but it's not the way things circulate. They say Leonid Andreyich accepted a position at the bank; six thousand a year . . . Except he won't last there; he's too lazy . . .

ANYA [*At the door*]: Mama is asking you: do not chop down the orchard until after she leaves.

TROFIMOV: Yes, really, how tactless . . . [*Exits through the entry way*]

LOPAKHIN: Yes, yes . . . So touchy. [*Exits after him*]

ANYA: Have they taken Fiers to the hospital?

YASHA: I told them this morning. I imagine they have.

ANYA [*To Epikhodov, who crosses the room*]: Semyon Panteleyevich, please find
out if they took Fiers to the hospital.

YASHA [*Offended*]: I told Egor this morning. What's the point of asking ten
times!

EPIKHODOV: In my conclusive opinion, the aged Fiers isn't worth mending;
he needs to join his forefathers. And I can only envy him. [*Puts a suitcase on a hatbox and squashes it*] Well, of course. I knew it. [*Exits*]

YASHA [*Derisively*]: Twenty-two disasters . . .

VARYA [*From behind the door*]: Have they taken Fiers to the hospital?

ANYA: Yes, they have.

VARYA: Then why didn't they take the letter for the doctor?

ANYA: We'll have to send it after . . . [*Exits*]

VARYA [*In the next room*]: Where's Yasha? Tell him his mother's here and wants
to say good-bye.

YASHA [*Waving his hand*]: Trying my patience.

*Dunyasha has been busy with the luggage. Now that Yasha is alone, she
goes up to him.*

DUNYASHA: You've not once looked in my direction, Yasha. You're leaving . . .
abandoning me . . . [*Weeps and throws herself around his neck.*]

YASHA: Why cry? [*Drinks champagne*] In six days I'll be back in Paris. Tomorrow we get on the express train and off we go. I can hardly believe it. Vif
la Frantz![25] . . . I don't like it here, I can't live here . . . there is nothing
to be done. I've seen plenty of ignorance—enough . . . [*Drinks champagne*] Why cry? If you behave yourself, you won't need to cry.

DUNYASHA [*Powders her face while looking in a handheld mirror*]: Send me a
letter from Paris. I loved you, Yasha, you know, loved you so much! I'm
a delicate creature, Yasha!

YASHA: Somebody's coming. [*He bustles around the suitcases, singing softly*]

Enter Liubov Andreyevna, Gaev, Anya, and Charlotta Ivanovna.

GAEV: We'd better go. There isn't much time left. [*Looking at Yasha*] Who
smells of herring?

LIUBOV ANDREYEVNA: In about ten minutes, let's go down to the carriages . . .
[*Looks round the room*] Farewell, dear house, dear old grandfather. After
the winter, the spring will come, and you'll no longer be here, you'll be
all broken down. These walls have seen so much! [*Fervidly kisses her*

daughter] My treasure, you're radiant, your eyes sparkle like two diamonds! Are you glad? Very much?

ANYA: Very much! A new life is beginning, Mama!

GAEV [*Cheerfully*]: Yes, really, everything is good now. Before the cherry orchard was sold, we were all worried and tormented, but then, once the question was resolved irrevocably, once and for all, we all calmed down and cheered up even . . . I'm an old hand at the bank now, a financier . . . the yellow into the middle, and you, Liuba, despite it all, you're looking much better, no doubt about that.

LIUBOV ANDREYEVNA: Yes. My nerves are better; that's true.

She is handed a hat and coat.

I sleep well. Bring out my luggage, Yasha. It's time. [*To Anya*] My little girl, we'll see each other soon . . . I'm off to Paris, and I'll live there on the money that your Yaroslavl grandmother sent us for the purchase of the estate—Long live Grandmother!—but the money won't last long.

ANYA: Mama, you'll come back soon, soon . . . won't you? I'll study, take the high school exam, and then I'll work and help you. Together, we'll read all sorts of books . . . Won't we? [*Kisses her mother's hands*] We'll read during autumn evenings; we'll read many books, and a beautiful new world will open up before us . . . [*As if dreaming*] Come back soon, Mama . . .

LIUBOV ANDREYEVNA: I'll come back, my treasure. [*Embraces her*]

Enter Lopakhin and Charlotta, who is softly singing a song.

GAEV: The happy Charlotta: singing!

CHARLOTTA [*Takes a bundle that looks like a swaddled baby*]: My little baby, bye-bye.

The baby's crying is heard, "Oua! Oua!"

Be quiet, my dear little boy.

"Oua! Oua!"

I feel so sorry for you! [*Throws the bundle down*] So, please, find me a place. I can't go on like this.

LOPAKHIN: We'll find you one, Charlotta Ivanovna, don't you worry.

GAEV: Everybody's leaving us. Varya's going away . . . suddenly nobody needs us.

CHARLOTTA: I have nowhere to live in town. It's time to leave . . . [*Hums*] All the same . . .

Enter Pischik.

LOPAKHIN: God's gift! . . .

PISCHIK [*Out of breath*]: Oh, let me catch my breath . . . I'm worn out . . . My
dears . . . Give me some water . . .

GAEV: Asking for money, huh? Your humble servant, I'm moving away from
temptation . . . [*Moves away*]

PISCHIK: It's been a while . . . my dearest madam. [*To Lopakhin*] You're here . . .
glad to see you . . . man of immense intellect . . . take this . . . here, take
it . . . [*Hands Lopakhin money*] Four hundred rubles . . . I still owe you
eight hundred and forty . . .

LOPAKHIN [*Shrugging his shoulders in surprise*]: I must be dreaming . . . Where
did you get it from?

PISCHIK: Wait . . . It's hot here . . . A most unusual thing happened. These
Englishmen came and found some kind of white clay on my land . . .
[*To Liubov Andreyevna*] And for you . . . my beautiful and wonderful . . .
here four hundred . . . [*Gives her money*] The rest later . . . [*Drinks the
water*] Just now, on the train, a young man was telling that some . . .
great philosopher advises to jump off the roof. "Jump!" he says, and
that's the whole point. [*Astonished*] Imagine that! More water! . . .

LOPAKHIN: Who are these Englishmen?

PISCHIK: I've leased them the lot with clay for twenty-four years . . . Now, excuse me, I'm late . . . I must trot along . . . I have go to Znoikov . . . and
to Kardamonov . . . I owe everybody money . . . [*Drinks*] All the best . . .
I'll stop by Thursday . . .

LIUBOV ANDREYEVNA: We're moving into town, and tomorrow I go abroad . . .

PISCHIK [*Alarmed*]: Really? Why into town? No wonder I see . . . the furniture . . . suitcases . . . Well, never mind. [*Through tears*] Never mind.
These Englishmen are men of great intellect . . . Never mind . . . I wish
you happiness . . . With God's help . . . Never mind . . . Everything in
this world comes to an end . . . [*Kisses Liubov Andreyevna's hand*] And
when the news of my departure reaches you, think of this very . . . horse
and say: "There lived this so and so . . . Simyonov-Pischik, may he rest
in peace . . ." Most remarkable weather . . . Well . . . [*Exits deeply confused and embarrassed, but returns at once and from the doorway says*]
Dashenka sends her regards! [*Exits*]

LIUBOV ANDREYEVNA: We can go now. I leave with two things on my mind. The first is Fiers, who is ill. [*Looking at the watch*] We still have five minutes . . .

ANYA: Mama, they sent Fiers to the hospital. Yasha sent him off this morning.

LIUBOV ANDREYEVNA: The second thing is Varya. She's used to getting up early and working, and now without work she's like a fish out of water. She's lost weight, looks pale, and is crying, poor thing . . .

A pause.

You know very well, Ermolai Alexeyevich, that I dreamed . . . of marrying her off to you, and it looked as if you were going to. [*Whispers something to Anya, who nods to Charlotta, and the two leave the room*] She loves you, you like her, and I don't understand, I really don't, why you are keeping away from each other. I really don't understand why!

LOPAKHIN: To tell you the truth, I don't understand it either. It's all a little strange . . . If there's still time, I'm ready right now . . . Let's get it over with right away—and basta, but I feel that I'll never propose without you.

LIUBOV ANDREYEVNA: Excellent then. It only takes a minute. I'll go call her . . .

LOPAKHIN: We even have the champagne. [*Looking at the tumblers*] They're empty, somebody's drunk it.

Yasha coughs.

I call that lapped it up . . .

LIUBOV ANDREYEVNA [*Animated*]: Wonderful. We'll go out. Yasha, *allez.*[26] I'll get her . . . [*Through the door*] Varya, leave everything and come here. Come! [*She leaves with Yasha*]

LOPAKHIN [*Looking at his watch*]: Well . . . [*A pause.*]

Muted laughter and whispering is heard behind the door, then Varya comes in.

VARYA [*Surveying the luggage in silence*]: So strange, I can't find it . . .

LOPAKHIN: What are you looking for?

VARYA: I packed it myself and can't remember where.

A pause.

LOPAKHIN: Where will you go, Varvara Mikhailovna?

VARYA: Me? To the Ragulins. . . . I've agreed to look after their household . . . like a housekeeper, I guess.

LOPAKHIN: Is that in Yashnevo? It's about seventy miles.

A pause.

So life in this house has come to an end . . .

VARYA [*Looking over the luggage*]: Where is it . . . Did I put it in the trunk? . . . Yes, life has come to an end in this house . . . and there won't be another one . . .

LOPAKHIN: And I'm off to Kharkov now . . . taking this train. I have a lot of work. I'm leaving Epikhodov to look after . . . I've hired him.

VARYA: Well, then!

LOPAKHIN: Last year, if you remember, at this time, it was already snowing, and now it's still and sunny. Only it's very cold . . . Three degrees below freezing or so.

VARYA: I haven't looked.

A pause.

Our thermometer's broken anyway . . .

A pause.

Voice from the outside coming in through the door. "Ermolai Alexeyevich!"

LOPAKHIN [*As if waiting a long time for this call*]: Coming! [*Exits quickly*]

Varya is sitting on the floor with her head on a bundle of clothes and weeping softly. The door opens slowly and Liubov Andreyevna enters carefully.

LIUBOV ANDREYEVNA: What?

A pause.

We have to go.

VARYA [*Wiped her eyes and not crying anymore*]: Yes, it's time, Mamochka. I'll make it to the Ragulins today if we don't miss the train . . .

LIUBOV ANDREYEVNA [*Through the door*]: Anya, put on your coat!

Enter Anya, then Gaev, and Charlotta Ivanovna. Gaev is wearing a heavy overcoat with a hood. The servants and drivers all gather in. Epikhodov busies himself around the luggage.

Well, now we can go.

ANYA [*Joyfully*]: Let's go!

GAEV: Friends, my dear friends! As I bid farewell to this home, I cannot restrain myself, I cannot remain silent, and in parting not express the emotions that fill my whole being . . .

ANYA [*Imploringly*]: Uncle!

VARYA: Dear Uncle, don't!

GAEV [*Dolefully*]: A bank shot with the yellow in the middle . . . I'll be quiet . . .

    Enter Trofimov, then Lopakhin.

TROFIMOV: Well, ladies and gentlemen, it's time to go!

LOPAKHIN: Epikhodov, my coat!

LIUBOV ANDREYEVNA: I'll sit here another minute. It's as if I'd never really seen the walls and ceilings of this house, and now I look at them ravenously, with tender love . . .

GAEV: I remember, when I was six years old, on Trinity Sunday, sitting in this window and watching my father walk to church . . .

LIUBOV ANDREYEVNA: Have we taken all the luggage?

LOPAKHIN: It seems so. [*To Epikhodov, as he is putting on his coat*] Epikhodov, make sure everything is all right.

EPIKHODOV [*Speaking in a hoarse voice*]: Rest assured, Ermolai Alexeyich!

LOPAKHIN: What's with your voice?

EPIKHODOV: I was just drinking water and I must have swallowed something.

YASHA [*Disdainfully*]: The ignorance . . .

LIUBOV ANDREYEVNA: We'll leave and there won't be a soul left here . . .

LOPAKHIN: Till the spring.

VARYA [*Pulls an umbrella out of a bundle; it looks like she is about to strike him. Lopakhin pretends to be frightened*]: No, no, no . . . I wasn't even thinking of doing that.

TROFIMOV: Ladies and gentlemen, let's take our seats in the carriages . . . It's time! The train is about to arrive!

VARYA: Petya, your galoshes are right here, by the suitcase. [*In tears*] Look how old and dirty they are . . .

TROFIMOV [*Putting them on*]: Let's go, ladies and gentlemen! . . .

GAEV [*Deeply moved, afraid that he might start crying*]: The train . . . the station . . . *Croiser* to the middle, a bank shot with the white to the corner . . .

LIUBOV ANDREYEVNA: Let's go!

LOPAKHIN: Is everyone here? Is anybody there? [*Locks the side door on the left*] This is where the things are stored; need to lock it up. Let's go! . . .

ANYA: Good-bye, home! Good-bye, old life!

TROFIMOV: Hello, new life! . . . [*Exits with Anya*]

    Varya looks over the room and slowly walks out. Yasha and Charlotta with her little dog walk out.

LOPAKHIN: Till the spring, then. This way, ladies and gentlemen ... Till we meet again! ...[*He leaves*]

Liubov Andreyevna and Gaev are left alone. It's as if they had been wait-ing for that. They fall into each other's arms sobbing quietly, with restraint for fear of being overheard.

GAEV [*In despair*]: My sister, my sister ...

LIUBOV ANDREYEVNA: My dear, tender, beautiful orchard! ... My life, my youth, my happiness, farewell! ... Farewell! ...

Anya's voice calling cheerfully: "Mama!" Trofimov's excited voice: "Yoo-hoo!"

LIUBOV ANDREYEVNA: For the last time I glance at these walls, windows ... Our late mother liked to walk about in this room ...

GAEV: My sister, my sister! ...

Anya's voice: "Mama!" Trofimov's voice: "Yoo-hoo!"

LIUBOV ANDREYEVNA: We're coming! ...

They leave.

The stage is empty. You can hear all the doors being locked, then carriages pulling away. Then quiet. Amidst the quiet, a dull tapping of an axe against a tree; it sounds sad and lonely. Footsteps are heard ... From the door on the right, Fiers emerges. He is dressed, as always, in a jacket and white waist-coat, and on his feet—slippers. He is ill.

FIERS [*Walks over to the door and tries the handle*]: It's locked. They've left. [*Sits down on a sofa*] They forgot about me ... Never mind, I'll sit here a bit... I s'pose, Leonid Andreyich didn't put on a fur coat, and left wear-ing an overcoat ... [*He sighs all worried*] And I didn't see to it ... Oh, too young and green to know! [*Mumbles something unintelligible*] Life's over and it's as if I never lived. [*Lying down*] I'll lie down a bit ... No strength left in you, nothing's left at all ... Oh, you ... nincompoop! ... [*He lies there without moving*]

A distant sound is heard as if coming from the sky; the sound of a string breaking; a dying and sad sound. Silence falls and from deep inside the or-chard the only sound heard is the sound of an axe rapping against a tree.

Curtain.

NOTES

IVANOV

1. A carriage drawn by a team of three horses abreast.

2. From a popular song in the 1880s.

3. Shurochka is a diminutive and/or endearing form of Alexandra. Other diminutives include Shura and Sasha.

4. In the original, *merlekhliundia*—a made-up word used to describe a personal state of gloom, doom, boredom, and general malaise. The word has entered the vernacular and is sometimes spelled slightly differently as *merikhliundia*.

5. Marfusha is a diminutive of Marfa.

6. *Gevalt* (Yiddish), "Oh my goodness"; used to display surprise or shock.

7. "Come here" (German).

8. In literature, this relatively isolated area in Greece was often referred to as the example of a simple, pastoral life.

9. The area by the Black Sea known for its mild climate and therefore considered favorable for those with tuberculosis. In 1898, Chekhov, who also had tuberculosis, moved to Yalta, Crimea, on the Black Sea.

10. *La fille de Madame Angot* (*The Daughter of Madame Angot*) is an opéra comique in three acts by Charles Lecocq, first premiered in 1872 in Paris.

11. Conversion from Judaism to Russian Orthodoxy was a rare event in nineteenth-century Russia, and marriages between Jews and ethnic Russians were also very unusual. Discrimination against Jews spiked during the reign of Alexander III (1845–1894), who enacted a law forcing Jews to live in the Pale of Settlement. The Pale included neighboring provinces stretching from Riga to Odessa, from Silesia to Vilna and Kiev. A number of cities within the Pale were excluded from it. Some Jews were allowed to live outside the Pale; exceptions were made for rich business people, and for certain professions.

12. "Who is this Marfusha?" (French)

13. "A pig in a skullcap . . . *mauvais ton*" are alluding to a letter that the main character, Khlestakov, writes in the last act of N. V. Gogol's *The Inspector General* (1842).

14. In Russian folk belief, the hooting one hears predicts the number of years one has left to live.

15. Homemade brandy, a common drink in the country in those times. It is still made today.

16. A popular ditty. In 1994, the municipal authorities of St. Petersburg installed a tiny bronze statue to this legendary bird Чижик-Пыжик (Chizhik-Pyzhik).

17. Watchmen would tap at night, in sequences, to keep the burglars away.

18. In Russian Mushkino sounds like a cross between *muzh* (husband), *mushka* (a gun-sight), and a bitty fly also used for bait in fishing.

19. *Zaimishche* (flood plains, forestry, and also a village in Smolensk district where Kutuzov took the command of the Russian Army from Barclay de Tolly during the Napoleonic invasion of 1812). Also, a play of words: *zaim* (loan), *zaimishche* (a huge loan).

20. The card game played is *vint*, a popular card game in Russia and very similar to bridge.

21. Zuzi, Ziuziushka are pet names for Zinaida.

22 She spits three times over her left shoulder, a common Russian custom to ward off evil.

23. In Russian, the gesture is to flick the neck (under the chin) with two fingers.

24. Between us (French).

25. *Cicerone* (mentor, guide in Italian).

26. Another nickname for Alexandra. Both nicknames, Sasha and Shura, are used in the play.

27. From a poem by M. Yu. Lermontov.

28. Chekhov's name for journalists from *New Times*.

29. A line from N. V. Gogol's *Dead Souls* (Nozdrev speaking to Chichikov, the protagonist of the novel).

30. N. A. Dobroliubov (1836–1861), a literary and social critic who insisted that a work of literature comment on social conditions. His best-known essay "What is Oblomovism?" (1860) was a critique of Oblomov, the main character of I. A. Goncharov's novel (1859) by the same title. Its hero is a young, generous estate owner who rarely leaves his room or bed and is incapable of making important decisions or undertaking any significant actions.

31. Chatsky, a hero of the play *Woe from Wit*, also translated as *The Misfortune of Being Clever* (Горе от ума, 1831) by A. S. Griboedov. Chatsky, a young man, comes back to Moscow after a long stay abroad. He goes to the house of his relative, who is a high-ranked courtier. Chatsky manages to disrupt the household, upsets all the guests at the party, and eventually leaves with everyone considering him a madman.

32. A line from a song; music by an unknown composer, lyrics by V. Krasnov.

33. Rabies.

34. From a poem by D. V. Davydov (1784–1839), "An Old Hussar's Song." Baron Jomini (1779–1869) was a general in the French and later in the Rusian service. In the poem, an old Hussar complains that the young Hussars are discussing only Jomini and are not saying anything about the vodka. "Repeat" (Latin).

35. Gudgeon (a small, round-bodied, brown-backed freshwater fish of the minnow family that is very easy to catch).

36. Healer, and in ancient Greek mythology, a demigod of medicine and healing.

37. A paraphrased line from "Doctor's Serenade," by N. Kh. Davingof and A. M. Ushakova.

38. Milbach, possibly a reference to the first pharmacy set up in Russia under Ivan the Terrible.

39. From this point on, both Ivanov and Sasha are using *ty*, the familiar form of "you," instead of *vy*, the earlier, formal "you" in Acts One and Two. The switch alerts us to a closer, more intimate relationship between the two.

40. The line is from a song written by P. O. Pavlova (lyrics) and E. S. Shashina (music). The lyrics in the song are addressed to a man, and so Borkin adapts the words slightly to address Sasha.

41. One "of the best" in Spanish. There is also a possible pun and a reference to *makhorka*, a subgenus of tobacco plant used for making inexpensive cigarettes. In Chekhov's

plays and stories, characters sometimes pick up smoking when they have found a financial benefactor (like Babakina, who may have a particular reason for supporting Borkin).

42. In Russia, a wealthy peasant was called a *kulak* (fist).

43. Referring to a scene from *The Inspector General*, a play by N. V. Gogol (1809–1852), in which a policeman describes his unusual dream in which two rats came, sniffed around, and left.

44. In Russia, a hospital for the mentally ill was often referred to as a "yellow house." This referred to the color of the best-known hospital for the mentally ill in St. Petersburg.

45. The Museum of Curiosities, Kunstkamera, was established in St. Petersburg on the orders of Peter the Great and holds, among other things, a collection of malformed fetuses of animals and humans.

THE SEAGULL

1. N. A. Nekrasov (1821–1878), a Russian poet, publisher, and critic. His poetry tended to idealize Russian peasants.

2. Eleonora Duse—Italian and French opera singer, and the love of I. S. Turgenev. Duse would have been a contemporary of Arkadina.

3. Adapted for the stage from *La Dame aux camélias*, a novel by Alexandre Dumas (1848). The play premiered at the Theatre de Vaudeville in Paris in 1852.

4. A play by B. M. Markevich (1822–1884) based on his *roman à clef*.

5. A theater superstition that says that one should never have three candles burning simultaneously in one's dressing room.

6. A major city on the Black Sea.

7. The dog's name in the original text: Trezor (Treasure).

8. A song based on a poem by the poet N. A. Nekrasov.

9. From a very popular song based on a poem by V. Krasov (1810–1854), a poor schoolteacher and poet who died of consumption.

10. Poltava is a city in Ukraine, a possible reference to N. V. Gogol's birthplace as well as the Sorochinsky Fair, immortalized by Gogol as the setting of his collection of stories *Evenings on a Farm near Dikanka*.

11. Reference to *Krechinsky's Wedding: A Comedy in Three Acts* by A. V. Sukhovo-Kobylin (1854). A grotesque comedy, in which a father is looking for a suitor for his daughter, and Krechinsky, penniless, with the help of his sidekick Raspluev, creates a meticulous scheme to procure funds.

12. Shamraev is mixing up two Latin expressions: *de gustibus non est disputandum* (to each his own) and *de mortuis nil nisi bonum* (when speaking of the dead, speak kindly or not at all).

13. The rhythm of the line is the same as Queen Gertrude's line when she addresses her son, Hamlet.

14. Arkadina omits "Oh, Hamlet, speak no more" from the first line of her rendition of Hamlet's mother, Queen Gertrude. Chekhov uses Nikolai Polevoy's translation in *The Seagull*.

15. Translation from the Russian version back into English: "Nay, why did you give into wickedness and seek love / in the depths of crime?" Chekhov uses N. Polevoy's translation, a translation known for its inaccuracies and inoffensive language that, perhaps for that very reason, had become a staple of stage productions. Polevoy's translation makes Hamlet weaker compared to other translations and the language of the play is toned down considerably. Polevoy's emasculated Hamlet does confront his mother, but "making love," "rank sweat" and "enseamed bed" do not make it into Polevoy's translation.

16. The text bears a resemblance to *Songs of Maldoror* (*Les chants de Maldoror*) by the Uruguayan-born French poet Comte de Lautréamont (pseudonym of Isidore Lucien Ducasse 1846–1870).

17. An actor who plays the young male lead (French).

18. Shamraev recounts a story that was a popular one at the time. There were many variations of the anecdote, often involving different characters and different theaters, but the plot always remained the same. It is perhaps for that reason that the conversation stops, awkwardly.

19. From the opera *Faust* by Charles Gounod. The aria sung by Sibel when he wants to give Margarita a bouquet of flowers.

20. "As is proper" (French).

21. Commonly prescribed sedative drops made from valerian root.

22. "Thank you very much" (French).

23. "Rudd," a freshwater fish.

24. Reference to the madman from "Diary of a Madman" by N. V. Gogol, in which Poprishchin suffers from the persistent delusion that he is the King of Spain.

25. Elisavetgrad, or Elizabethgrad, a city in Ukraine; present name Kirovgrad. *Grad* means town or city.

26. Arkadina is very tight with her money.

27. From *molchat* (to be silent) (Russian).

28. The price is given in Ukrainian currency. The pood, about 37 pounds, was part of the Imperial Russian weight measurement system abolished in 1924.

29. "Месяц плывет по ночным небесам"—the opening line of a then-popular serenade by K. S. Shilovsky (1849–1893).

30. Opera by A. S. Dargomyzhsky based on a poem of the same name by A. S. Pushkin (1799–1837). The opera is about a miller's daughter who is seduced and abandoned by a local prince. Her daughter, a water nymph, avenges her mother's death by taking the prince's life. The opera was first performed in 1856.

31. A city in the northeast of Ukraine, formerly part of the Russian Empire. It's about four hundred miles from Moscow.

32. Nina is quoting from the novel *Rudin* (1855) by I. S. Turgenev.

33. *Muzhik* (Russian)—peasant, uncouth, uncultured man.

34. See note 9.

UNCLE VANYA

1. From a poem by I. I. Dmitriev (1760–1837), "Чужой толк" ("Other People's Views"), 1794. The poet Dmitriev belonged to the school of Sentimentalism. He wrote elegies, satire, and songs in a style imitating folk fables and ballads.

2. "As much as needed" (Latin). Prescription terminology still in use today as the abbreviation *q.s.*

3. Kharkov is the second largest city in Ukraine.

4. The Russian upper class conversed in French among themselves in the late eighteenth and early nineteenth centuries. However, using the French *Jean* instead of the very common Russian name Иван (Ivan, the equivalent of John), or its diminutive Ваня (Vanya, the equivalent of Johnny) is made to sound pretentious in the play that takes place at the end of the nineteenth century.

5. "Nonstop mechanism" (Latin).

6. Allusion made, most likely, to General Krititski, a character in Alexander Ostrovsky's comedy *На всякого мудреца довольно простоты* (*Enough Stupidity in Every Wise Man*). The play is a satire and follows the rise of a double-dealer who tries to manipulate others.

7. See note 17 to *Ivanov*.

8. Konstantin Batiuhkov (1787–1855), a Russian poet, was one of the founders of a new school in Russian poetry that is usually defined as Romantic or pre-Romantic.

9. I. S. Turgenev (1818–1883) was a Russian novelist and playwright, author of some of the best-known works of Russian literature, including *A Sportman's Sketches, Fathers and Sons, Rudin, Nest of the Gentlefolk, Smoke,* and *A Month in the Country. Gout* is chronic inflammatory arthritis.

10. A common folk remedy. The tea is made from the blossoms of the linden tree.

11. "Ходи хата, ходи печь, хозяину негде лечь . . ." A folk song that exists in other variations as well—for example, where a young miss has no place to go.

12. A line from "Сказка о мёртвой царевне и семи богатырях" ("The Tale of the Dead Princess and the Seven Knights"), a fairytale in verse by A. S. Pushkin (1833). The story is based on "Snow White," by the brothers Grimm. The line is said to the wicked stepmother by a mirror that she is holding. Astrov changes the pronoun from *you* to *she*.

13. Elena, when she addresses Sonya by the French variant *Sophie,* is acting a little pretentious and like Voinitsky's mother when she calls him *Jean* instead of Vanya.

14. In the original Russian, this is where Elena and Sonia alter their relationship and switch from the formal way of addressing each other (*Vy* for "you") to the informal *ty.* This brings them closer and makes having intimate conversations possible.

15. The Russian word русалка is the equivalent of *water nymph.* A water nymph is different from a mermaid and not part fish. Mythological water nymphs are females who live in the water and mate with men at will.

16. Elena must have been very good to be accepted to the prestigious St. Petersburg Music Conservatory.

17. Astrov switches here from the formal *vy* (you) to the informal *ty* (you) as if announcing a greater intimacy between him and Elena. Elena, on the other hand, never switches to the informal *you* when addressing Astrov.

18. Voinitsky, as if trying to mock Serebriakov and appear exceedingly polite, uses the formal *you* to address the professor. The next time Voinitsky poses the question, he is back to using the informal *you* and a less polite phrasing of the question.

19. The professor uses one of the most recognizable opening lines in Russian literature, from *The Inspector General,* a very funny and poignant comedy of errors by N. V. Gogol that showcases greed, stupidity, and the underlying corruption among officials in nineteenth century Russia.

20. "Night awaits us all," from Horace's *Odes.*

21. *Dacha* in the original.

22. Referring to Turkey's nineteenth-century law that allowed the husband to keep the dowry even if the wife dies.

23. A. Schopenhauer (1788–1860), the German philosopher. F. M. Dostoyevsky (1821–1881), the Russian novelist.

24. A diminutive of мать (mother).

25. I. K. Aivazovsky (1817–1900) is a Russian artist of Armenian descent, famous for his stormy seascapes. Chekhov visited his estate in the Crimea in 1888 and met the painter and his beautiful wife. At the time of their marriage, Aivazovsky was sixty-five and his bride was twenty-two.

26. "The comedy is over!" (from the Italian *È finita la commedia*). The same phrase, but with a misspelling of the word 'commedia' (a single *m* as opposed to a double *m*) occurs in M. Yu. Lermontov's *A Hero of Our Time*. The hero Pechorin says it after his duel with Grushnitsky. The phrase is also the last line in Ruggero Leoncavallo's opera Pagliacci, first premiered in Milan in 1892, only the word order is different: "La commedia è finita!"

27. Kissing three times on alternate cheeks is an old custom that can still be seen today.

28. One of the three horses in a troika, a three-horse carriage.

29. Diminutive of Petya, which itself is a diminutive of Peter.

30. The name of the place can be translated as Christmas Village.

THREE SISTERS

1. In the Russian Orthodox tradition, именины (*imeniny*, name-day) is celebrated on the birthday of one's patron saint. Russian Orthodox people are named after saints, so that their saints' birthdays become their name-days. The name-day is considered more important than a person's actual birthday.

2. See note 30 to *Ivanov*.

3. The opening lines of A. S. Pushkin's poem *Ruslan and Ludmilla*. Published in 1829, it is an epic fairytale in verse that tells the story of the abduction of a prince's daughter, Ludmilla, by an evil wizard and the brave knight Ruslan's attempts to rescue her. Schools routinely make their students memorize many of Pushkin's poems.

4. In the text: *merlekhliundia*—a word Chekhov made up and which has entered the vernacular to mean feeling low.

5. I. Krylov's fable in verse, "The Peasant and the Workman," is based on Aesop's fable.

6. A kind of present considered somewhat inappropriate for a young woman, something customarily reserved for a bride to be or a wedding anniversary.

7. The name of the street translates to "German."

8. A more vernacular variation of the patronymic Vasilyevich.

9. The cemetery at the Novodevichy Convent is in Moscow. Many prominent writers, including Chekhov, are buried there.

10. A last name that can be translated from the Russian as "arch-priest."

11. Andriusha and Andriushka are both pet names of Andrey.

12. A line originally from an old French comic opera that was adapted by P. N. Kobiakov into Russian with the title *Werevolves, or Argue All You Want, but a Wager Is a Fool's Argument* ("Оборотни или Спорь до слез, а об заклад не бейся") (1808).

13. Although he addresses her as sister, Irina is his sister-in-law.

14. "I did what I could, those who can will do better" (Latin).

15. "A healthy mind in a healthy body" (Latin).

16. From the French, "a duelist," "a troublemaker." A reference to Turgenev's short story by the same name "Бреттер" (1846).

17. A cloying diminutive of another diminutive (Andriusha).

18. *Bliny* in the original—thin pancakes.

19. Refers probably to the first electrical wire in Moscow.

20. "Come here" (French).

21. From N. V. Gogol's short story "A Tale About How Ivan Ivanovich Quarreled with Ivan Nikiforovich" (1835).

22. In 1850, three months before his death, Honoré de Balzac, already in declining health, traveled to Berdichev, a predominantly Jewish town then in the Russian Em-

pire, to marry a Polish countess, Evelina Hanska, with whom he had corresponded for fifteen years.

23. City in northeast China.

24. A person's father's first name with a suffix: Ignat—Ignatievich.

25. The Panama Canal Scandal or Panama Affair—the largest monetary corruption scandal of the nineteenth century, linked to the building of the Panama Canal in 1892. The French government took bribes to keep quiet about the Panama Canal Company's financial troubles.

26. "Please excuse me, Marie, but your manners are a little crude" (French).

27. "Bobik is not asleep anymore" (translation of Natasha's bad French).

28. A. Griboyedov's *Woe from Wit*.

29. Aleko is a hero of Pushkin's "The Gypsies." Here, Solyony mixes up his literary references.

30. M. Yu. Lermontov (1814–1841) a Russian Romantic writer and poet, is sometimes referred to as "the poet of the Caucasus." He, like Pushkin, was killed in a duel.

31. "Enough!" (Italian).

32. In the original: *chekhartma* (a meat dish) versus *cheremsha* (a root vegetable in the onion family).

33. In Russian: "Ах вы сени, мои сени, / Сени новые мои …" A traditional folk song.

34. Proposes a toast to their new closeness, to the informal way of addressing each other (*ty* instead of *vy*).

35. "How vain are men's hopes" (Latin).

36. A diminutive of Olga.

37. "In wine the truth" (Latin).

38. A town in Siberia, founded in 1653 and located southeast of Irkutsk. Chita was a place of exile for the Decembrists, those who called for constitutional monarchy during an uprising in St. Petersburg in 1825.

39. "Любви все возрасты покорны, её порывы благотворны." The opening of Prince Gremin's aria in P. I. Tchaikovsky's opera *Eugene Onegin* (1879). The opera was based on a novel in verse by A. S. Pushkin (published serially between 1825 and 1832).

40. "I love," "you love," etc. (Latin).

41. "All my things I carry with me" (Latin).

42. Like the hero of N. V. Gogol's short story "Diary of a Madman," who is forced to suppress what he knows to be true.

43. Ferapont must have misheard Andrey's title and uses an even higher honorific when addressing Andrey.

44. "Dear" (Polish).

45. "The way of life" (Latin).

46. A subjunctive grammatical construction in Latin.

47. "La prière d'une vierge," a popular piano piece by Tekla Bądarzewska.

48. "А он мятежный ищет бури,/Как-будто в буре есть покой." From the poem "The Sail" by Lermontov.

49. Fermented drink made with bread; it is similar to ale.

50. "You should not make noise. Sophie is asleep. You are a bear." Natasha's French is unidiomatic and she makes mistakes.

51. Vershinin switches from the formal *vy* (you) to the intimate *ty* (you) in addressing Masha.

THE CHERRY ORCHARD

1. *Kvass*—a fermented drink, similar to ale, low in alcohol and made from rye bread.

2. *Как огурчик* (like a little cucumber) (Russian); it refers to somebody looking sprightly and fit. (Later, in Act Two, Charlotta is seen munching on a cucumber.)

3. According to Russian customs and superstitions, breaking dishes (accidentally) brings good luck.

4. In the original, "шаровары"—very wide men's pants that are gathered at the waist and ankles, and are a part of the Ukrainian national costume.

5. See note 31 to *The Seagull*.

6. University students wore uniforms in those days.

7. The forties—the fathers (German idealism); the sixties—the sons (positivism, utilitarianism, populism, terrorism—as in the assassination of Alexander II in 1881); the eighties—a period of political reaction, censorship, and, to some extent, intellectual stagnation.

8. "Deadly jump"(Italian), a flip in the air.

9. A type of sad romantic song, very popular at that time.

10. Henry Thomas Buckle (1821–1862).

11. The name refers to the late nineteenth-century writers and philosophers who, in opposition to Romantics, praised artifice over the naïve view of nature. Some of them proudly referred to themselves as Decadents.

12. A billiard term in French.

13. The serfs (peasant slaves) were freed in Russia in 1861 by Tsar Alexander II.

14. When angry, Trofimov switches to informal "you" in addressing Lopakhin.

15. The Volga is a major river in Russia. The passerby, intentionally or not, reads the first line, "Брат, мой страдающий брат . . . ," from S. Ya. Nadson (1862–1887), followed by the second line, "Выдь на Волгу чей стон . . . ," from N. A. Nekrasov. Both poets wrote about the suffering of the poor in Russia.

16. A popular dance tune from the Caucasus.

17. "One, two, three" (German).

18. Charlotta is purposefully using ironic grammar and pronunciation here.

19. "Good man but a bad musician" (German).

20. It was relatively common then for students to be expelled for political activity.

21. A moralistic poem by the poet Alexey Tolstoy (1817–1878) about the sinning Mary Magdalene who changes her wicked ways.

22. A more informal pronunciation of Andreyevich.

23. "Поймешь ли ты души моей волненье"—the opening line from the romance written by N. S. Rzhevskaya in 1869.

24. Lopakhin uses the informal "you" in addressing Trofimov, and Trofimov switches to the informal "you" as well.

25. Yasha says it with a Russian accent.

26. "Go" (French).